SHORTORDER

MICROSOFT® FrontPage® 2000

WAYNE BROOKS

Short Order Microsoft® FrontPage® 2000

International Standard Book Number: 0-7897-2050-7

Library of Congress Catalog Card Number: 99-65513

Printed in the United States of America

First Printing: September 1999

02 01 00 99 4 3 2 1

Trademarks

Warning and Disclaimer

EXECUTIVE EDITOR
Beth Millett

ACQUISITIONS EDITOR
Karen Whitehouse

DEVELOPMENT EDITOR
Laura Norman

MANAGING EDITOR
Thomas F. Hayes

PROJECT EDITOR
Heather Talbot

COPY EDITOR
Julie McNamee

INDEXER
Aamir Burki

PROOFREADER
Tricia Sterling

TECHNICAL EDITOR
Richard Bodien

TEAM COORDINATOR
Lori Morgan

INTERIOR DESIGNER
Karen Ruggles

COVER DESIGNER
Aren Howell

COPY WRITER
Eric Borgert

LAYOUT TECHNICIANS
Stacey DeRome
Ayanna Lacey
Heather Hiatt Miller
Mark Walchle

CONTENTS AT A GLANCE

CONTENTS

ABOUT THE AUTHOR

Mr. Brooks' diverse background encompasses 15 years in government and commercial information systems. In addition, he is a consultant in the areas of multimedia and Web-based application design and development. He is the author of the following:

- *The Access 2000 Programming Blue Book*, The Coriolis Group
- *Active Server: A Developer's Guide*, MIS Press/M&T Books
- *FrontPage Fundamentals*, DigitalThink (Online Technology Training Course)
- *FrontPage 97 Sourcebook*, John Wiley & Sons
- *Client/Server Fundamentals*, DigitalThink (Online Technology Training Course)

Mr. Brooks is also the co-author and technical editor of

- *Special Edition Using Asymetrix Multimedia ToolBook*, Macmillan Computer Publishing

He can be contacted at `waynebrooks@nolla.org`.

DEDICATION

This book is dedicated to the Spirit, to Wisdom, to the drive for perpetual learning, and to my mom, Frances B. Brooks, for instilling me with all three.

ACKNOWLEDGMENTS

As always, there are many to thank for their patience, perseverance, guidance, and understanding. Thanks again to Margot Maley-Hutchinson and the folks at Waterside Productions: Couldn't get it done without your unfailing support. Also, special thanks to Brian Gill, Laura Norman, Karen Whitehouse, and the entire *Short Order* team.

On a personal note, I would like to thank my wife Tanya for her love and support, to the kids for letting Dad write, and to all my friends and family for always being there. You guys are the greatest.

TELL US WHAT YOU THINK!

As the reader of this book, *you* are our most important critic and commentator. We value your opinion and want to know what we're doing right, what we could do better, what areas you'd like to see us publish in, and any other words of wisdom you're willing to pass our way.

As a publisher for Hayden, I welcome your comments. You can fax, email, or write me directly to let me know what you did or didn't like about this book—as well as what we can do to make our books stronger.

Please note that I cannot help you with technical problems related to the topic of this book, and that due to the high volume of mail I receive, I might not be able to reply to every message.

When you write, please be sure to include this book's title and author as well as your name and phone or fax number. I will carefully review your comments and share them with the author and editors who worked on the book.

Fax: 317-581-4666

Email: `hayden@mcp.com`

Mail: Publisher
Hayden
201 West 103rd Street
Indianapolis, IN 46290 USA

INTRODUCTION

Who This Book Is For

Short Order Microsoft FrontPage 2000 was created for people interested in quick solutions to the tasks and problems encountered every day. Using step-by-step examples and plenty of illustrations, you'll learn to put intermediate to advanced tasks and commands to work for you in short order.

If you have worked with FrontPage before and want to step up your skills, this book will teach you tricks used by professional Web designers that are sure to enhance your site. You will find this book particularly helpful as a quick reference, as well as a guide to expanding your FrontPage horizons to include cutting-edge techniques and learning the new features of FrontPage 2000.

About FrontPage 2000

FrontPage 2000 is a feature-rich redesign of its predecessors. Designed to facilitate professional Web development without programming, this application provides the tools to support the needs of the Web designer without compromising the desires of the Web application programmer. For this reason, you'll find that FrontPage 2000 is not so much a Web development tool, as it is a Web development environment.

What You Can Do with FrontPage 2000

FrontPage 2000 introduces enhancements to the standard FrontPage features you know and love, as well as a few new surprises. The list below provides a summary of what this new FrontPage version makes possible.

- Create Web sites without having a Web server installed on your computer.
- Precisely position and overlay objects on your Web pages using FrontPage 2000's Positioning feature.

- Use Dynamic HTML to create animation effects.
- Add consistency to your Web site with the application of Themes and Cascading Style Sheets.
- Use FrontPage 2000's built-in source control feature to manage changes to your Web site.
- Use Microsoft Office components like spreadsheets, pivot tables, and charts.

What's New in FrontPage 2000

Microsoft introduces a number of significant enhancements with this latest product version.

- The most obvious enhancement is the reworked user interface. Experienced FrontPage users will immediately notice that the FrontPage Explorer and the FrontPage Editor have been merged into a singular front-end. The new look and feel is an expression of FrontPage's integration as a component of the Microsoft Office 2000 Productivity Suite.
- FrontPage 2000 now offers you the benefit of incorporating Excel spreadsheets, charts, and pivot tables into your Web pages.
- You'll also find a feature set that extends the reach of your Web design creativity to the world, with enhanced foreign language support.
- You now have greater control over your Web development environment, as FrontPage 2000 introduces support for disk-based Webs. By using disk-based Webs, you no longer require the installation of a Web server on your local machine.
- Discover enhanced diagnostic support with the new Web Reports view. Using the Web Reports view, you'll be able to see the new Site Summary report, which provides statistical detail about your site's overall composition and integrity.

As you identify and execute specific tasks in each chapter, you'll become more familiar with the features that make FrontPage 2000 the premier Web development and site management application.

How to Use This Book

I've made an effort to keep things as simple as possible, yet jammed as much useful information as space allowed onto every page. Follow the straightforward step by steps to achieve a task (highlighted in the colored bar at the top of each page), but don't overlook the tips and notes in the corners of every page.

The tips should serve as memory joggers for the experienced user, and as points to commit to memory for the novice to intermediate Web developer. The notes, also placed throughout the book, offer explanations to clarify task-specific details, and provide commentary on some of FrontPage 2000's more challenging aspects.

If a picture is worth a thousand words, then you'll find no shortage of visual verbiage here. As is characteristic of the *Short Order* series, there are plenty of screenshots to guide you through the tasks, along with plenty of callouts that emphasize specific features of FrontPage 2000's dialog boxes and palettes.

About *Short Order*

Treat *Short Order FrontPage 2000* as your briefcase ready reference. Although this book is not meant to be read sequentially from cover to cover, there is a method to the way that the chapters have been organized, so you can find what you need quickly.

Refer to Chapters 1 through 4 during the preparatory phase of your Web development plan. These chapters guide you through those activities you'll need to consider before you begin development of your site content. Specifically, you'll find information on establishing network and database connectivity, configuring your Web host, setting default options, becoming familiar with the new FrontPage 2000 nterface, and performing general Web administration tasks.

Chapters 5 through 12 should be used when you're ready to begin your site content development activities. These chapters are designed for the novice, as well as the experienced FrontPage user. For this reason, you'll find material that offers insight into FrontPage fundamentals, while also orienting the more advanced user to the enhancements that FrontPage 2000 now enjoys. For example, you'll discover how to apply Cascading Style Sheets, as well as how to create your own custom HTML style tags. You'll find yourself designing pages with increased precision as you learn to use FrontPage 2000's new Positioning capability.

Refer to Chapters 13 through 16 when you're ready to extend the dimensions of your Web by integrating Microsoft Office 2000 components and applying multimedia elements such as audio, video, and banner ad animation. You'll also find useful material on the application of Dynamic HTML and scripting languages such as VBScript and JavaScript, along with insights on browser compatibility issues and how to use FrontPage 2000 to address them with ease.

From static pages to special effects, *Short Order FrontPage 2000* strives to break through the complexities of Web design with FrontPage and deliver what you really need, when you really need it.

CHAPTER 1

In this chapter you will learn how to...

Test Network Connectivity

Configure a Computer to Create Server-Based Webs

Configure Web Default Options

Configure Page Default Options

Customize the User Interface

Enable Source Control

Before you begin building Web sites with FrontPage 2000, you'll want to create a working environment conducive to the task. This means making sure that you can establish connectivity to a Web server, setting up default parameters for your Web and the pages you'll create, and customizing the look and feel of the FrontPage 2000 interface to suit your individual taste. For example, FrontPage 2000 displays the Views bar by default.

CONFIGURING A FRONTPAGE 2000 WORKING ENVIRONMENT

You may determine that you would rather have the Views bar hidden to provide a little more space in the Page view window. In addition, if you'll be working in a multi-user environment, you'll also want to invoke basic source control to make sure that only one person at a time is able to edit an active file.

This chapter also introduces the FrontPage MMC (Microsoft Management Console) snap-in utility. The FrontPage MMC snap-in utility is a program that replaces the Fpsrvwin.exe utility used to perform FrontPage Server Extension administration functions in earlier FrontPage versions. You'll find that you can also use the FrontPage MMC snap-in utility to perform some of the functions formerly associated with the FrontPage Explorer such as recalculating hyperlinks.

Testing Network Connectivity

Because FrontPage 2000 uses the TCP/IP protocol to support HTTP data transmissions, you'll need to be sure that your computer is TCP/IP ready before you start to work. You can make this determination by running the FrontPage 2000 Network Test utility using the following steps:

1. Open FrontPage 2000 from the Windows Programs menu to reveal the program's user interface **(1.1)**.

2. Choose Help→About Microsoft FrontPage from the FrontPage 2000 menu bar to open the About Microsoft FrontPage dialog box **(1.2)**.

FrontPage 2000 introduces a single integrated user interface, as opposed to the dual FrontPage Explorer and FrontPage Editor interfaces found in previous versions of the product.

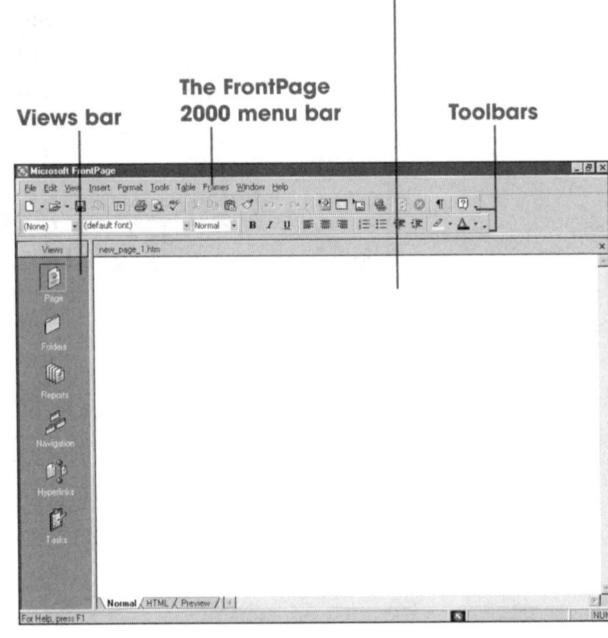

1.1

When you run the Network Test, FrontPage 2000 invokes a dynamic link library (.DLL) file called Wsock32.dll. This file allows FrontPage 2000 to use features of the Winsock Application Programming Interface (API) to browse and retrieve files. Winsock is the popular name for the Windows Sockets Interface Specification. This specification defines a standard Windows programming interface for network applications that use the TCP/IP protocol.

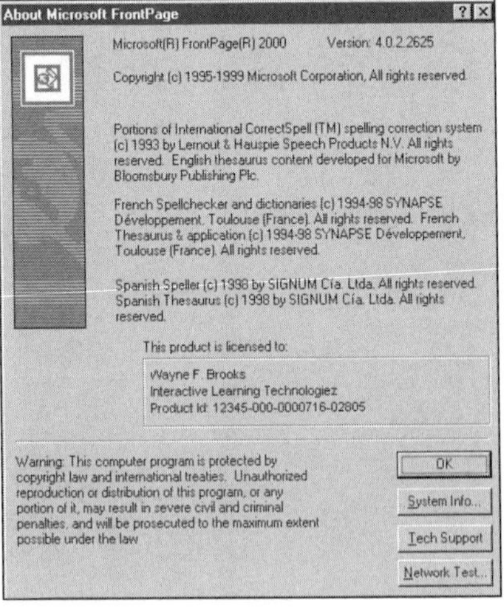

1.2

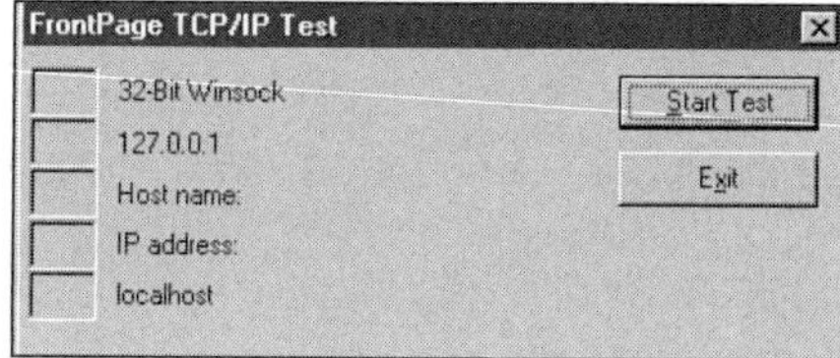

1.3

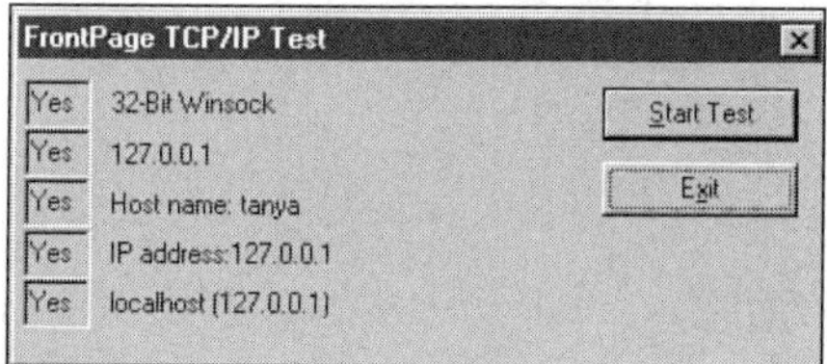

1.4

3. Click the Network Test button to open the FrontPage TCP/IP Test dialog box **(1.3)**.
4. Click the Start Test button to run the Network Test utility. A successful network test results in a Yes response in each cell of the FrontPage TCP/IP Test dialog box **(1.4)**.
5. Click the Exit button to close the TCP/IP Test dialog box, and then click the OK button to close the About Microsoft FrontPage dialog box.

TCP/IP (Transmission Control Protocol/Internet Protocol) is a suite of standard protocols, tools, and diagnostics used to connect network devices.

If you happen not to get a Yes response during the TCP/IP test, check the configuration of your TCP/IP stack and then run the test again. If the problem persists, refer to article q205466 in the Microsoft Knowledgebase entitled FP2000: TCP/IP Test Fails But Other Internet Programs Run.

Configuring a Computer to Create Server-Based Webs

With FrontPage 2000, the need to have an installed Web server to create a new FrontPage Web is eliminated. This means you can now specify a folder on your hard drive as the staging area for Web creation and storage, giving you the option to publish your Web to a production Web server at a later time. However, if you choose to use a Web server to stage your Webs rather than saving your Webs to disk, and you don't have a Web server installed, then you'll need to configure your computer for the task by performing the following steps:

1. Install the Web server software of your choice (for example, Microsoft Personal Web Server or Internet Information Server).
2. Run the FrontPage Microsoft Management Console (MMC) snap-in utility **(1.5)**.

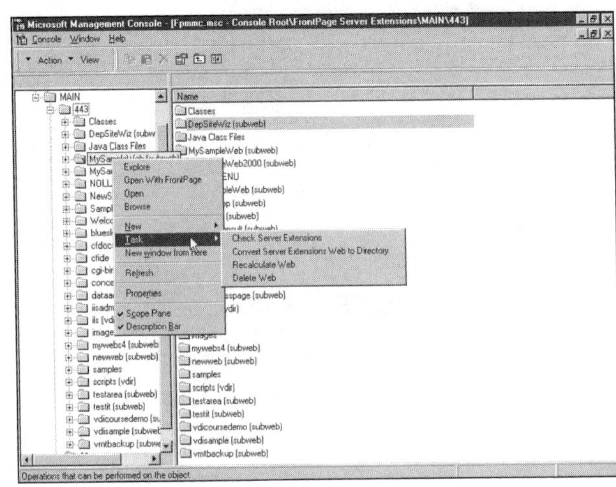

1.5

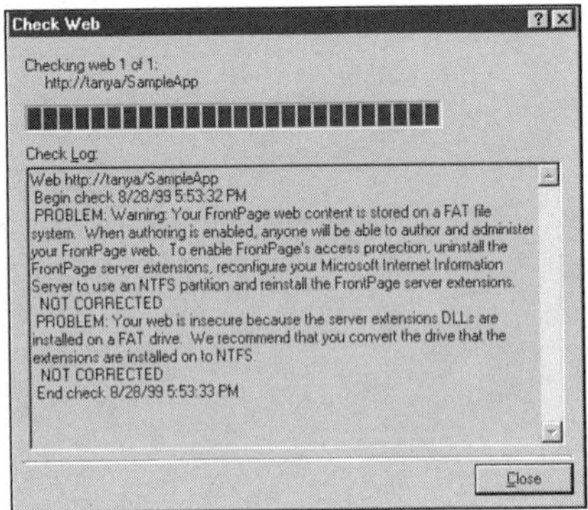

1.6

The FrontPage MMC snap-in adds its functionality directly to the Microsoft Management Console and is called the Server Extensions Administrator on the Windows Program menu, if you're running a Web server other than IIS 4.0. Use the FrontPage MMC snap-in to configure, remove, upgrade, or check the state of the FrontPage Server Extensions (1.6). You can also convert server-based Webs to directories.

Configuring Web Default Options

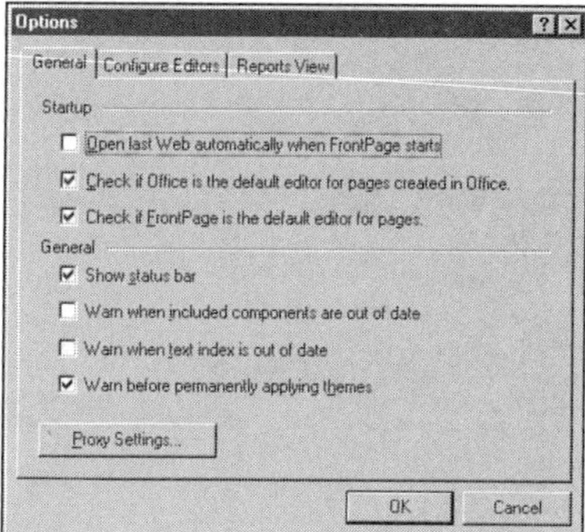

1.7

The Configure Editors tab lets you associate a specific file type with its source application. In addition, it presents options for modifying or deleting the same.

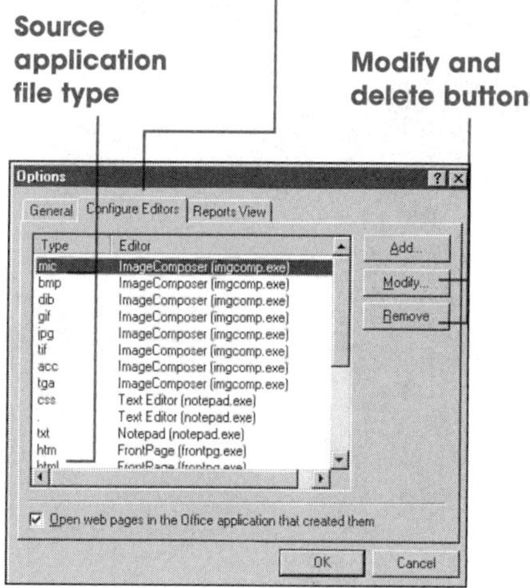

1.8

Web defaults are those settings that specify how FrontPage interacts with the user, for instance, the use of external file editors and report parameters for site analysis. You can configure these settings by performing the following steps:

1. Choose Tools→Options to open the Options dialog box.
2. The Options dialog box contains three tabs: the General tab **(1.7)**, the Configure Editors tab **(1.8)**, and the Reports View tab. The General tab presents options for checking a default page editor at startup, determining Status bar display, setting specific warnings, and establishing proxy settings. Apply user-defined values on the General tab as needed.

continues

FrontPage 2000 calculates the Site Summary reports from the settings in Reports view.

If you're running Windows NT instead of Windows 95 or Windows 98, you can use the Microsoft Management Console snap-in to configure your computer with the FrontPage Server Extensions.

Configuring Web Default Options continued

3. Select the Configure Editors tab and choose the Add button to open the Add Editor Association dialog box **(1.9)**.
4. In the Add Editor Association dialog box, enter a file extension in the File Type field, enter a title for the file's source application in the Editor Name field, and enter the path and filename for the source application in the Command field.
5. Click OK to close the dialog box and add the new file type and source application to the Configure Editors tab list box.
6. The Reports View tab **(1.10)** presents options for checking a default page editor at startup, determining Status bar display, setting specific warnings, and establishing proxy settings.

Choosing the Browse button gives you the option of locating the path and filename for the source application on your host machine.

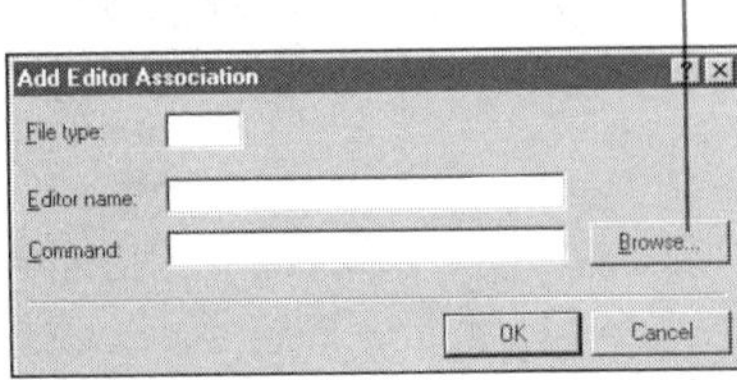

1.9

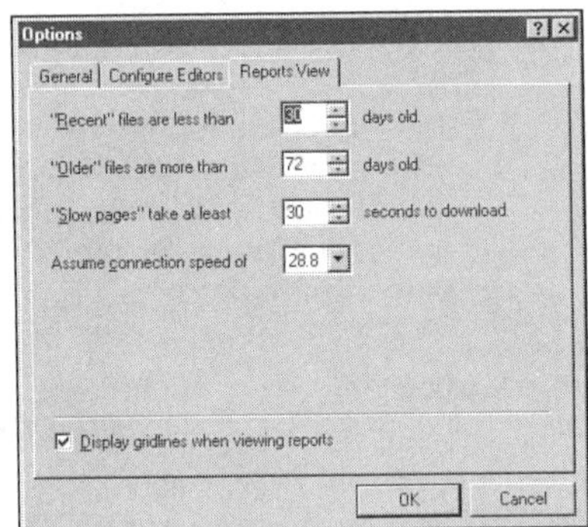

1.10

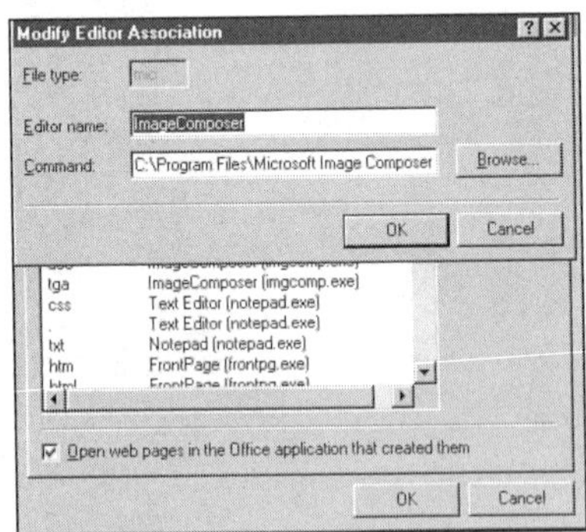

1.11

TIP

The Modify button presents a dialog box exactly the same as the Add Editor Association dialog box (1.11). The difference is that the fields are populated for editing purposes rather than being blank. Changing a populated entry and clicking OK causes the modification to occur.

Configuring Page Default Options

The Page Options dialog box contains six tabs that allow you to configure all aspects of your page setup.

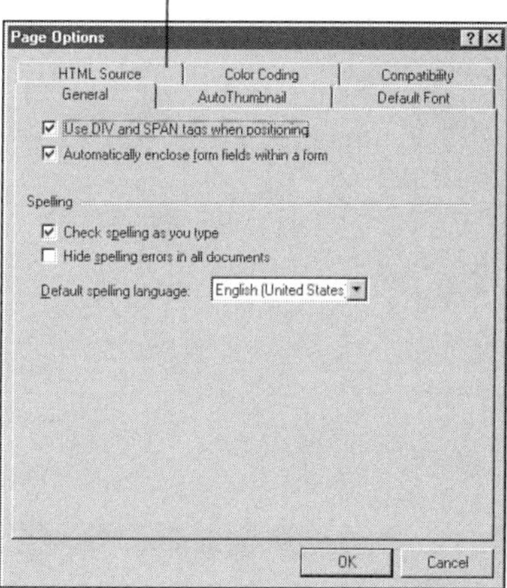

1.12

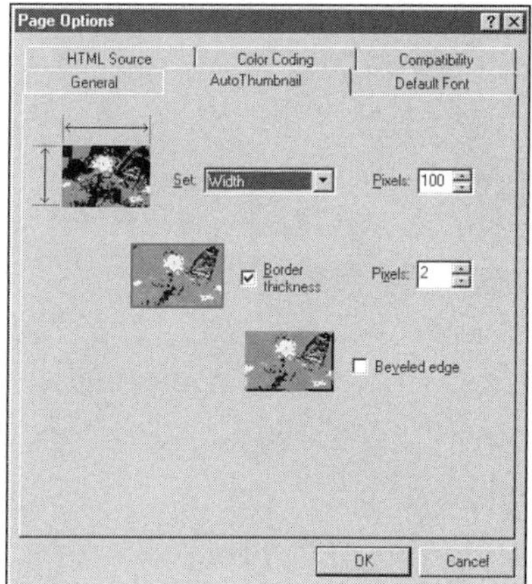

1.13

Page default options are settings that specify how FrontPage influences and displays various page design elements (for example, spelling errors, thumbnail image properties, HTML presentations, and proportional and fixed font specifications). As with the Web default options, you can configure these settings by performing the following steps:

1. Choose Tools→Page Options to open the Page Options dialog box **(1.12)**.
2. Choose the General tab in the dialog box to set options for enabling content positioning tags and spelling management.
3. Choose the AutoThumbnail tab to set sizing parameters for image files converted to thumbnails **(1.13)**.

continues

If you find that the features on the Compatibility tab don't support the way you want to handle browser compatibility, you might want to consider testing for specific browser types using code.

Configuring Page Default Options continued

4. Choose the Default Font tab to set options for specifying language specific proportional and fixed font styles **(1.14)**.
5. Choose the HTML Source tab to select options for specifying how to save, format, and display HTML source code **(1.15)**.

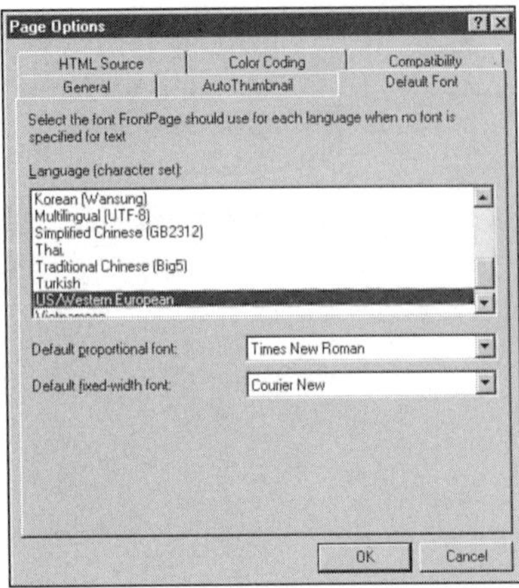

1.14

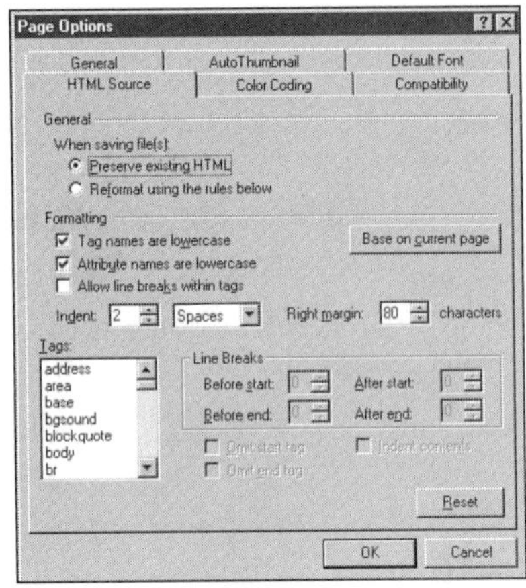

1.15

If you select the Preserve Existing HTML option, be aware that checking any of the Formatting on the HTML Source tab of the Page Options dialog box will still apply the selected formatting changes to your HTML source code.

You can specify particular technologies or features rather than browser versions, by selecting Custom from the Browser versions drop-down menu, and then selecting or deselecting specific technology check boxes. Commands not supported by certain browser technologies appear dimmed on FrontPage 2000 menus when you begin Web development.

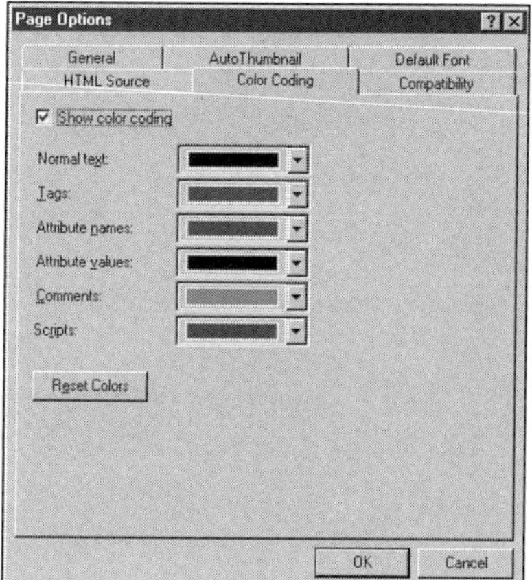

1.16

FrontPage now offers you the ability to make your Web site compatible across multiple browsers and versions. Select from a list of available browsers in the Browsers drop-down list.

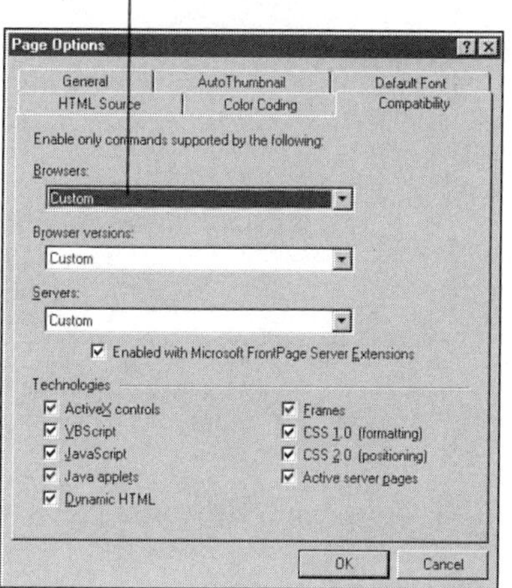

1.17

6. Choose the Color Coding tab if you want to select options for setting HTML color defaults **(1.16)**. This can be very helpful when debugging your HTML code.

7. Choose the Compatibility tab to select from options for specifying a unique publishing environment in which certain FrontPage features are disabled when published or viewed in the specified environment **(1.17)**. Web browsers, Web servers, FrontPage Server Extension presence, and technology type, that is ASP, DHTML, CSS, or Java, specify selectable values.

Customizing the User Interface

You can give the FrontPage 2000 user interface a personal look and feel by designing custom toolbars that offer point-and-click access to commands that you use most frequently.

1. Choose Tools→Customize to open the Customize dialog box **(1.18)**.
2. Click the New button to open the New Toolbar dialog box **(1.19)**.
3. Enter a name for your new toolbar in the Toolbar Name field.
4. Click OK to close the dialog box. This action adds the new toolbar name and its associated check box to the Toolbars tab list box, and displays a blank toolbar object **(1.20)**.

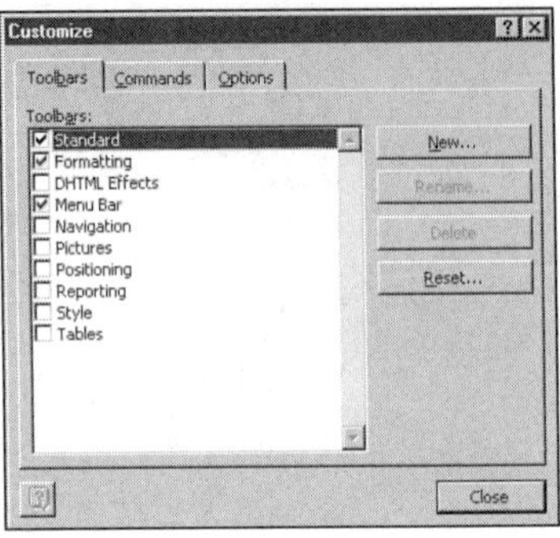

1.18

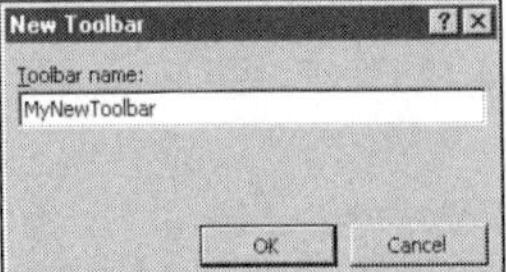

1.19

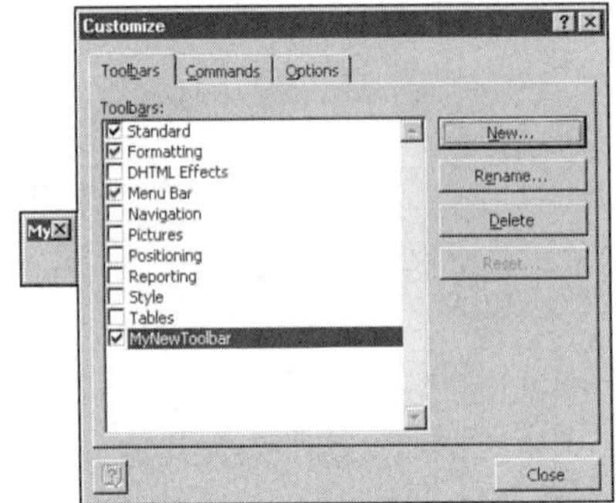

1.20

The Customize dialog box contains three tabs: the Toolbars tab, the Commands tab, and the Options tab. The Toolbars tab presents 10 standard FrontPage toolbars. You can display or hide each of these toolbars by selecting or deselecting the toolbar's associated check box.

Custom toolbar

The Commands tab contains FrontPage 2000 commands organized by Command category. Selecting a command category from the tab's scrolling Categories list box displays the commands for that category in the right pane of the dialog box.

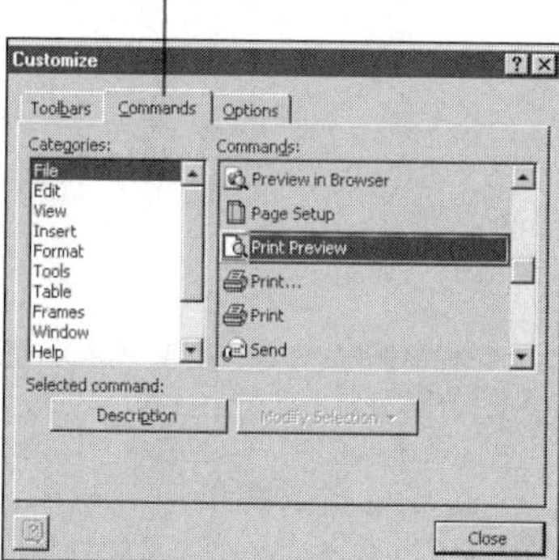

1.21

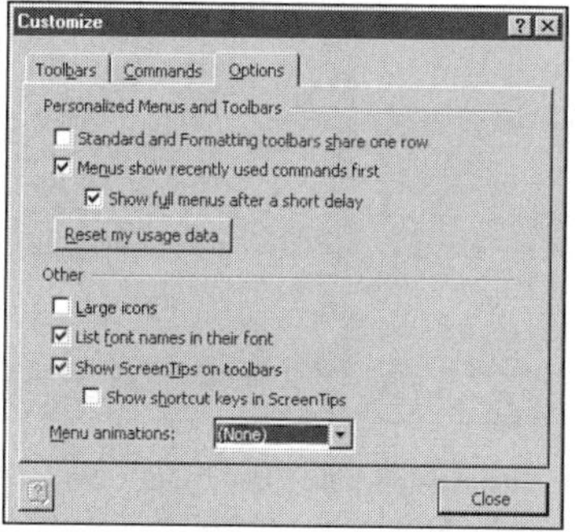

1.22

5. Select a command category from the scrolling Categories list box, and then drag a command from the scrolling Commands list box to your custom toolbar **(1.21)**.
6. Repeat step 5 for each additional command icon you want to add to your custom toolbar.
7. Use the Options tab to further customize the FrontPage 2000 interface by enabling display parameters for toolbars, menus, toolbar icon size, toolbar screen tips, and menu animation **(1.22)**.
8. Click the Close button to exit the dialog box.

TIP

Toolbars can float in the FrontPage editing window, or they can be docked along side other toolbars.

Enabling Source Control

Source control is the mechanism by which you maintain the integrity of different versions of your Web site, as you apply changes or updates. You can invoke basic source control in FrontPage using the Web Settings dialog box.

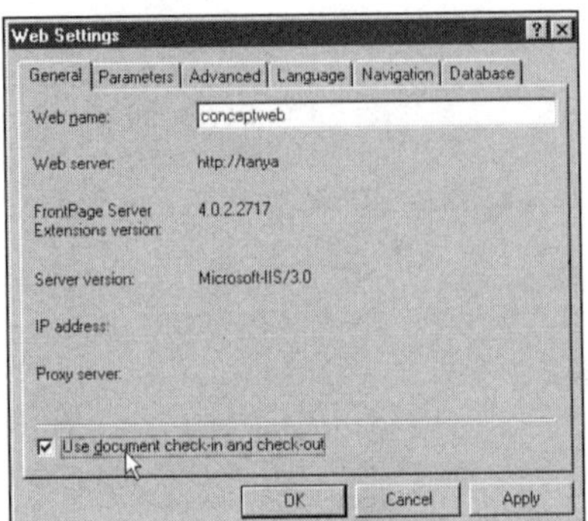

1.23

1. Choose Tools→Web Settings from the FrontPage 2000 menu bar.
2. Select the Use document check-in and check-out check box on the General tab.
3. Click OK to close the dialog box.

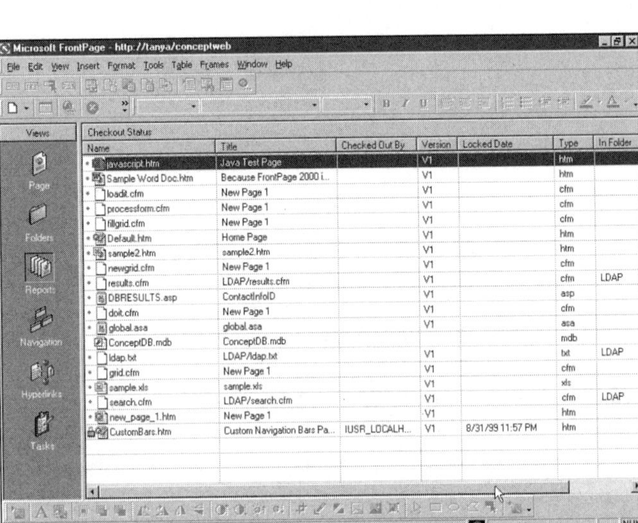

Ⓝ O T E

If you're inclined to implement a more robust change management mechanism, you might want to consider using Microsoft's Visual SourceSafe (VSS) (1.23). By using change management tools like FrontPage's source control or Microsoft's VSS, you can insure that no one else is able to make changes to the file you're working on in the process of your making changes. This feature is especially useful in environments where a Web project is being produced by multiple developers.

1.24 **If you have invoked source control, you can select View, Reports, Checkout Status to see a listing of all files that are either available for checkout or that are checked out. Files available for checkout are listed with a green dot in front of the filename. Files that are checked out are listed with a lock icon in front of the filename (1.24).**

CHAPTER 2

In this chapter you will learn how to...

- Create a New Web
- Open a Pre-Existing Web
- Import a Web
- Convert a Disk-Based Web to a Server-Based Web
- Populate a Web
- Import Web Content from Other Applications

A Web structure is a FrontPage generated folder stored on a Web server or a computer's hard drive that serves as a container for your site's content. This content is typically comprised of HTML files, graphics, multimedia, and other file types. With FrontPage 2000, you can choose from several options when it comes to establishing a Web structure. For example, you can use FrontPage's Corporate Web Wizard to build a

ESTABLISHING WEB STRUCTURES

site containing elements predesigned to support a corporate intranet. In addition, you can use the Discussion Web Wizard to create a Web structure for a threaded discussion group with article search capabilities, or you can use the Import Web Wizard to build a site from documents stored on a local or remote machine.

FrontPage 2000 Webs can be either server-based or disk-based. Server-based Webs can even be created to do information transfer over a secure connection by selecting the Secured Connection Required check box on the New dialog box. FrontPage 2000 uses the Secure Socket Layer (SSL) protocol to effect secured connections. SSL not only provides secure data transmissions, but also supports data and server authentication. SSL works by initiating a data transmission using public key encryption to set up a secure socket through which data can be transmitted. It then sends data using private key encryption, which allows the data being sent to be encrypted by the sender and decrypted by the receiver. The point of all this is that producing a FrontPage 2000 Web site begins with establishing a proper Web structure. This chapter shows you how to accomplish just that.

Creating a New Web

When it comes to creating a new Web structure, you can use a Web template or a Web wizard. If you have access to a pre-existing Web, using the Import Web Wizard is a great way to increase productivity by saving you a few development steps.

1. Choose File→New→Web to open the New dialog box **(2.1)**.
2. Select the template or wizard of your choice.
3. If you'll be developing server-based Webs, enter a URL and the name of your Web in the Specify the Location of the New Web field, under the Options section in the New dialog box. If you'll be creating disk-based Webs, enter a directory path on your hard drive and the name of your Web.
4. Click OK to close the New dialog box and create a new copy of the selected Web template. If you selected a Web wizard, click OK to close the New dialog box and follow the instructions for the Web wizard.

The Web Sites tab of the New dialog box offers a choice of nine Web templates and three Web wizards to begin your site building activity.

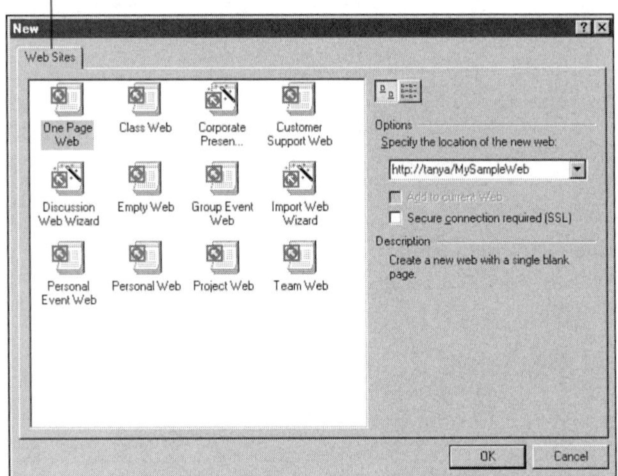

2.1

If you already have a Web structure open, and you want to add a new Web to it, check the Add to Current Web check box before you click OK to close the New dialog box.

Opening a Pre-Existing Web

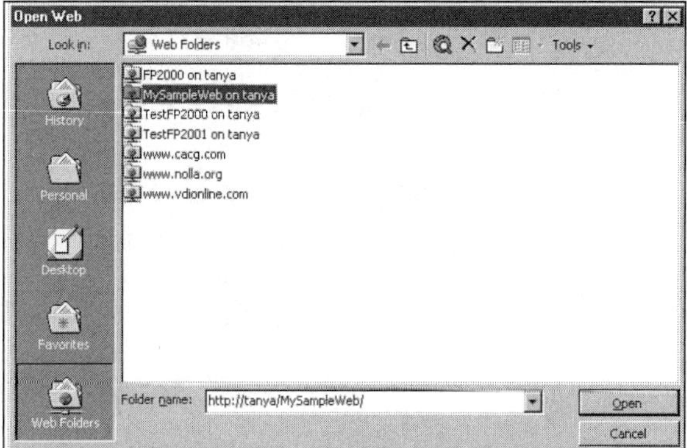

2.2 **The Choose Source panel prompts you for the file source that will be used to populate new Web structure.**

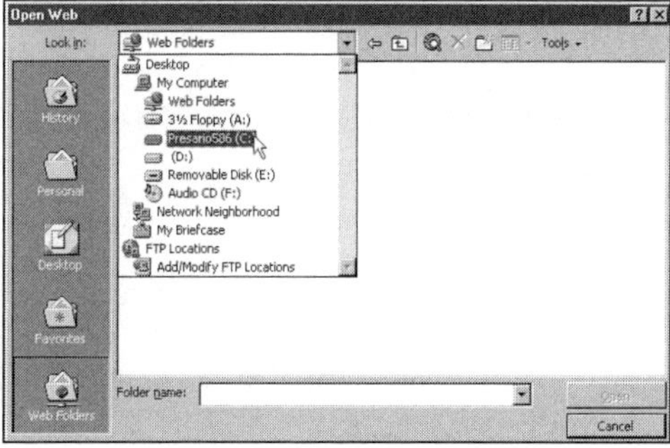

2.3

Because Web development is a dynamic process, chances are you'll be updating your site constantly. The Webs you work on may be stored on either a Web server or your local hard drive and the technique for opening from either location are outlined in the steps that follow.

1. To open a Web from a Web server, choose File→Open Web to open the Open Web dialog box (2.2).
2. Select the Web that you want to open, and then click the Open button.
3. If the Web is stored in a directory on your hard drive, in the Folder Name field of the Open Web dialog box, enter the path to the directory where your disk-based Web is stored. Or, you can navigate your local drive by using the **Look In** drop-down menu at the top of the Open Web dialog box (2.3). Click the Open button.

The Choose Download Amount panel prompts with options to limit the volume of content included in the new Web structure. You may choose to limit the content import ed to your new Web structure by number of hyperlink levels below the first page, by number of kilobytes, or by text and image file types.

Importing a Web

From time to time, you may want to reuse existing work to create a new Web. In these cases, you'll want to employ the Import Web Wizard.

1. Choose File→New→Web to open the New dialog box.
2. Select the Import Web Wizard icon from the New dialog box, enter a location for the new Web in the dialog box's Options section, and then click the OK button to open the Choose Source panel of the Import Web Wizard **(2.4)**.
3. Select or enter a file source location, and then click the Next button to open the Choose Download Amount panel **(2.5)**.
4. After establishing your content import limits, click Next and then click Finish to complete the Web import process.

The Choose Source panel prompts you for the file source that will be used to populate new Web structure.

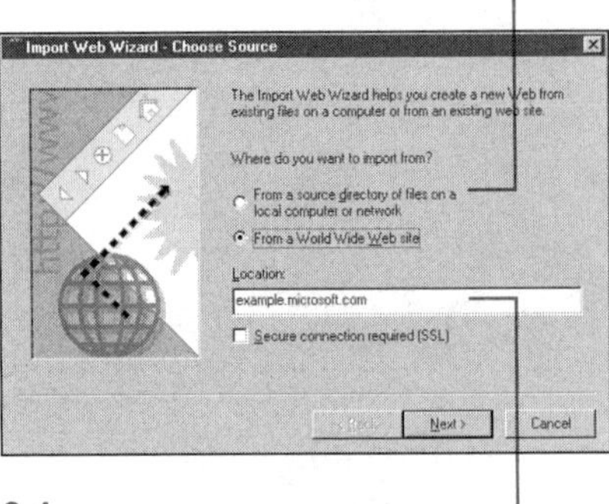

2.4

You may designate a location on your local drive or on the Web.

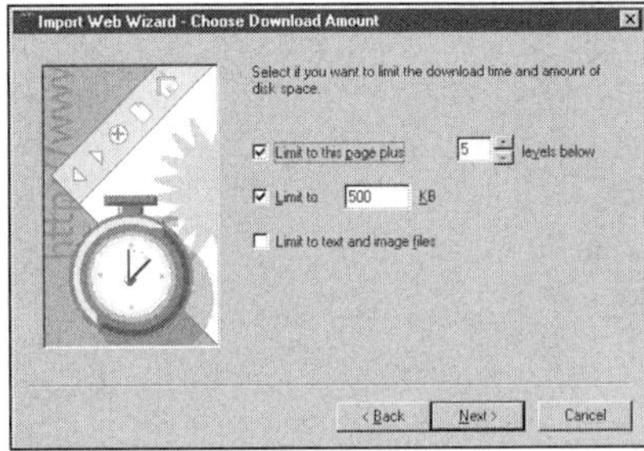

2.5

If the Web being imported is a FrontPage Web, you'll be alerted that the attributes of the imported Web will be maintained to avoid potential conflicts.

Converting a Disk-Based Web to a Server-Based Web

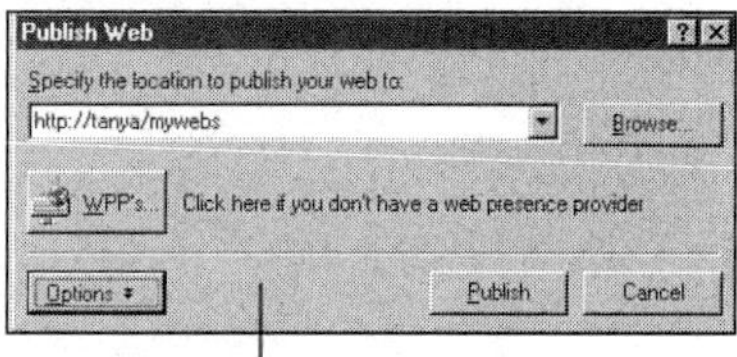

2.6 **Converting a Web or subweb to a folder may cause Web settings for the converted Web to be lost.**

If you have chosen to create disk-based Webs rather than configure your machine with a Web server, you'll need to convert your disk-based Webs to server-based Webs when you're ready to publish them to a Web server.

1. Choose File→Open Web to open the Web to be converted.
2. Choose File→Publish Web to open the Publish Web dialog box **(2.6)**.
3. Enter the URL of the destination Web server and Web name for the disk-based Web. For example, the disk-based Web `c:/myweb` would be published to `http://www.hostname.com/myweb`.
4. Click the Publish button.

FrontPage 2000 also lets you convert a folder to a Web. You can accomplish this by right-clicking a folder in Folder List view, and then selecting Convert to Web from the shortcut menu. Be advised, however, that you should NEVER convert a root folder such as a drive letter to a Web. This action could severely corrupt the drive's usability. You can also convert a server-based subweb to a disk-based Web. All you have to do is locate the server-based subweb you want to convert. Right-click the Web folder, and then select Convert to Folder.

Populating a Web

After you've established a structure for your Web site, you'll need to begin adding content. Populating a Web with content is accomplished by using FrontPage 2000 to create new Web pages, and by importing content from external sources using the Import command.

1. Open a FrontPage Web, and then choose File→New→Page, or right-click the first folder in the Folder List window and select New Page from the shortcut menu to open the New dialog box **(2.7)**.
2. Choose a page template from the General tab, and then click the OK button.
3. Choose File→Save to open the Save As dialog box **(2.8)**.
4. Enter a name for the page in the File Name field, and then click the Save button to add the new page to the Web structure hierarchy.

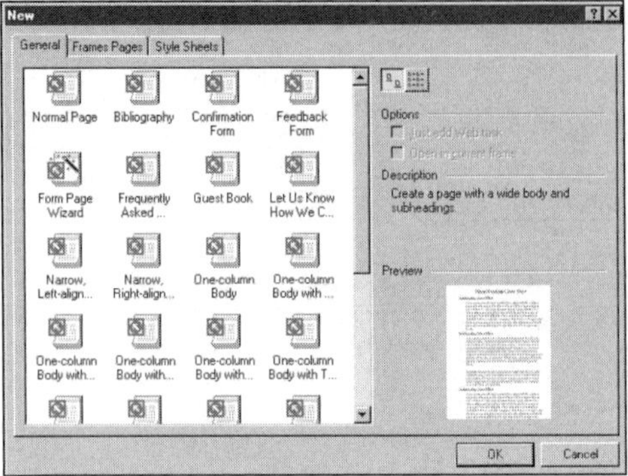

2.7

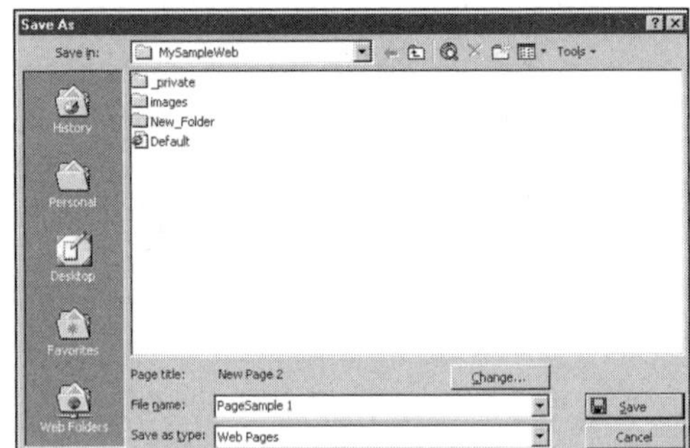

2.8

NOTE

The New dialog box for the New Page command contains three tabs: the General tab (2.7), which presents 26 page templates and 1 page template wizard; the Frames Pages tab, containing 10 frame styles, and the Style Sheets tab, containing 13 style sheet themes.

Importing Web Content from Other Applications

Use the dialog box's Look In drop-down menu to navigate to the location of the file or files you want to import.

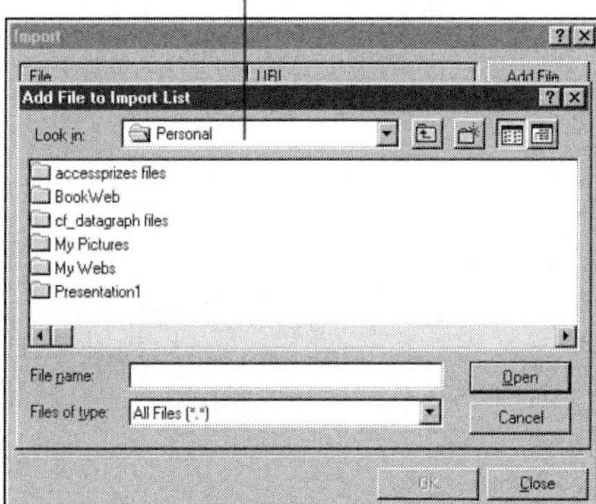

2.9

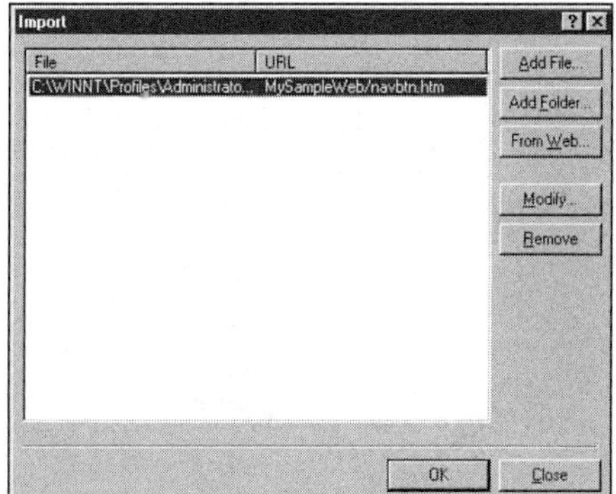

2.10

If you've created content using applications other than FrontPage 2000, you can add those files to your Web. For example, you can add a few files at a time using the Import command or use the Import Web Wizard to bring in an entire Web site.

1. Open the FrontPage Web that will host the files you want to add.
2. Choose File→Import to open the Import dialog box.
3. On the Import dialog box, click the Add File button to open the Add File to Import List dialog box **(2.9)**.
4. After locating the file or files you want to import, click a file to select it, or hold down the Ctrl key while clicking to select multiple files.
5. Click the Open button to load the files in the dialog box's list box **(2.10)**.
6. Click the OK button to have the selected content added to the Web structure hierarchy.

Clicking the Add Folder button on the Import dialog box lets you import an entire folder of content at once, while clicking the From Web button opens the Import Web Wizard.

CHAPTER 3

In this chapter you will learn how to...

Copy a Web

Rename a Web

Publish a Web Via HTTP

Publish a Web Using FTP

Generally, when you speak of managing Web structures, or Webs as these structures are called in FrontPage terminology, you're talking about those activities concerned with Web file manipulation. Specifically, these tasks involve the processes used to copy, rename, close, delete, and publish a Web structure. Each of these tasks is performed at different stages in the Web development process. For example, you might

MANAGING WEB STRUCTURES

copy a Web as a means of creating a backup of your site for disaster recovery purposes, or copy a file to export it to another location. Closing or deleting a Web or a file lets you do housekeeping as your production Web begins to evolve into a ready-to-publish production site. Publishing then makes your site available to the masses.

Be aware of the difference between a Web site and a Web structure. A Web site is a location on the Internet's World Wide Web that contains one or more Web pages. A Web structure is a reference to the way that FrontPage uses the term Web to represent a collection of Web pages and media files stored in a folder on your Web server. Therefore, visitors to your Web site are requesting pages from your Web structure.

Copying a Web

Copying a FrontPage 2000 Web is accomplished using the Publish Web command. However, a distinction should be made between using Publish Web to copy a Web and using Publish Web to in fact publish a Web to the Internet. Publish Web to copy a Web is intended to preserve the integrity of a complete Web structure and all of its content for backup purposes, while using Publish Web for publishing purposes is directed at making a fully developed and tested site available for production use.

1. Using an open FrontPage Web, choose File→Publish Web to open the Publish Web dialog box (3.1).
2. In the Specify Location to Publish Your Web To field, enter the directory path to the folder where you want to store the copied Web.
3. On the Publish Web dialog box, click the Options button to expose the available publishing options (3.2).
4. Select the option button for Publish All Pages, overwriting any already on the destination, and then click the Include Subwebs check box.
5. Click Publish to create a copy of the active Web's entire Web structure and content in a folder on your local machine.

You can also use the Publish Web command to create a new Web using the hierarchy of an existing Web.

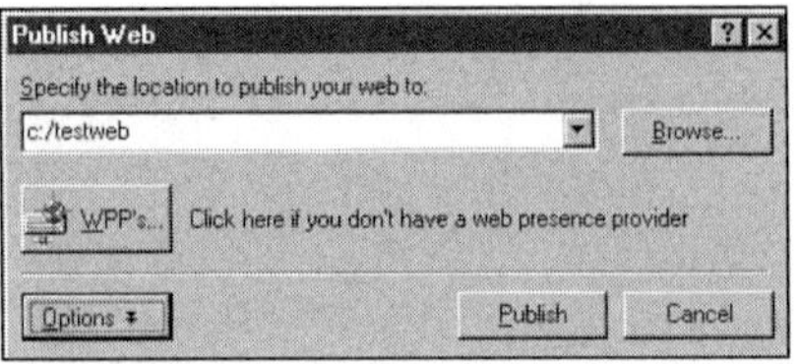

3.1

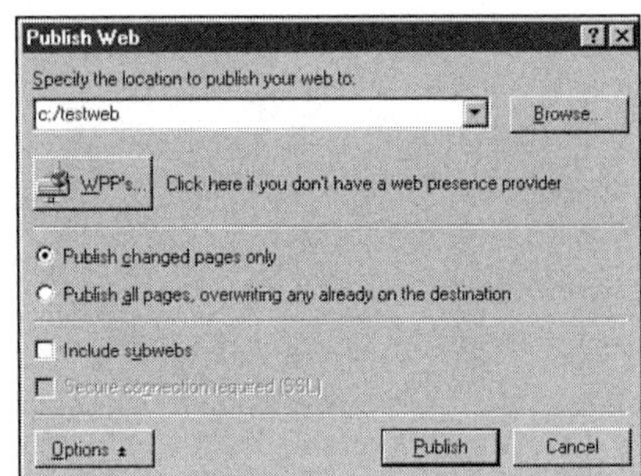

3.2

Renaming a Web

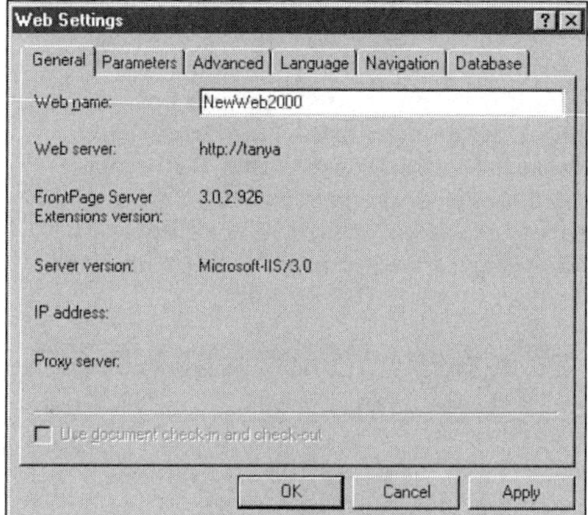

3.3

Renaming a Web is simply a technique for giving an active Web a new name. This is useful when a master Web must be duplicated and hosted in the same environment, or when your development Web has been created with a cryptic name and you want to make it more understandable to your development team. Be aware that renaming a disk-based–Web changes the Web's path on your local machine or local network, and renaming a server-based–Web changes the Web's URL on the server. In addition, if you rename a Web after publishing it, you'll need to republish the entire Web under the new name, as hyperlinks from other Web sites to your old Web will no longer work.

1. Choose Tools→Web Settings to open the Web Settings dialog box **(3.3)**.
2. On the Web Settings dialog box, click the General tab, and enter a new Web name in the Web Name field.
3. Click the Apply button to execute the name change.
4. Click the OK button to close the Web Settings dialog box.

Renaming a FrontPage Web automatically updates all internal hyperlinks and Web settings to the new name.

Publishing a Web Via HTTP

When you're ready to publish your FrontPage Web, you can do so via HTTP or via FTP. Publishing your Web via HTTP is generally used when the FrontPage Server Extensions are installed on a destination Web server.

1. Using an open FrontPage Web, choose File→Publish Web to open the Publish Web dialog box.
2. In the Specify Location to Publish Your Web To field, enter the URL of the Web server where you want to publish the completed Web.
3. On the Publish Web dialog box, click the Options button to expose the available publishing options **(3.4)**.
4. Select the option button for Publish All Pages, overwriting any already on the destination, and then click the Include Subwebs check box.
5. Click the Publish button.

When you select an option to publish only changes, or to exclude subwebs, FrontPage 2000 automatically publishes the correct pages. You don't need to worry about republishing the entire Web.

Be aware that behind the scenes of your Web lies the FrontPage Server Extensions. The FrontPage Server Extensions are three executable programs installed on your Web server when you install FrontPage 2000. These executable programs, author.exe, admin.exe, and shtml.exe run on most HTTP server platforms, and are what extends FrontPage 2000's capabilities beyond the limits of basic HTML editing.

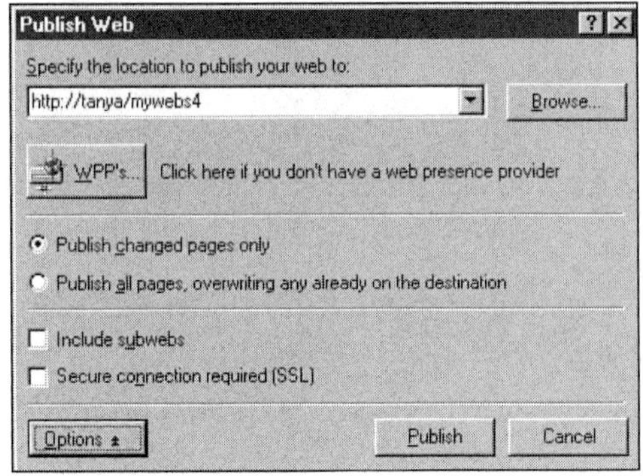

3.4

Publishing a Web Using FTP

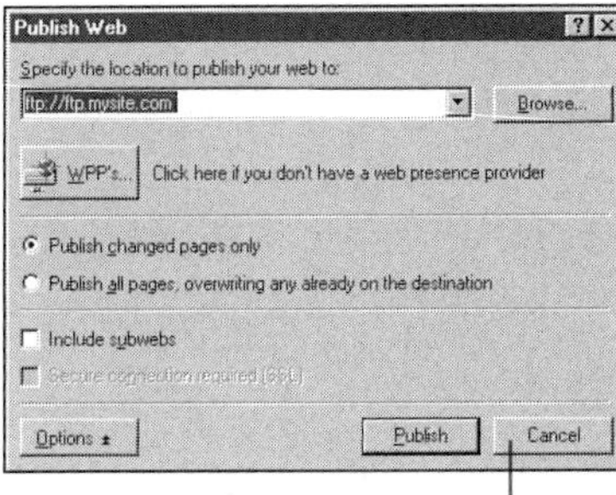

3.5 **Canceling a publishing operation prior to completion results in files that have already been published remaining on the destination Web server.**

When FrontPage Server Extensions are not installed on a destination Web server, you'll need to publish your Web using File Transfer Protocol (FTP). You may also need to publish to an FTP server, if you simply want to make the files stored in your Web available for purposes other than viewing in a browser. For example, you may want to exchange files with members of your Web development team.

1. Using an open FrontPage Web, choose File→Publish Web to open the Publish Web dialog box.
2. In the Specify Location to Publish Your Web To field, enter the location of an FTP Web server (for example, `ftp://ftp.ftpserver.com/myweb`) where you want to publish the completed Web.
3. Click the Options button to expose the available publishing options (3.5).
4. Select the option button for Publish All Pages, overwriting any already on the destination, and then click the Include Subwebs check box.
5. Click the Publish button.

CHAPTER 4

In this chapter you will learn how to...

Define Substitution Variables

Establish Access Permissions

Add Users

Customize Navigation Bar Labels

Modify Server Message Language Settings

Establish Database Connections

Web administration is the process of performing those tasks that affect the user's ability to interact with the site, and the site's response to that interaction. Typically, these tasks involve issues with configuration variables, site security, file management, server management, and database connectivity. You might be shielded from some of these activities, if you host your Web with an Internet service provider (ISP). However, it

PERFORMING WEB ADMINISTRATION

never hurts to know a little about what goes on behind the scenes. For example, take the case of establishing Web access permissions. If an ISP is hosting your Web on a Windows NT Server machine running Internet Information Server, you should understand that your ability to use FrontPage 2000's security features may be limited because user rights and privileges are likely to be controlled by your NT host. Furthermore, if you plan to build database-driven applications, understanding a little about how FrontPage 2000 supports database connections over the Web is a necessity.

Be aware that the FrontPage Server Extensions must be installed on the machine that hosts your Web site if you want to take advantage of FrontPage 2000 Web administration features such as security management. This is a consideration because using FrontPage 2000's security not only lets you establish access rights and permissions, but it also lets you encrypt all content transfer via a secure Web server. In this scenario, FrontPage 2000 can encrypt content transferred between the secure Web server and the client browser, as well as the content between the FrontPage client and the Web server.

Defining Substitution Variables

With FrontPage 2000, you have the option of using substitution variables. Substitution variables, also called configuration variables, are placeholders containing information about a Web or Web page. They are stored with the Web and are displayed at runtime when used in conjunction with Substitution Components or Form Results.

1. Choose Tools→Web Settings to open the Web Settings dialog box.
2. Choose the Parameters tab on the Web Settings dialog box **(4.1)**.
3. Click the Add button to open the Add Name and Value dialog box **(4.2)**.
4. Enter a name for the substitution variable in the Name field, and then enter a variable value in the Value field.
5. Click OK to close the Add Name and Value dialog box to add the newly defined variable to the Name/Value list box on the Parameters tab **(4.3)**.

You can delete a substitution variable by selecting it from the Parameter's tab list box, and then clicking the Remove button in the dialog box.

The Parameters tab lets you add, modify, or remove the name/value pairs that represent the contents of a substitution variable.

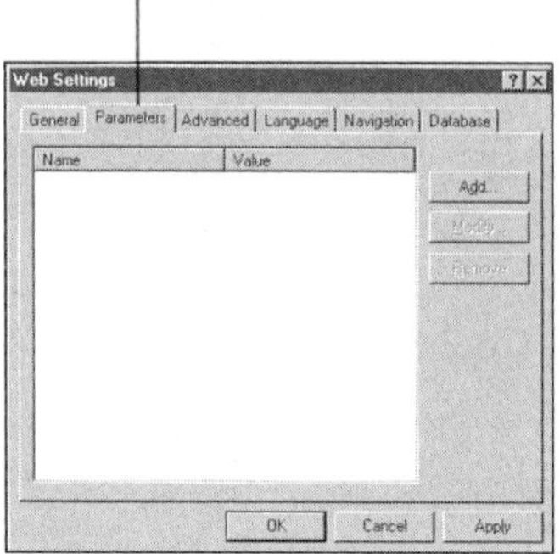

4.1

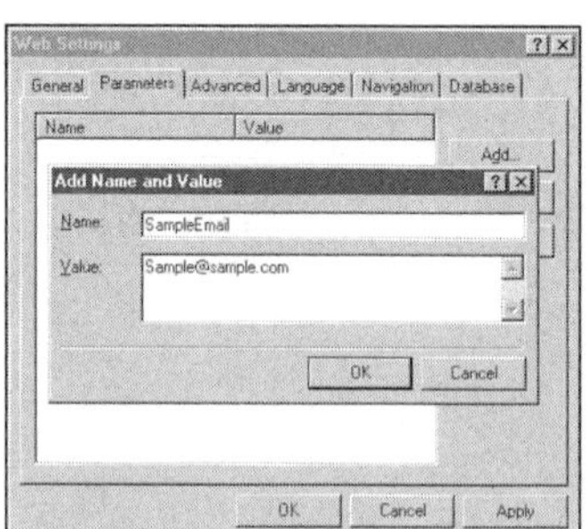

4.2

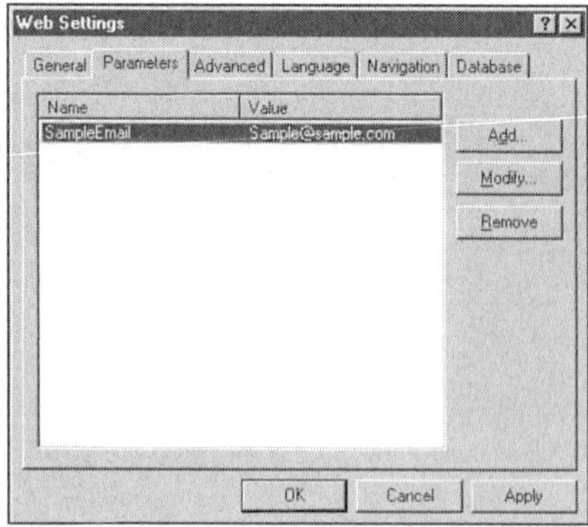

4.3

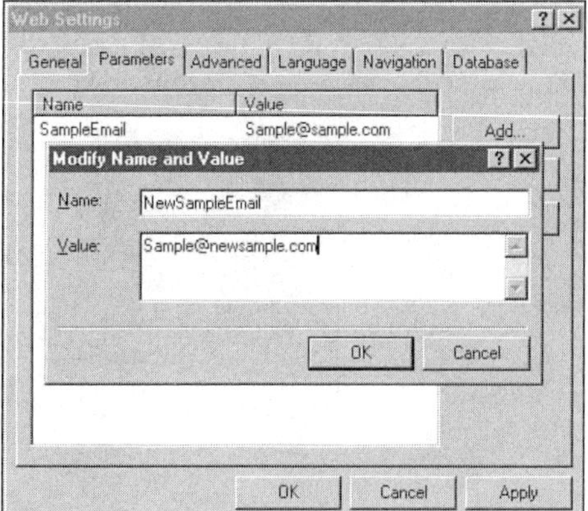

4.4

6. Click OK to close the Web Settings dialog box and complete the substitution variable definition process.
7. Select a substitution variable to modify from the Parameter's tab list box, and then click the Modify button to open the Modify Name and Value dialog box **(4.4)**.
8. Enter the changes you want to make, and then click the OK button to close the Modify Name and Value dialog box.
9. Click OK to close the Web Settings dialog box and complete the substitution variable modification process.

There are four predefined substitution variables: Author, Description, Modified By, and Page URL. The values for Author, Description, and Modified by: correspond to the values Created by, Modified by, Comments, and Location. These corresponding values may be viewed by right-clicking a filename in the Page View Folder List, and then choosing Properties. The Location value is shown on the General tab of the Properties dialog box, while the other values are shown on the Summary tab of the Properties dialog box. The Comments scrolling list box is typically blank.

Establishing Access Permissions

The extent to which others are authorized to view and interact with your Web is determined by the access permissions that you establish. If you're an ISP or an intranet administrator, you'll typically establish Web server access permissions as part of your NT Server security setup. Consequently, if you want to take advantage of FrontPage 2000's security features, you'll need to retain Administrator privileges to your hosting Web server.

1. Choose Tools→Security→ Permissions to open the Permissions dialog box **(4.5)**.
2. If you choose to establish access permissions by group rather than having the active Web inherit the permission parameters of its parent Web, select the Use Unique Permissions for This Web option button located on the Settings tab **(4.6)**, and then select the Groups tab **(4.7)**.

NOTE

The Permissions dialog box typically contains three tabs: the Settings tab seen in Figure 4.5, which lets you define root Web access privileges for all users or unique access privileges for specific users; the Groups tab, which lets you add, edit, or remove specific user categories; and the Users tab, which lets you add, edit, or remove specific users by name.

If the active Web is the Web server's root Web, the Settings tab will not appear on the Permissions dialog box. This is because the root Web already has unique permissions.

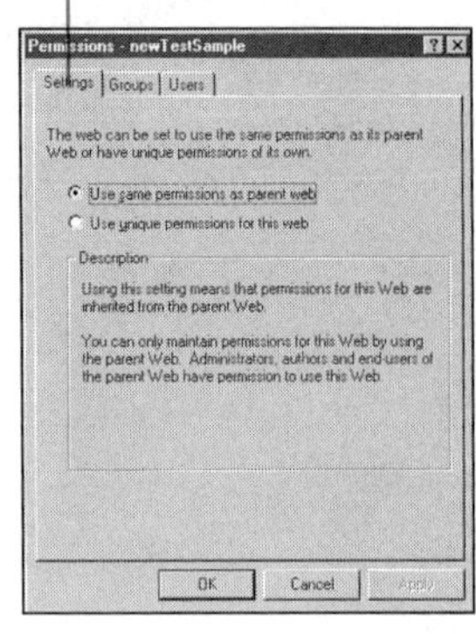

4.5

You can remove a specific user group by selecting it from list box on the Groups tab, and then clicking the Remove button.

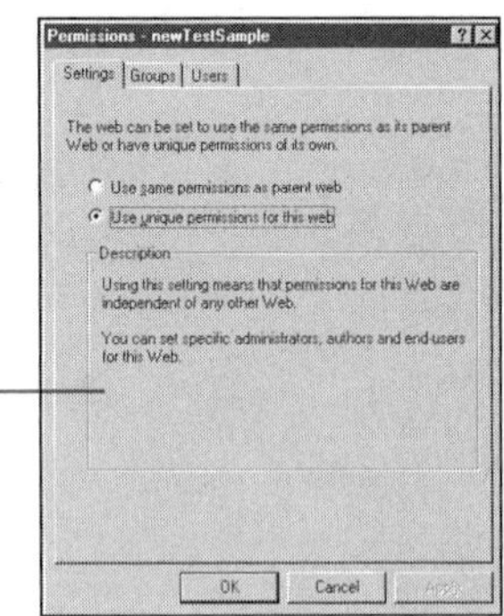

4.6

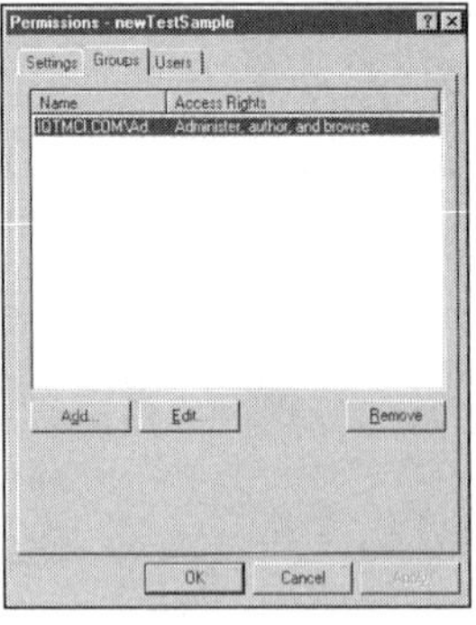

4.7

Just as individuals can be assigned specific user access rights and privileges/permissions, multiple users requiring the same access rights and privileges/permissions can be configured as a named set called a Group. User groups are typically built by the Web administrator.

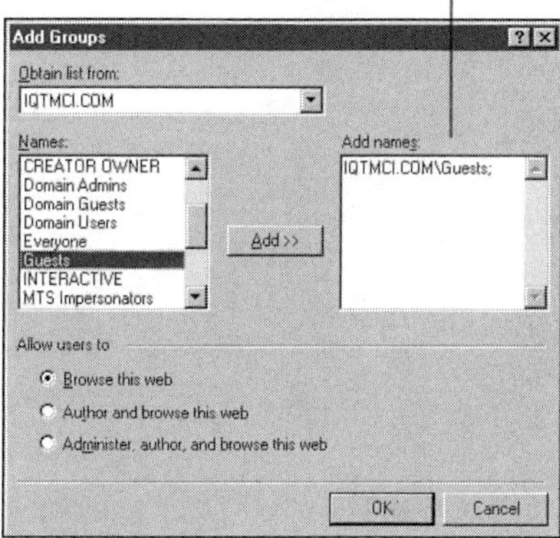

4.8

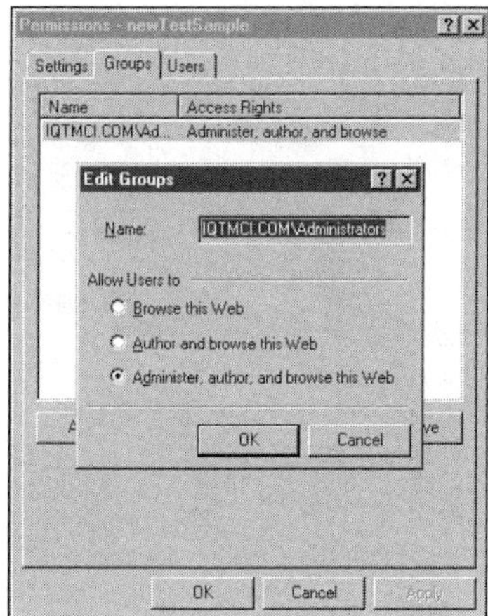

4.9

3. Select the Add button on the Groups tab to open the Add Groups dialog box (4.8).
4. Select a specific user's group from the Name list box.
5. Click the Add button to have the group name appear under the Add Names list box.
6. Click the OK button to close the Add Groups dialog box, and then click the OK button to close the Permissions dialog box.
7. To change the permissions assigned to a specific user group, select the Edit button on the Groups tab to open the Edit Groups dialog box (4.9), make your permission reassignments, and then click the OK button to close the Edit Groups dialog box.

NOTE

Under Windows NT, by establishing your server as an NTFS file system, you gain the ability to control user access down to the file level, the ability to recover data in the event of a system shutdown, and the ability to implement case-sensitive filenames. I highly recommend doing your serious Web development on the Windows NT platform. In addition, NT servers running Internet Information Server gain default Administrator access to FrontPage 2000 Webs.

Adding Users

You can also assign permissions to individual users who comprise a user group or who stand alone. If you're running Windows NT and are connected to a local area network, chances are you'll be able to assign user permissions by selecting names from existing NT network user accounts.

1. Choose Tools→Security→Permissions to open the Permissions dialog box.
2. Select the Use Unique Permissions for This Web option button located on the Settings tab, and then select the Users tab, or select the Users tab directly, if you're working with a subweb **(4.10)**.
3. Select the Add button on the Users tab to open the Add Users dialog box **(4.11)**.
4. Select a specific user from the Name list box.
5. Click the Add button to have the username appear under the Add Names list box.
6. Click the OK button to close the Add Users dialog box, and then click the OK button to close the Permissions dialog box.

To change the permissions assigned to a specific user, select the Edit button on the Users tab (4.12), make your permission re-assignments, and then click the OK button.

You can remove a specific user with access permissions to your Web by selecting the user from the Users tab list box and clicking the Remove button.

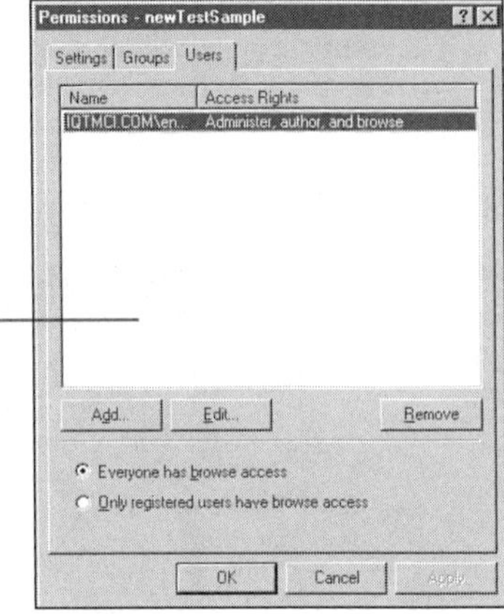

4.10

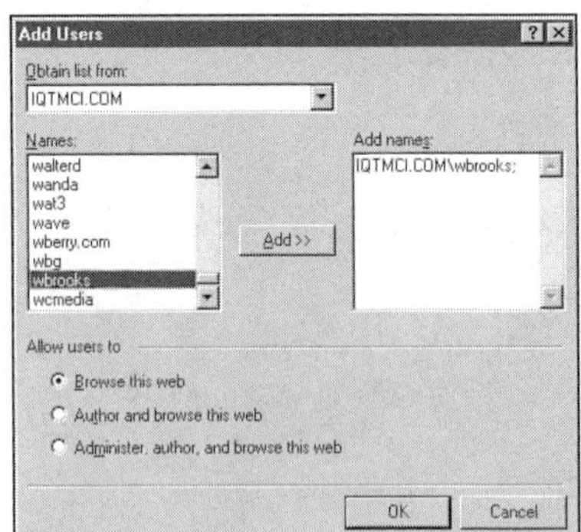

4.11

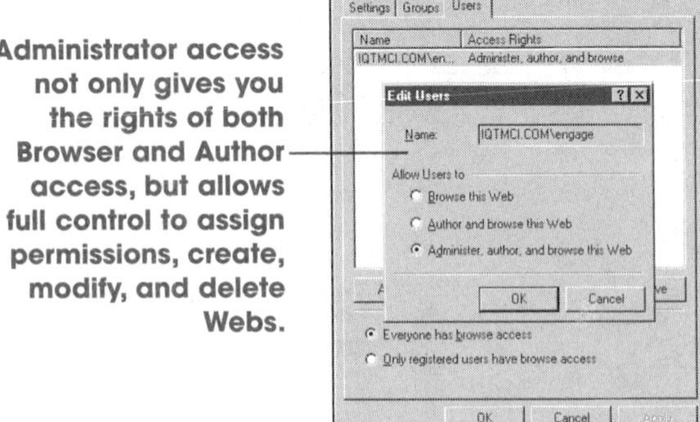

4.12

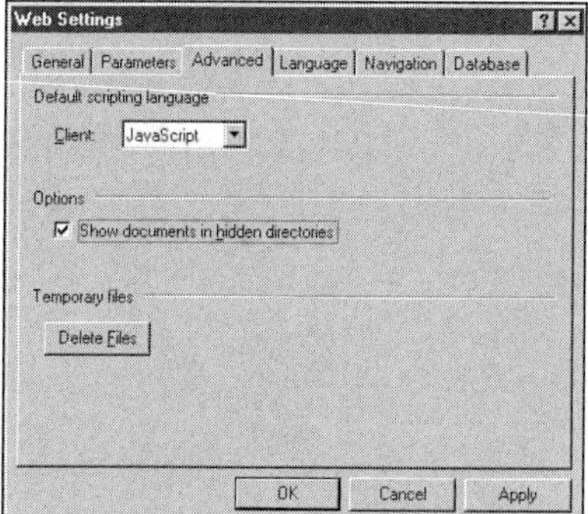

4.13

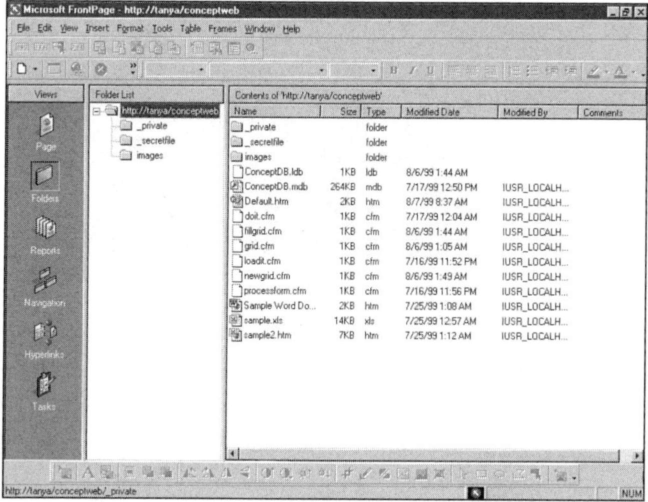

4.14

In a FrontPage Web, if an underscore precedes a folder name, the folder and its contents, although available for browsing, are not visible using FrontPage views. The exception to the "available for browsing" rule is the _private folder generated each time you create a new FrontPage 2000 Web. Hidden directories like _private and others that you create are generally used as housekeeping folders for the files that support your Web front-end. For instance, themes, borders, and Java class files are stored in hidden directories.

1. Choose Tools→Web Settings to open the Web Settings dialog box.
2. Select the Advanced tab **(4.13)**.
3. Select the Show Documents in Hidden Directories check box, and then click OK to close the Web Settings dialog box. Completing this step causes any hidden folders to be visible in FrontPage Folder view **(4.14)**.

Navigation view lets you see your Web graphically as an object hierarchy, while allowing you to manipulate its contents in Folder view. Access Navigation view by choosing View→Folders.

Customizing Navigation Bar Labels

FrontPage 2000 provides a set of four textual default labels when navigation bars are applied to a page. However, you can customize these default labels to fit your unique design needs. Customizing the labels of your navigation bars can be useful if you want to maintain a certain thematic context for your Web. For example, if your site were of a baseball-related motif, Home might be named Home Plate or Up might be labeled Pop Up.

1. Choose Tools→Web Settings to open the Web Settings dialog box.
2. Choose the Navigation tab **(4.15)**.
3. Change the default labels to labels of your choice, and then click OK **(4.16)**.

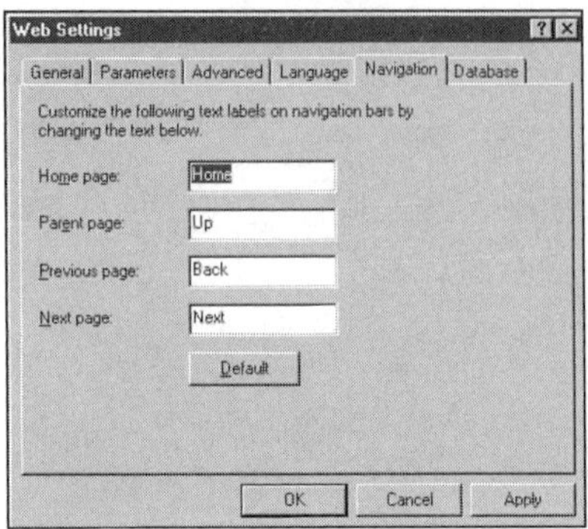

4.15

4.16

FrontPage 2000 generates navigation bars automatically when you're working with a Web as a whole, not when you're working with individual pages. You'll find more about navigation bars in Chapter 6, "Developing Static Web Pages."

Modifying Server Message Language Settings

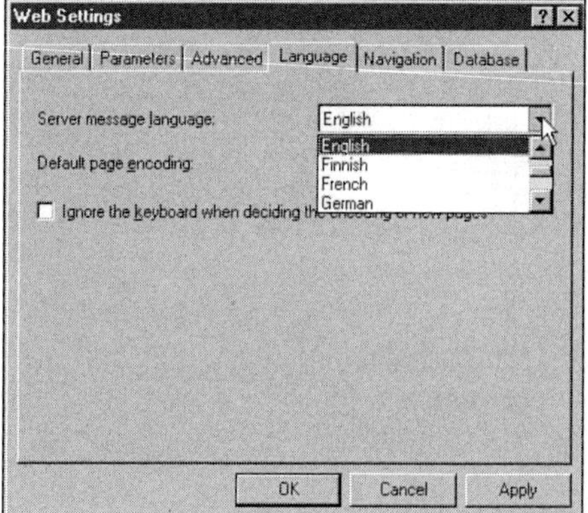

4.17

FrontPage 2000 is able to present server messages in 15 different languages. You can set the language that you want to have these messages presented in by using the Web Settings tool.

1. Choose Tools→Web Settings to open the Web Settings dialog box.
2. Choose the Language tab (4.17).
3. Select the language of your choice from the Server Message Language drop-down menu, and then click OK.

Language-specific messages also include error messages and form validation warnings.

You can create Web pages in a different language by changing the keyboard. Changing the keyboard setting in the Windows Control Panel automatically sets the language and encoding for new pages. By installing additional keyboards and code pages, FrontPage 2000 is able to create pages in other languages that your computer might not otherwise support. Default page encoding is set for each Web, and is used by FrontPage 2000 to specify the initial language encoding for new pages, if the encoding is compatible with the current keyboard setting. If the encoding is not compatible with the keyboard, the keyboard's encoding is used instead.

Establishing Database Connections

Database connections specify the name, location, and type of database that you want to access via the Web. FrontPage lets you establish a database connection using the Database Results Wizard; however, you can also create a database connection manually by following the steps outlined here.

1. Choose Tools→Web Settings to open the Web Settings dialog box.
2. Choose the Database tab **(4.18)**.
3. Select the Add button on the Database tab to open the New Database Connection dialog box **(4.19)**.
4. Select the type of connection you want to establish, and then click OK.

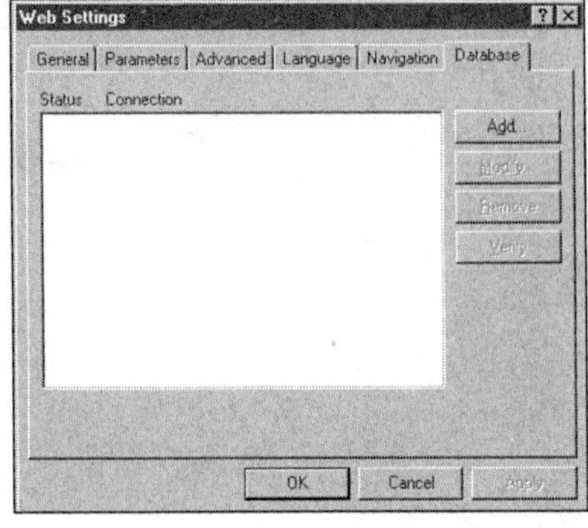

4.18

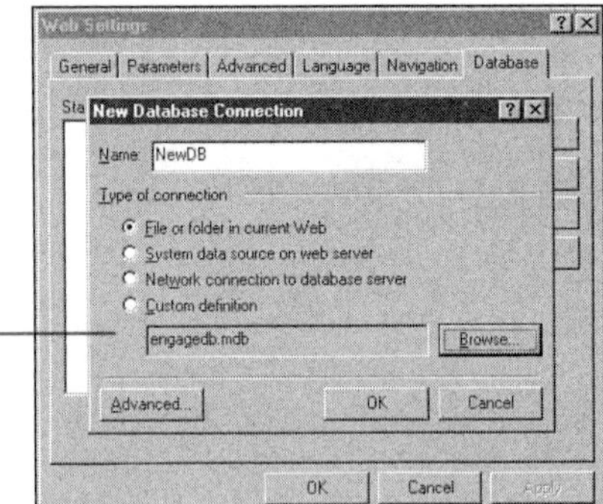

Using a custom database connection definition calls for you to enter the path of a user-defined database connection definition. User-defined connection definitions typically include parameter settings that dictate how long an open connection will remain available before timing out.

4.19

FrontPage 2000 provides several ways to establish a database connection—using a file or folder in the current Web, using a System Data Source on a Web server, using a Network connection to a database server, or using a custom database connection definition.

CHAPTER 5

In this chapter you will learn how to...

Create New Tasks

Associate Tasks to Web Pages

Prioritize Tasks

Modify Tasks

Perform Tasks

Mark Task Completions

Delete Tasks

When you're ready to begin adding content to your Web, doing so in an organized fashion can be beneficial. FrontPage 2000 facilitates an organized Web development process by allowing you to identify, assign, prioritize, and maintain a list of development activities using its integrated task management features. Users of previous FrontPage versions will find the capabilities available via Tasks view are actually

MANAGING WEB DEVELOPMENT TASKS

enhancements to the old To Do List feature. For example, Tasks view provides a status of the items on the task list, as well as a date/time stamp indicating when the task was last modified. Each of these enhancements is designed to support a more collaborative approach to Web development by providing data that informs other developers about the state of a task being performed, and the amount of work that remains to be done. As you begin to work in Tasks view, you'll discover how its accessiblity and versatility make it very easy to use. You'll find that FrontPage 2000 lets you add new tasks to the Tasks view automatically as it performs certain processing functions. You'll be able to sort tasks by Tasks view column name, and even access a list of uncompleted tasks via Report view. This chapter shows you how to use FrontPage 2000's task management features to organize your Web development activities.

Creating New Tasks

In FrontPage 2000, *tasks* are defined as items associated with a Web that represent the actions you must take to complete or maintain that Web.

1. Open a FrontPage 2000 Web, and then choose File→New→Task to open the New Task dialog box **(5.1)**.
2. Enter a name for the activity you want to perform in the Task Name field.
3. Enter a name or title for the person responsible for performing the task in the Assigned to field, or select a previously entered name from the field's drop-down menu.
4. Select an option button indicating the task priority from the Priority section.
5. Enter a brief description of the task being recorded in the Description text box.
6. Click the OK button.

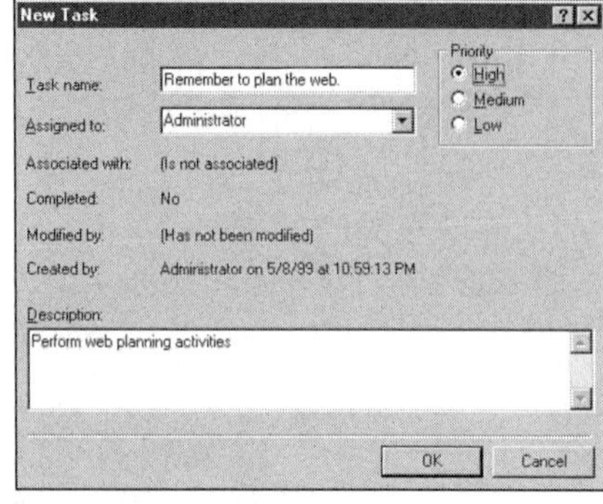

5.1

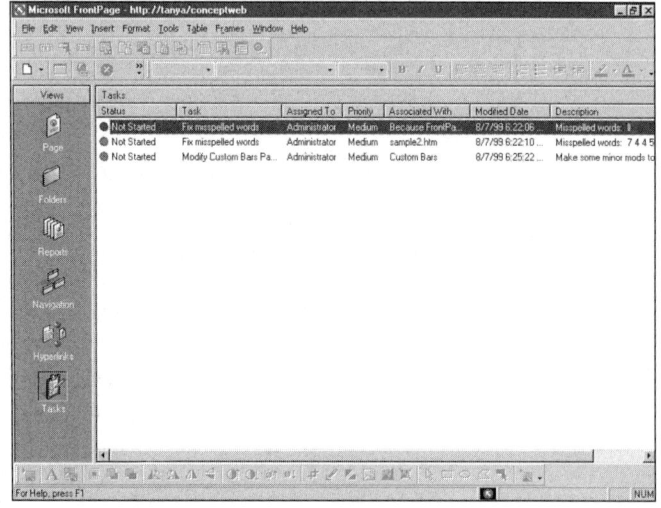

5.2

Tasks view gives you a list of tasks to be performed for your Web (5.2). Tasks displayed are listed by status, task identifier, assigned party, priority, related associations, date modified, and task description. Tasks view is accessible by choosing View→Tasks from the FrontPage 2000 menu bar or by clicking on the Tasks icon from the View bar.

Associating Tasks to Web Pages

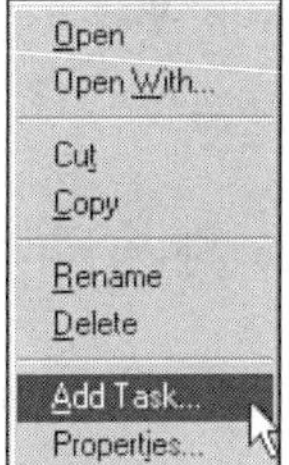

5.3

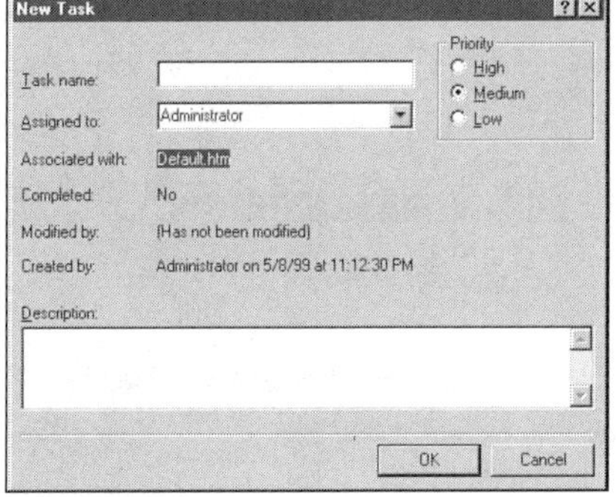

5.4

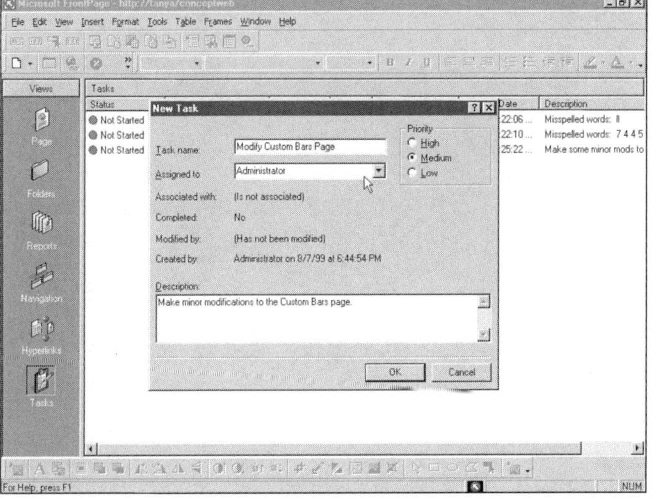

5.5

Tasks are usually associated with activity for a given Web page, and serve to organize the scope of work that must be performed to complete an entire Web development project. When it comes to associating Web development tasks, running a spell check or performing a verification of hyperlinks lets you assign tasks as a result of errors found with either of these processes. This section outlines the general steps required to associate any given task with a Web page.

1. Open a FrontPage 2000 Web in Page view, right-click a specific Web page in Page view's Folder List pane, and then choose Add Task from the shortcut menu **(5.3)** to open the New Task dialog box. Notice that the dialog box item labeled Associated with contains the name of the page you selected **(5.4)**.

2. Enter a name for the activity you want to perform in the Task name field **(5.5)**.

continues

Associating Tasks to Web Pages continued

3. Enter a name or title for the person responsible for performing the task in the Assigned to field.
4. Select an option button indicating the task priority from the Priority section.
5. Enter a brief description of the task being recorded in the Description text box.
6. Click the OK button.
7. Select the Tasks icon on the Views bar to see that a page is now associated with the task you just created (5.6).

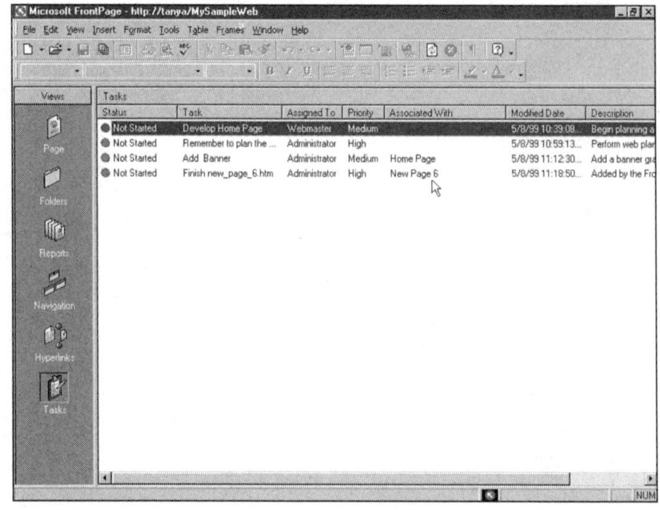

5.6

You can also create a new task when you first create a page by selecting the Just Add Web Task check box on the New dialog box, and then clicking the OK button.

In Tasks view, double-click any task with a status of Not Started to open the Task Details dialog box (5.7). Click the Start Task button to launch the page associated with the given task. However, be aware that if you open the Task Details dialog box for a task that has no associated page, the Start Task button does not appear (5.8).

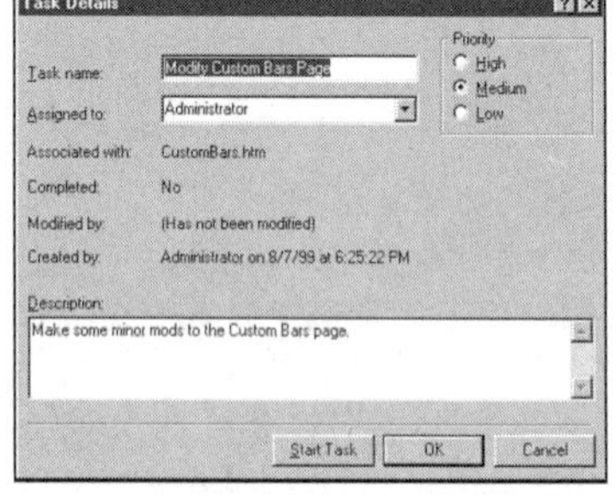

5.7

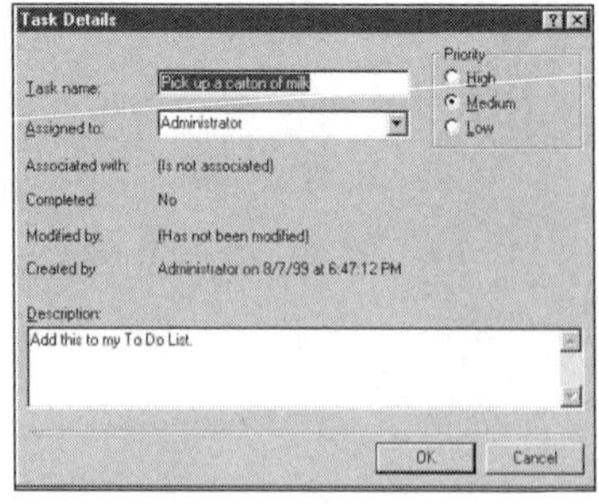

5.8

Prioritizing and Modifying Tasks

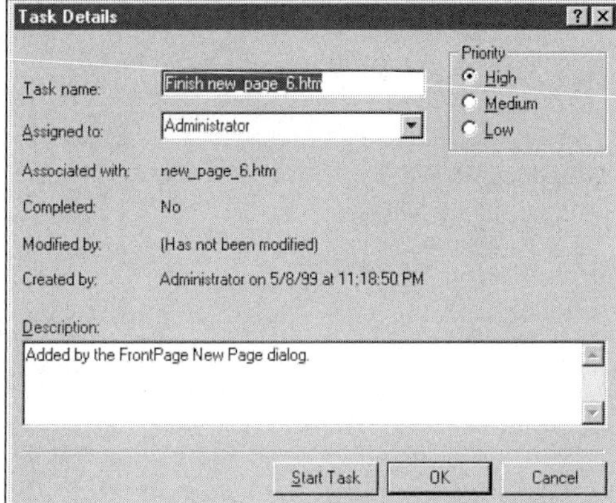

5.9

5.10

FrontPage 2000 lets you prioritize tasks as High, Medium, and Low when you create a new task; however, you can also modify the priority of a current task:

1. Select the Tasks icon on the Views bar of the FrontPage 2000 user interface.
2. Right-click a listed task, and then choose Edit Task from the shortcut menu to open the Task Details dialog box **(5.9)**.
3. Select an option button indicating the task priority from the Priority section.

FrontPage 2000 lets you modify a task and its assignment, making it simple to keep Web development projects organized and current among multiple team members.

1. Select the Tasks icon on the Views bar of the FrontPage 2000 user interface, right-click a listed task, and then choose Edit Task from the shortcut menu to open the Task Details dialog box.
2. Enter a new name or title for the person responsible for performing the task in the Assigned to field, or select a previously entered name from the field's drop-down menu **(5.10)**.

Performing Tasks and Marking Task Completions

When you're ready to perform a task listed under the Tasks view task list, perform the following steps:

1. Select the Tasks icon on the Views bar of the FrontPage 2000 user interface to open the task list.
2. Right-click a listed task with a status of Not Started **(5.11)**, and then choose Start Task from the shortcut menu to open the task's associated Web page.

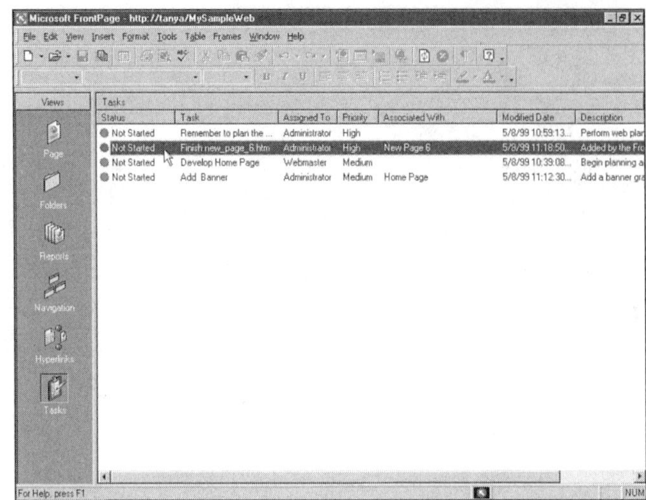

5.11

When you've completed a task on the Tasks view task list, you can mark that task as complete by performing the following steps:

1. Select the Tasks icon on the Views bar of the FrontPage 2000 user interface.
2. Right-click a listed task, and then choose Mark As Completed from the shortcut menu. Performing this action changes the status of the task from Not Started preceded by a red dot to Completed preceded by a green dot **(5.12)**.

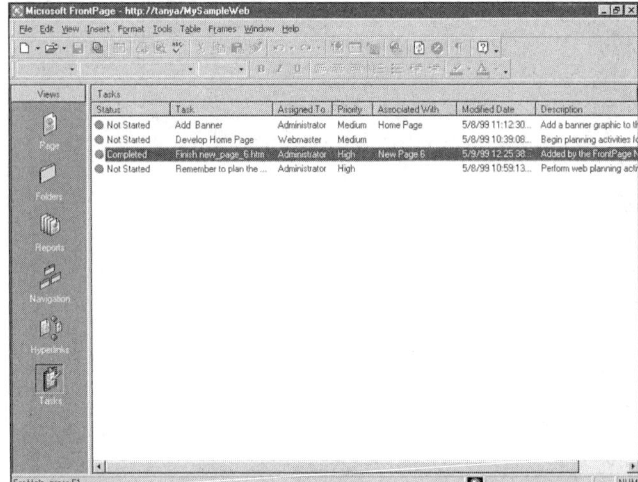

5.12

Deleting Tasks

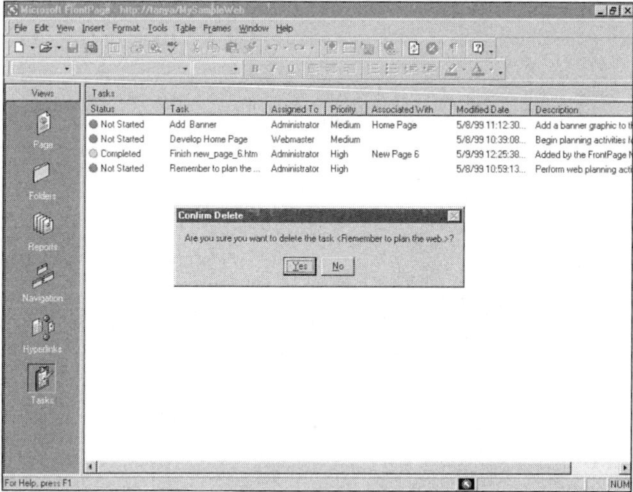

5.13

Should you ever want to remove a task from the Tasks view task list, you can perform the following steps:

1. Select the Tasks icon on the Views bar of the FrontPage 2000 user interface, right-click a listed task, and then choose Delete from the shortcut menu to open the Confirm Delete dialog box **(5.13)**.
2. Click the Yes button on the Confirm Delete dialog box to remove the selected task from the list.

You can hide completed tasks rather than delete them by right-clicking inside the Tasks view window and then unchecking the Show Talk History option on the shortcut menu.

Tasks listed on the Tasks view task list may be ordered by status, task name, assigned party, priority, associated page, date modified, or description. You can sort the task list by clicking any of the column headers in the Tasks window.

CHAPTER 6

In this chapter you will learn how to...

- Add Horizontal Lines and Line Breaks
- Apply and Modify Themes
- Modify Colors in a Theme
- Modify Graphics in a Theme
- Modify Text Styles in a Theme
- Apply Cascading Style Sheets
- Apply Shared Borders and Navigation Bars
- Create HTML Tag Styles
- Customize HTML Formatting Preferences
- Display HTML Tags in Page View
- Edit HTML
- Apply a Background Color or Picture
- Apply Comments
- Preview a Web Page

The foundation of any Web site is the content that comprises it. In its formative stages, this content most often takes the form of static Web pages designed to provide information to the user about the site. Sometimes referred to as brochure pages because of their early use as Web-based brochures. Static Web pages focus on presenting information in a variety of interesting layouts, rather than emphasizing

DEVELOPING STATIC WEB PAGES

interactivity or data processing. These pages typically make use of design features such as background colors or pictures, horizontal lines of different sizes, varying font styles and sizes, and combinations of page elements applied as a theme to enhance the message the page is attempting to deliver. FrontPage 2000 offers several new features to enhance the development of static pages such as absolute positioning and layering of page elements, support for Cascading Style Sheets to facilitate consistent look and feel between pages, and Shared Borders to assist in the development of Web navigation schemes. This chapter shows you how to use FrontPage 2000 and its page enhancement features to develop static Web pages.

Adding Horizontal Lines and Line Breaks

When developing a Web page, horizontal lines help to structure your page layout by dividing the page into discrete sections. Page breaks, on the other hand, let you accomplish much the same using whitespace. By following the steps outlined here, you can quickly apply and customize horizontal lines on a page using FrontPage 2000.

1. Open or create a page in Page view.
2. With the blinking cursor in the Editing window, choose Insert→Horizontal Line to apply the line to the page **(6.1)**.
3. Select the line, and then choose Format→Properties to open the Horizontal Line Properties dialog box **(6.2)**.
4. Enter a value in the Width field to specify the span of the line from left to right.
5. Enter a value in the Height field to specify the thickness of the line from top to bottom.

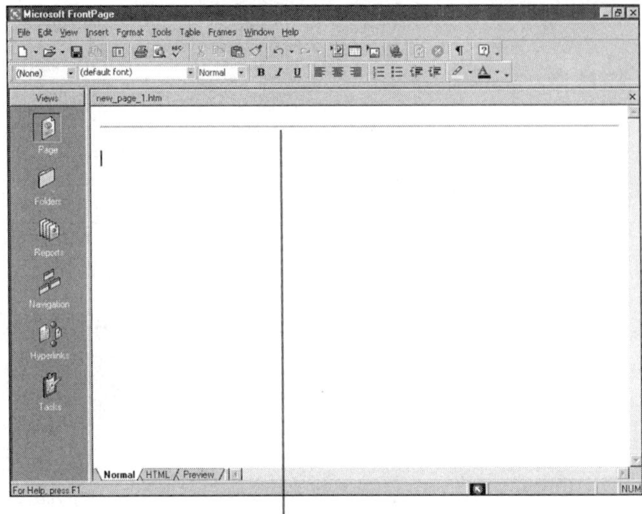

6.1 **You can right-click the line and select Horizontal Line Properties from the shortcut menu to access the Horizontal Line Properties dialog box.**

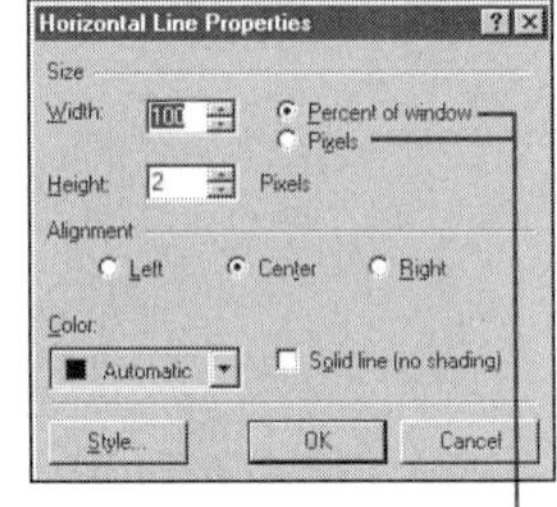

6.2 **You can adjust horizontal line width by percent of window used or in pixels, by selecting the appropriate option button.**

You can also use the indent tools to size the horizontal line. Simply select the horizontal line, and then click the Increase Indent icon on the Format toolbar to extend the line or the Decrease Indent icon to shorten the line.

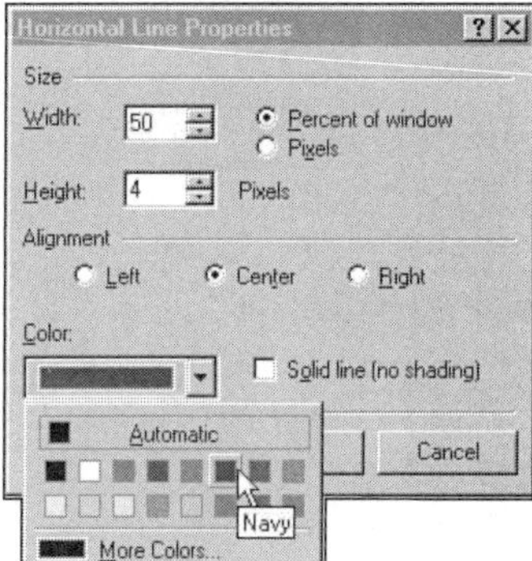

6.3

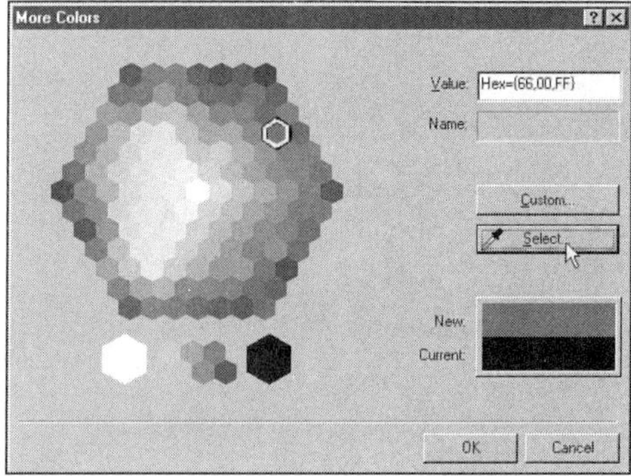

6.4

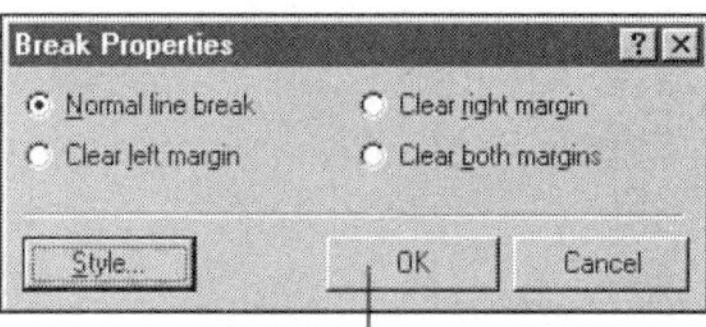

6.5

You could press the Enter key for a full line break or press Shift + the Enter key to add a line break without leaving whitespace.

6. Select how the horizontal line is positioned on the page by choosing from the three alignment options: Left, Center, and Right.
7. Select a line color by picking from the color options on the Color drop-down menu **(6.3)**, or select a custom color by selecting the More Colors option to open the More Colors dialog box **(6.4)**.
8. Select the Solid line (no shading) check box to prevent FrontPage 2000 from adding shading to the applied horizontal line, and then click the OK button.
9. To add a line break between horizontal lines, choose Insert→Break to open the Break Properties dialog box **(6.5)**, choose the break type, and then click OK.

The alignment setting only works if the width of the horizontal line is less than 100%.

The Style button lets you apply or change inline styles for a specific page element. An inline style is a method of applying Cascading Style Sheet properties and values to an element on a page like a horizontal line. This is a new feature in FrontPage 2000.

Applying and Modifying Themes

A theme is a set of predesigned graphics and page elements used to apply a consistent look and feel to the pages and navigation bars in your FrontPage Webs.

1. Open a FrontPage 2000 Web.
2. Choose Format→Theme, or right-click the page and select Theme from the shortcut menu to open the Themes dialog box **(6.6)**.
3. Select an option button to have the theme applied to all pages or only to a selected page or pages.
4. Select the theme of your choice from the scrolling list box.
5. Select the theme customization check box of your choice to make theme colors more vivid, to use dynamic graphic elements for effect, to use a predefined background image, or to have the theme applied using a Cascading Style Sheet.
6. Click the OK button to apply the theme **(6.7)** and close the Themes dialog box.

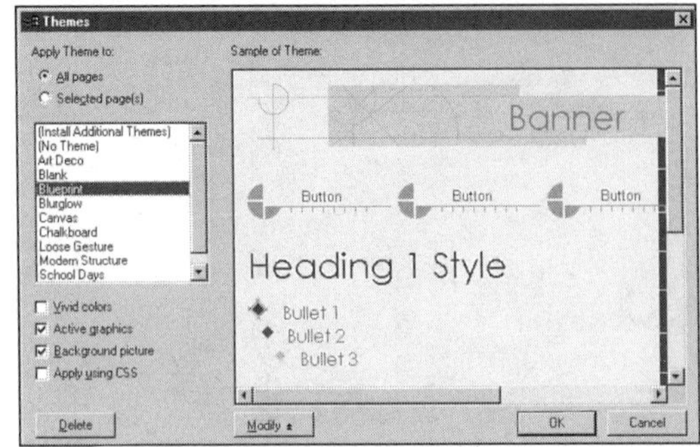

6.6 **With the general steps here, you can apply any one of FrontPage 2000's 50 plus themes to an existing Web.**

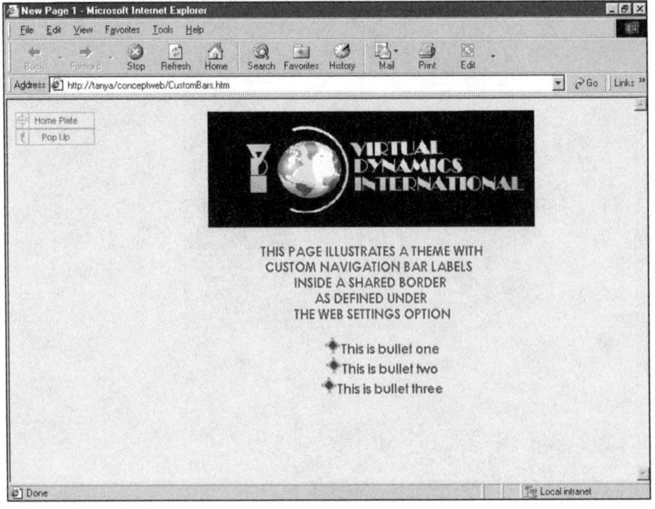

6.7

Currently, both IE4 and Netscape Navigator support the Level One Cascading Style Sheet standard. This standard defines the specification for style sheet notation, and the syntax for formatting Web page elements like fonts, borders, margins, and so on.

Modifying Colors in a Theme

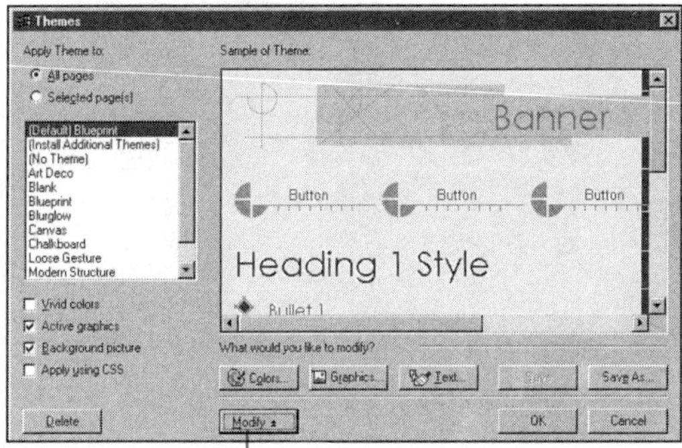

6.8

The Modify button presents a button bar that lets you modify a theme's color scheme, the image and font of its background graphic, and text style. You can also save the changes made to the theme, and see a dynamic preview. Theme editing is a new feature in FrontPage 2000.

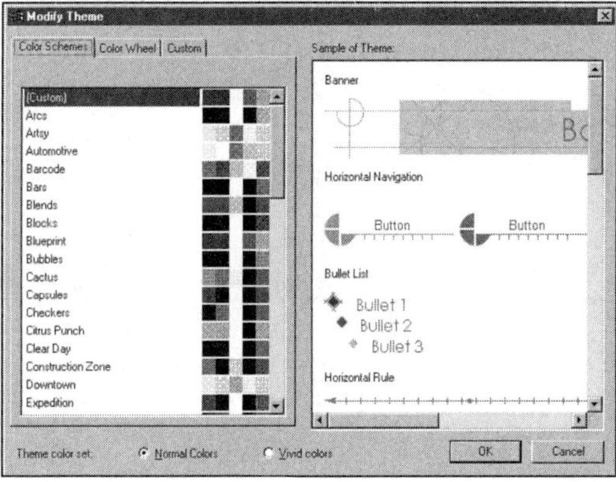

6.9

If you decide to customize a theme color or background, understand that you can define either a background color or a background image for a theme, but not both. In addition, you need to make the choice about background prior to doing any other theme customization. When you modify a theme, save your changes to a new theme, as you cannot overwrite a predefined theme.

1. Open a FrontPage 2000 Web containing a theme.
2. Choose Format→Theme, or right-click the page and select Theme from the shortcut menu to open the Themes dialog box.
3. Select the Modify button on the Themes dialog box to display the button bar of available modification options **(6.8)**.
4. Select the Colors button on the Themes dialog box to display the Modify Theme dialog box **(6.9)**.
5. Modify a theme's default color scheme by selecting an alternative from the Color Schemes tab (shown in Figure 6.9) scrolling list box, and then clicking the OK button.

continues

You can modify a theme without opening a Web, by selecting Format→Themes from the FrontPage 2000 menu bar.

Modifying Colors in a Theme continued

6. Modify a theme's default color mix and brightness by selecting the Color Wheel tab **(6.10)** on the Modify Theme dialog box. Use the mouse to move the color pointer inside the color wheel to select a new color, and to move the Brightness adjustment slider.
7. Click the OK button to apply the color mix and brightness adjustments.
8. Modify the color of a theme's individual page elements by selecting the Custom tab **(6.11)** on the Modify Theme dialog box, choosing an item and color from both the Item drop-down menu and the Color drop-down menu, and then clicking the OK button.

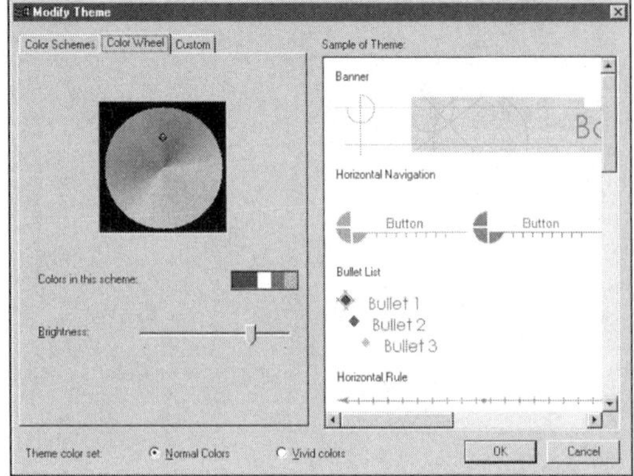

6.10

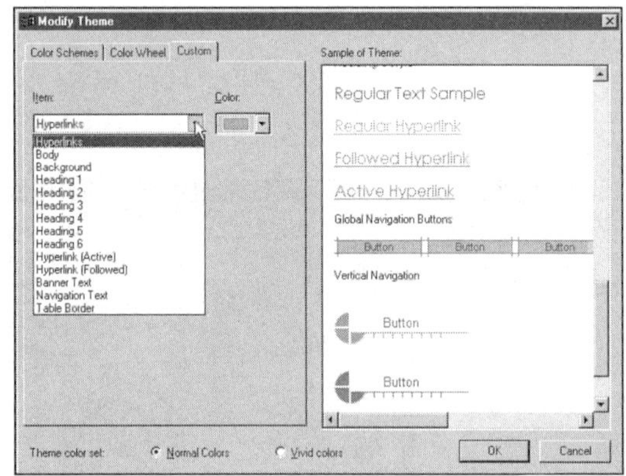

6.11

Themes can be applied to Webs, subwebs, and pages in both Folders and Page views.

Modifying Graphics in a Theme

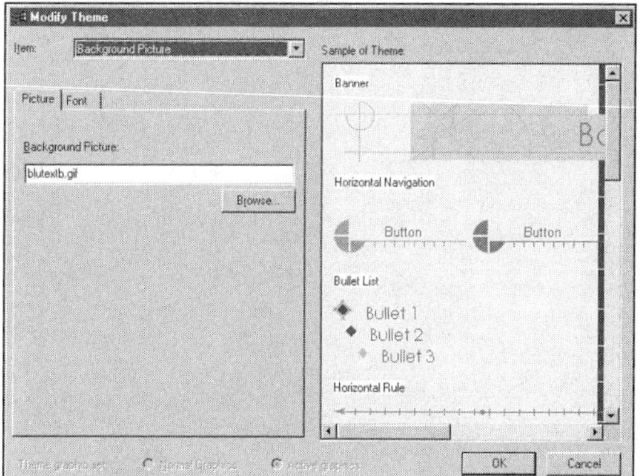

6.12

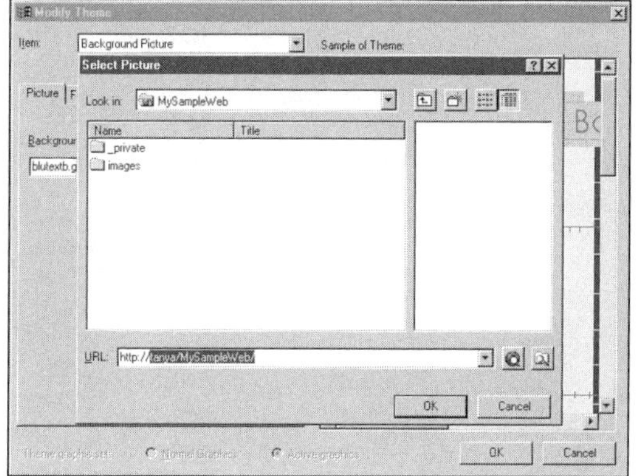

6.13

When it comes to customizing theme graphics, you're talking about the basis of what makes a theme a theme. In other words, modifying theme graphics has a potential impact on the appearance of page banners, horizontal lines, navigation buttons, bulleted list icons, background images, and navigation controls.

1. Open a FrontPage 2000 Web containing a theme and then select Format→Theme to open the Themes dialog box. Click the Modify button to access the Modify button bar. Click the Graphics button to open the Modify Theme dialog box **(6.12)**.
2. Modify a theme's default background image by entering a new image filename in the Background Picture field, and then clicking the OK button. You may also click the tab's Browse button to open the Select Picture dialog box **(6.13)**, select an alternative image from the active Web, and then click the OK button.

continues

Modifying Graphics in a Theme continued

3. Modify a theme's default picture font by selecting the Modify Theme Font tab **(6.14)**. Then select the image item containing the font to be changed from the Item drop-down menu, select a new font from the scrolling list box, make adjustments to style, size, horizontal and vertical alignment, and then click the OK button.

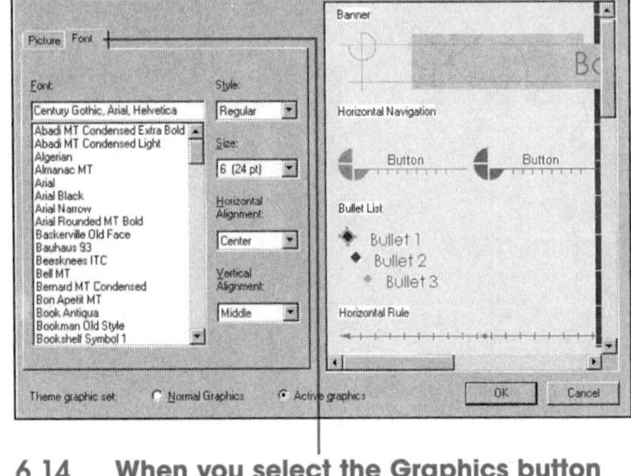

6.14 **When you select the Graphics button on the Themes dialog box, and choose the Font tab, you'll find that it allows you to do fine adjustments to the style, size, and horizontal and vertical alignment of image bound fonts.**

The alternative image file can come from any source. Consequently, you can create a new image or download an image of your choice from the Internet, store it on your hard drive, and then select it during the browse operation.

Be aware that there are two sets of theme graphics—Normal and Active. The Normal theme graphics are like static Web pages in that there is nothing dynamic about them. The Active theme graphics set, on the other hand, makes your theme navigation buttons hover buttons which respond to mouseover and click events.

Modifying Text Styles in a Theme

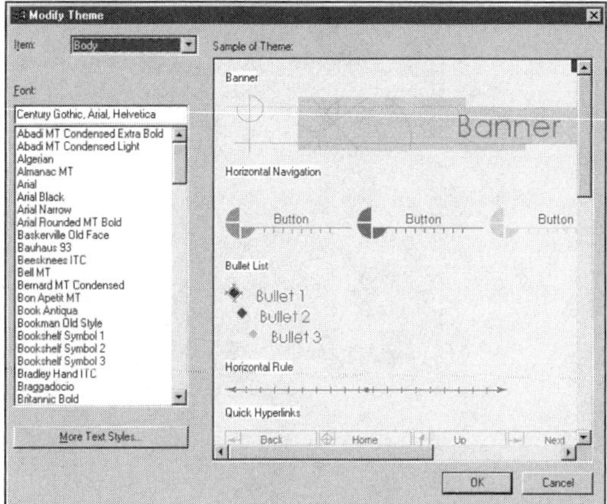

6.15

Modifying a theme text style means that you can define your own HTML style tags similar to Normal, Heading 1 through 6, and so on. Modifying a theme text style with your own custom text style has the advantage of allowing you to mix your own design ideas with the pre-existing design enforced by the theme.

1. Open a FrontPage 2000 Web containing a theme and then select Format→Theme to open the Themes dialog box. Click the Modify button to access the Modify button bar. Click the Text button to open the Modify Theme dialog box **(6.15)**.
2. Modify the font for a theme's default text style by selecting a text style from the Item drop-down menu, selecting a new font from the scrolling list box of font styles, and then clicking the OK button.

continues

 I P

Navigation button font styles for a theme can be modified by selecting the Graphics button and accessing the Modify Theme dialog box. However, if you want to assign font color for the same theme, you'll need to select the Colors button on the Themes dialog box, and then select the Custom tab on the Modify Theme dialog box.

Modifying Text Styles in a Theme continued

3. Select the More Text Styles button to open the Style dialog box **(6.16)**.
4. Select the New button on the Style dialog box, and then enter a name for your custom text style.
5. Select the Format button, and choose Font from the menu of options.
6. Establish Font properties for your custom style, and then click OK twice. Notice that your custom style is added to the Styles list box **(6.17)**.

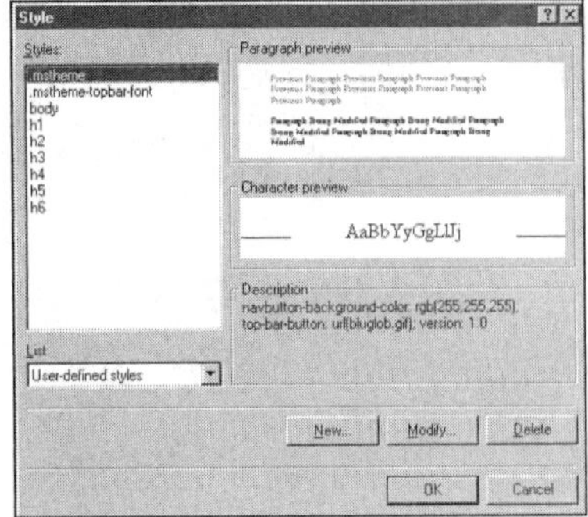

6.16

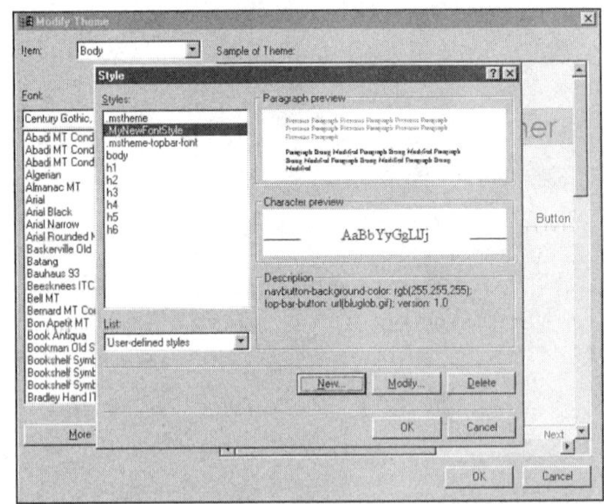

6.17

After you create a new custom font style, you can access it by selecting the styles drop-down menu on the FrontPage 2000 Formatting toolbar.

When deciding what font style to use, consider the font shape. Font shape is key if you intend to mix different fonts on the same page. For example, bold sans serif fonts work well with serif fonts if the shapes are similar. Serif fonts are characterized by stroke enhancements at the base like a Times New Roman font. Sans serif fonts are not stroke enhanced, as in the case of the Arial font.

Applying Cascading Style Sheets

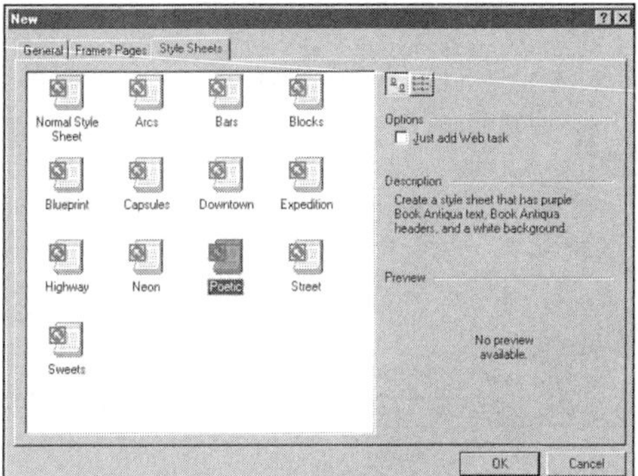

6.18

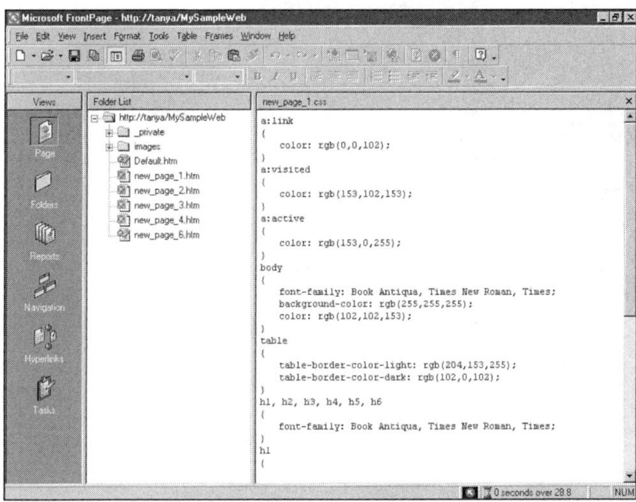

6.19

Cascading Style Sheets (CSS) is an HTML specification that enables Web authors to attach a set of defined style parameters to HTML documents. These defined style parameters, commonly known as style sheets, dictate the appearance of Web page elements and the look and feel of the Web itself. FrontPage 2000 supports the application of Cascading Style Sheets giving you more control over elements than was previously possible.

1. Open a FrontPage 2000 Web.
2. Choose File→New→Page to open the New dialog box.
3. Click the Style Sheets tab on the New dialog box **(6.18)**, select a style sheet of your choice, and then click the OK button to close the dialog box and have the Cascading Style Sheet syntax appear in the FrontPage 2000 Editing window **(6.19)**.

continues

I P

Cascading Style Sheets support requires IE or Netscape 4.0 or later.

Applying Cascading Style Sheets continued

4. Choose File→Save from the FrontPage 2000 menu bar to open the Save As dialog box **(6.20)**.

5. Enter a name for the Cascading Style Sheet in the File name field, and then click the Save button to close the dialog box, and to have the file listed in the file hierarchy in the Folder List pane of Page view **(6.21)**.

6. Choose File→Close to remove the .css file from the FrontPage 2000 Editing window.

7. From the Folder List pane in Page view, select the page that you want to apply the style to and then choose Format→Style Sheet Links to open the Link Style Sheet dialog box **(6.22)**.

6.20

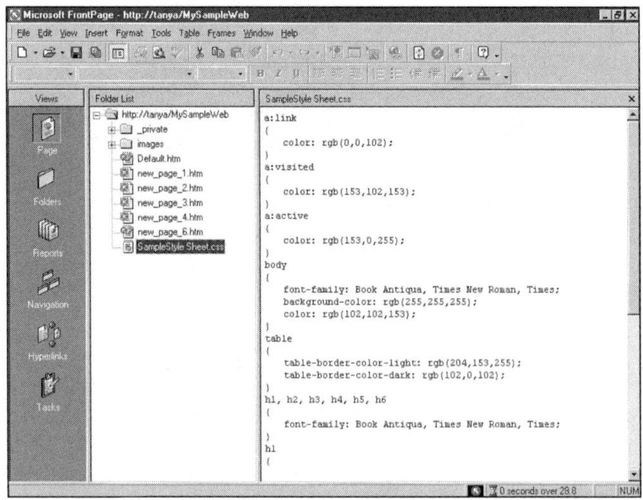

6.21

Applying a style sheet to a page by linking to a .css file differs from using styles, in that traditional styles are characterized by the HTML tag that defines them, and are therefore a standard entity. Style sheets are customized as defined by the Web developer and are non-standard entities.

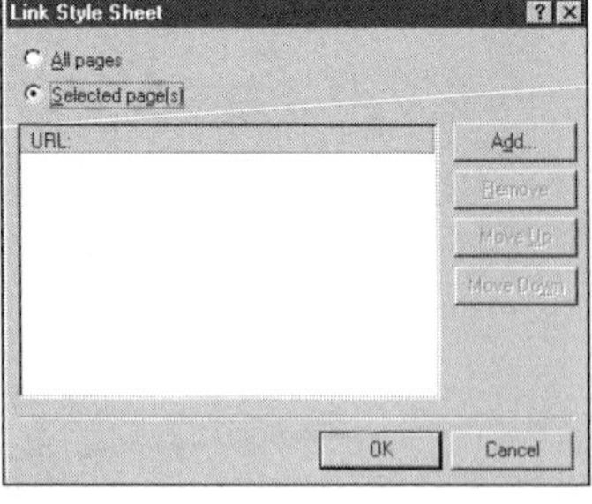

6.22

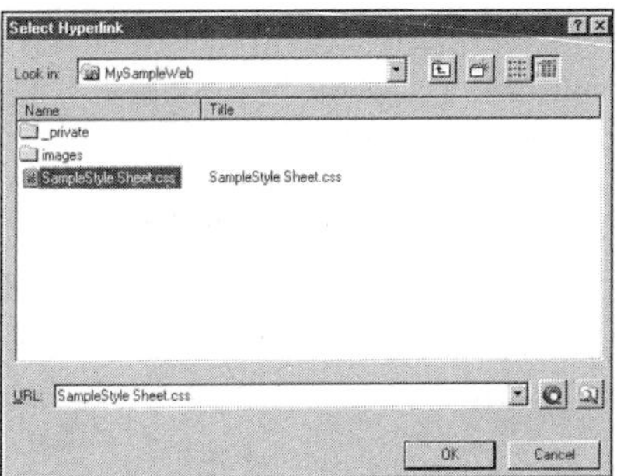

6.23

The Link Style Sheet dialog box lets you add the style to All pages or to Selected pages.

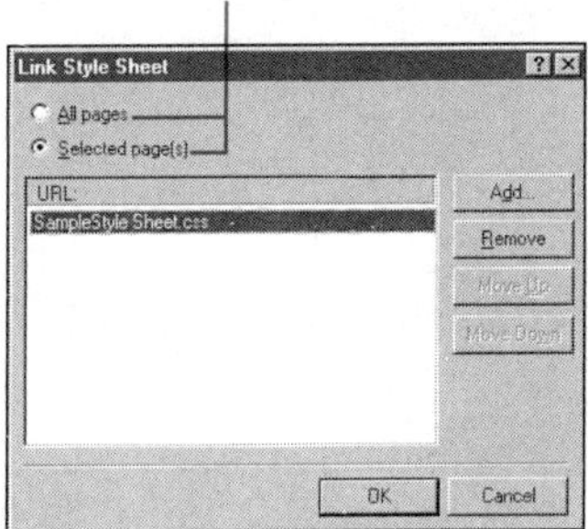

6.24

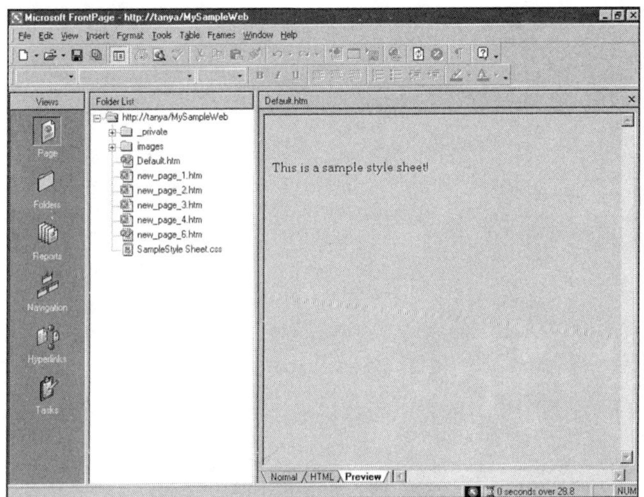

6.25

8. Click the Add button to open the Select Hyperlink dialog box **(6.23)**, select the file with the .css extension, and then click the OK button to close the dialog box and add the style sheet link to the Link Style Sheet dialog box **(6.24)**.
9. Click OK to close the Link Style Sheet dialog box.
10. Select the Preview tab on the FrontPage 2000 Editing window to see the application of the linked style sheet **(6.25)**.

 **I P**

Any style sheets that you apply to your pages will override any user-defined browser style settings.

 **I P**

You can edit the attributes of the .css file by double-clicking the file in the Folder List hierarchy. Effectively, this allows you to use FrontPage 2000 to create your own custom .css files.

Applying Shared Borders and Navigation Bars

Shared borders are Web page regions reserved for content that you want to appear consistently throughout your pages, as well as a device for adding symmetry to the Web page layout. Because shared borders typically host navigation bars, there is a synergy in the way that each of these page elements is applied. You can place shared borders along any page margin, and be assured that any modifications to the Web structure will automatically update shared border content.

1. Open a FrontPage 2000 Web in Page view.
2. Choose Format→Shared Borders to open the Shared Borders dialog box **(6.26)**.
3. Select the page borders you want to share by clicking the Top, Left, Right, or Bottom check boxes, and notice that your selection is previewed in the dialog box **(6.27)**. You also can select to Reset borders for current page to web default.

Select the Current page option to restrict shared borders to a selected page, or select the All pages option to have shared borders appear on all pages in the Web.

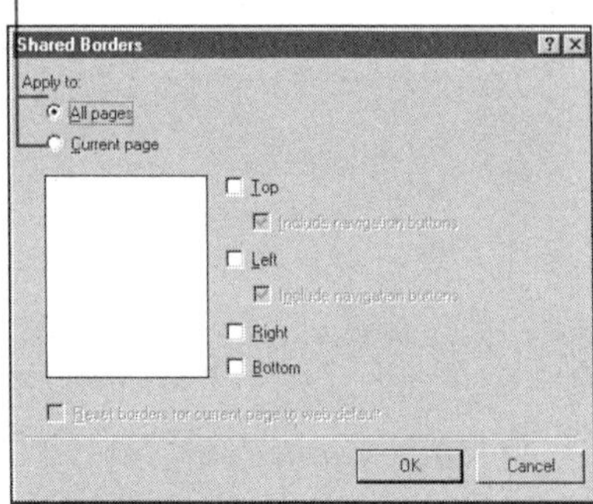

6.26

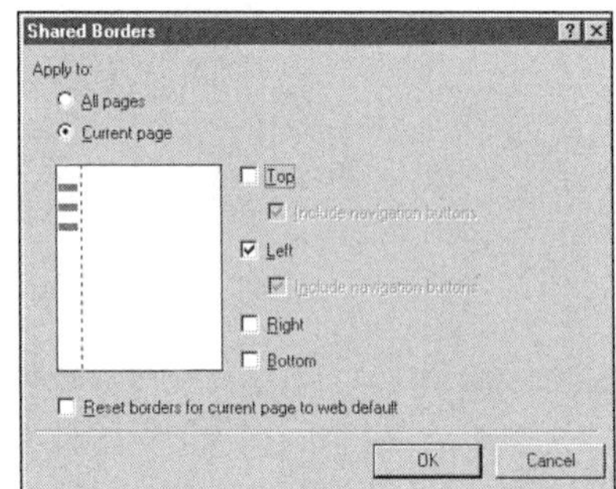

6.27

Navigation bars are not exclusive to shared borders, as they may be added directly to your Web page(s).

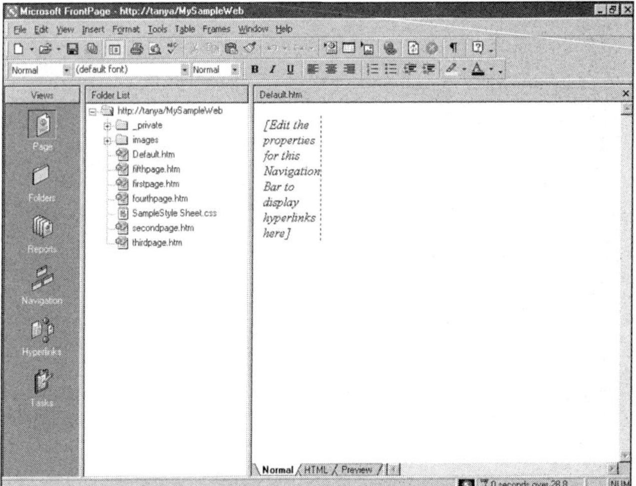

6.28

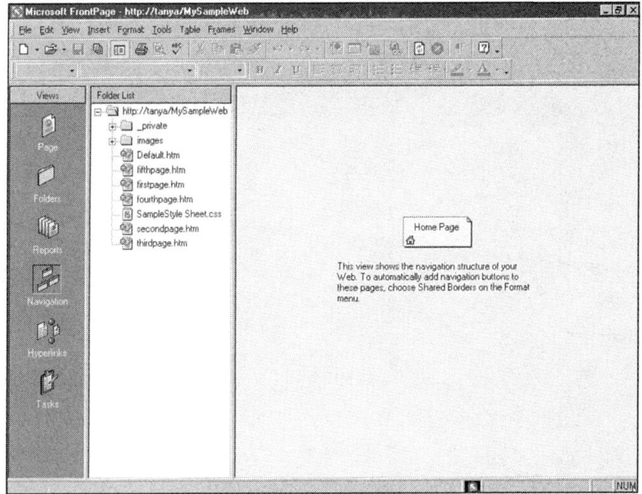

6.29

4. Click the OK button to close the dialog box and have the shared border appear on the page displayed in the FrontPage 2000 Editing window **(6.28)**.

5. Add a navigation bar to your shared border by selecting the Navigation icon on the FrontPage 2000 Views bar to enter Navigation view **(6.29)**.

continues

I P

You can define up to four shared borders for a Web site—Top, Bottom, Left, and Right.

Applying Shared Borders and Navigation Bars continued

6. Drag the pages that will comprise your navigation bar from the Folder List pane to the Navigation view window, placing each added page side by side beneath the Home Page **(6.30)**.

7. Select the Page icon under the Views bar to return to Page view where your navigation bar has been automatically set **(6.31)**.

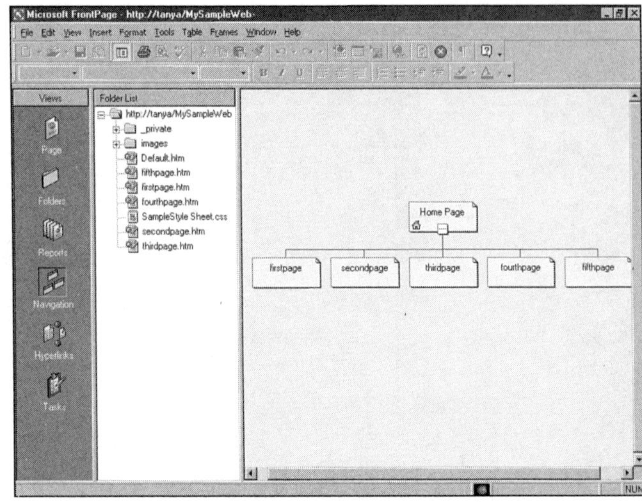

6.30

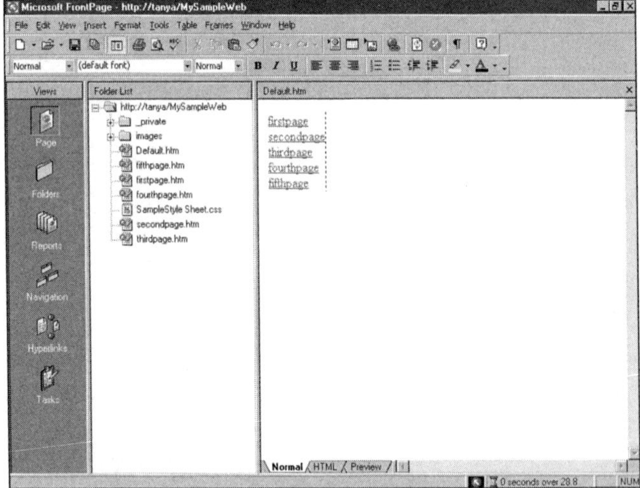

6.31

You can always locate a specific page in the Navigation view block hierarchy, by right-clicking the filename in the Navigation view's Folder List, and then selecting Find in Navigation from the shortcut menu.

You can see shared border pages in Folder view by selecting Tools→Web Settings, and then selecting the Advanced tab. On the Advanced tab, click the Show documents in hidden directories check box. You will then see a folder called "_borders". This folder contains your shared border page files.

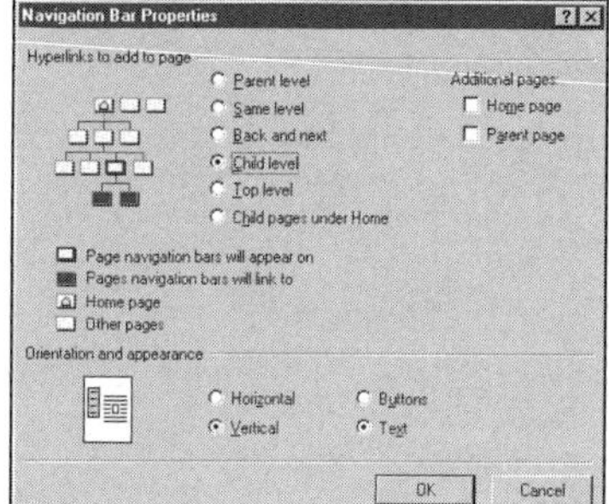

6.32

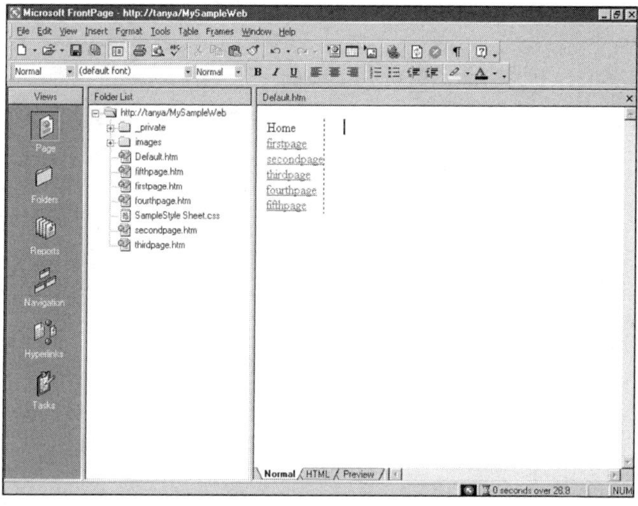

6.33

8. Right-click inside the shared border in Page view, and then choose Navigation Bar Properties from the shortcut menu to open the Navigation Bar Properties dialog box **(6.32)**.

9. Select the Home page check box under Additional pages, select the Child pages under Home option button, and then click the OK button to close the dialog box. This places a link to the home page on the page containing the shared border, and lists links to all child pages beneath the home page **(6.33)**.

If you apply shared borders via the Shared Borders dialog box, any shared borders assigned by a theme will be superceded.

Shared borders are similar in function to page headers and footers, as they present an information constant across documents.

Creating HTML Tag Styles

From time to time you may find yourself applying personal nuances to your page elements again and again. In these cases, having an HTML tag to support these little nuances saves you a few steps. FrontPage 2000 lets you create custom HTML tags or modify existing tags by creating styles.

1. With an open page in the FrontPage 2000 Editing window, create a custom HTML style tag by selecting Format→Style to open the Style dialog box **(6.34)**.
2. Select the New button to open the New Style dialog box **(6.35)**.
3. Enter a name for your new style in the Name (selector) field, and then click the Format button to select the page element to which your style will apply **(6.36)**.

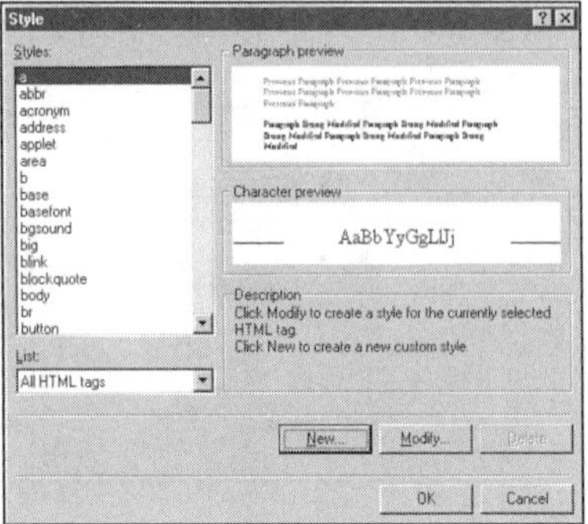

6.34

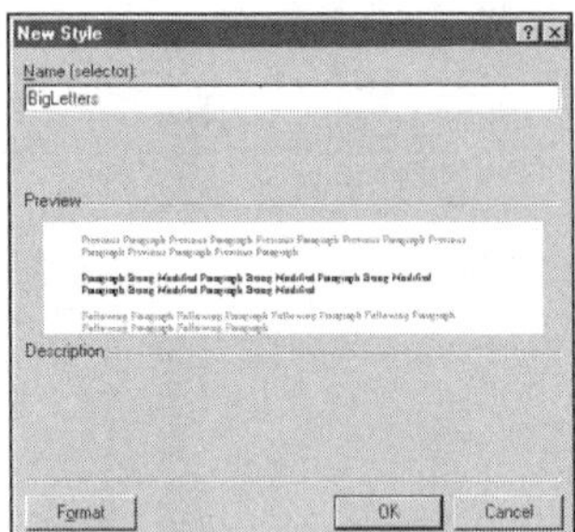

6.35

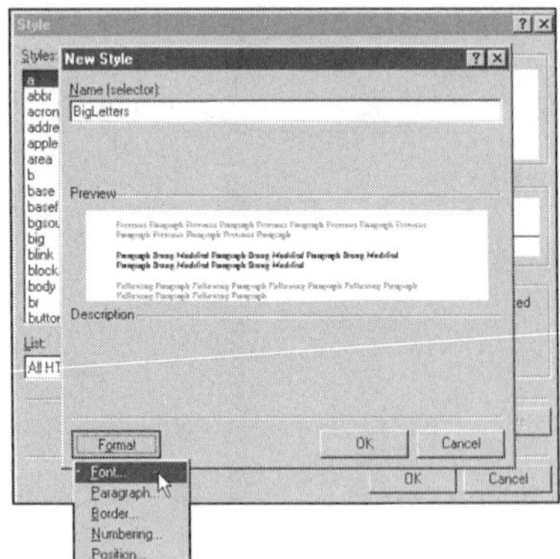

6.36

NOTE

There are browser compatibility issues with the application of styles. Be aware that you'll need Internet Information Server with FP Extensions and IE 4.0 or Netscape Navigator 4.0 or better to take advantage of FrontPage 2000's user-defined style and style sheet support features.

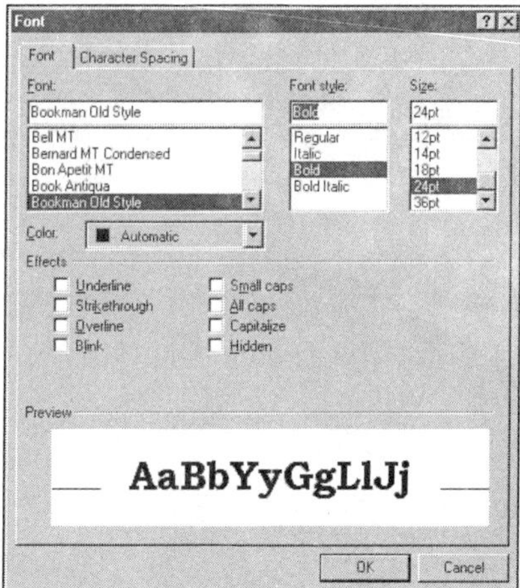

6.37

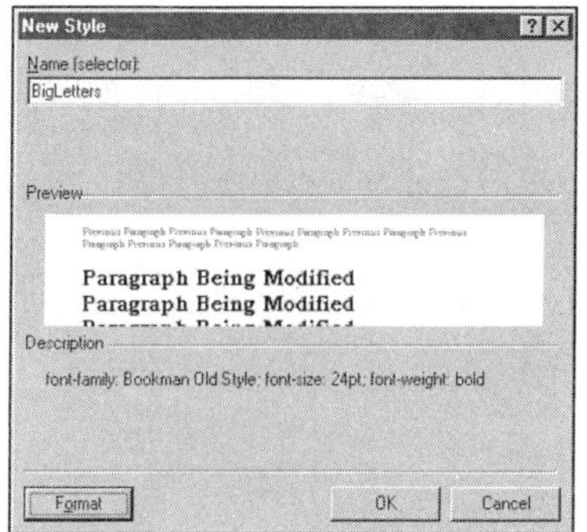

6.38

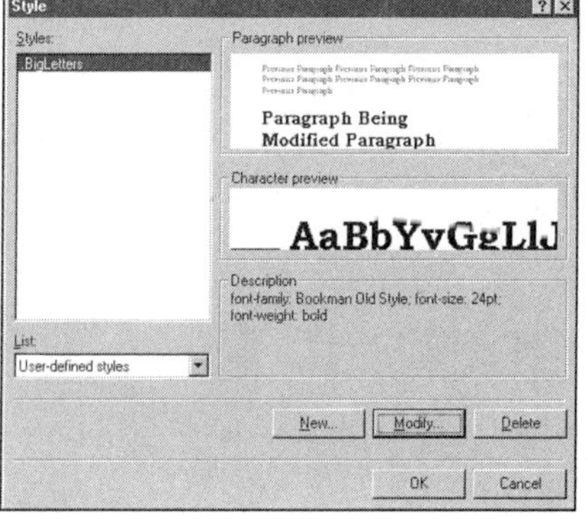

6.39

4. Set the parameters that will characterize your new style **(6.37)**, and then click OK to close the applicable dialog box.

5. Preview the attributes of your new style in the New Style Preview box **(6.38)**, and then click OK to close the New Style dialog box.

6. Click OK to close the Style dialog box **(6.39)**.

continues

 I P

When a dot (.) appears in front of a user-defined style, it means that the style represents a style class. Style classes can be applied to any HTML element.

 I P

You can also apply formatting styles using the Format Painter. Select the page element containing the style you want to copy, and then click Format Painter and the page element to which you want to apply the style.

Creating HTML Tag Styles continued

7. Apply your new style tag by selecting it from the FrontPage 2000 Style drop-down menu on the Format toolbar **(6.40)**. Notice the result of applying the example custom HTML tag on the Normal tab **(6.41)**. Also, notice that the custom tag appears in the HTML source code for the page **(6.42)**.

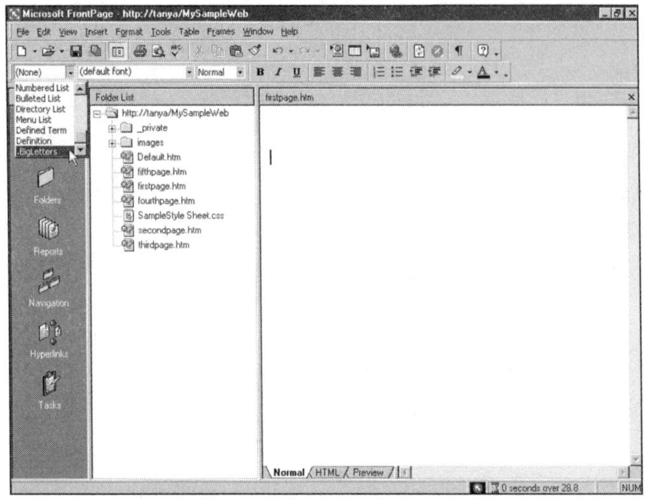

6.40

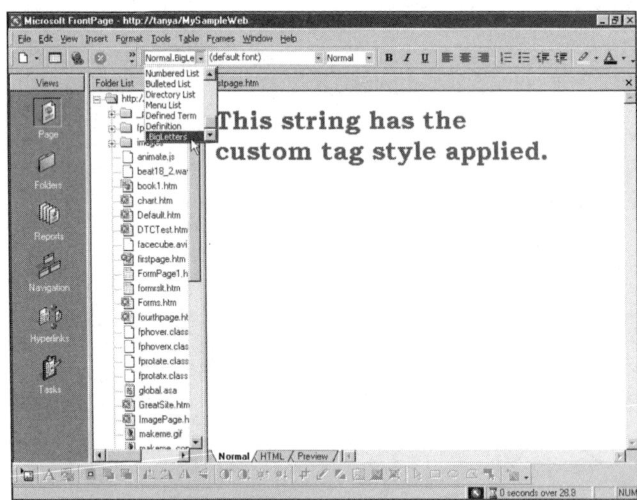

6.41

User-defined style names should be single strings without spaces.

User-defined styles override default styles applied by a browser.

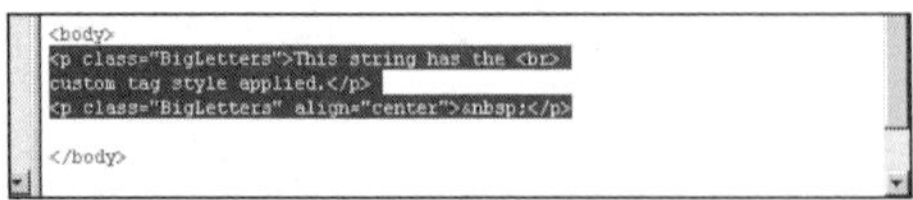

6.42

Customizing HTML Formatting Preferences

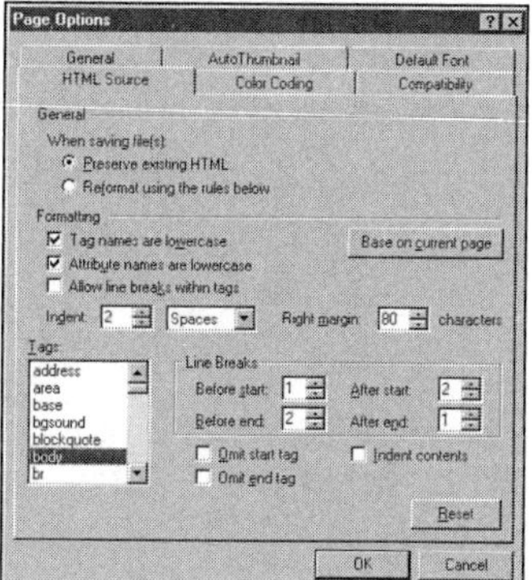

6.43

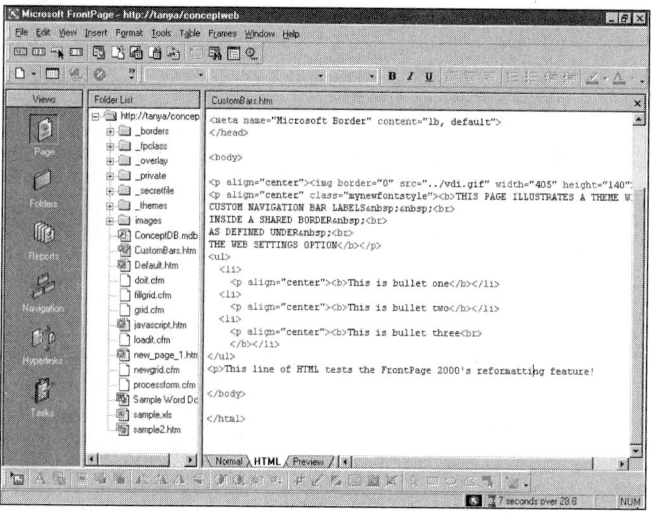

6.44

One of the complaints in previous versions of FrontPage had to do with the fact that FrontPage changed HTML code that you entered manually. With FrontPage 2000, this is no longer a problem. FrontPage 2000 lets you determine how you want it to format HTML.

1. Choose Tools→Page to open the Page Options dialog box, and then select the HTML Source tab **(6.43)**. Notice that all HTML tags in the body page are lowercase and not indented **(6.44)**.

2. Change line break defaults for any given HTML tag by selecting the tag from the Tags scrolling list box, and then enter a value of your choice to specify new parameters such as line breaks, right margin, or indent.

continues

Customizing HTML Formatting Preferences continued

3. Preserve your changes by selecting the Reformat option using the rules in the General section at the top of the HTML Source tab.

4. Click OK to close the dialog box. Notice that all HTML tags in the page body are now uppercase and indented according to the reformatting rules specified **(6.45)**, **(6.46)**.

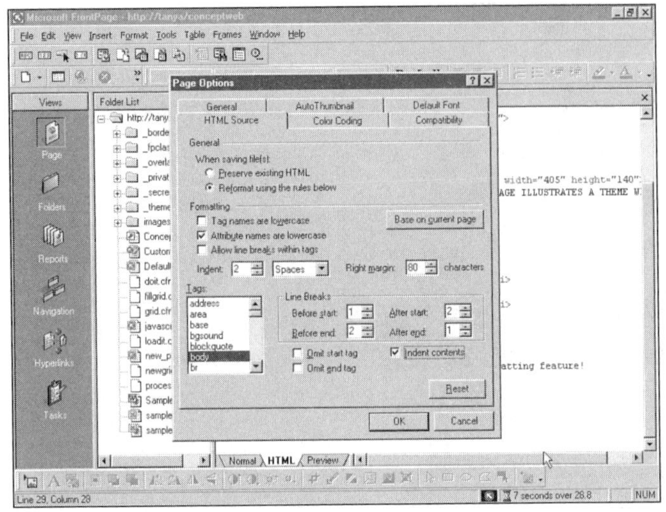

6.45

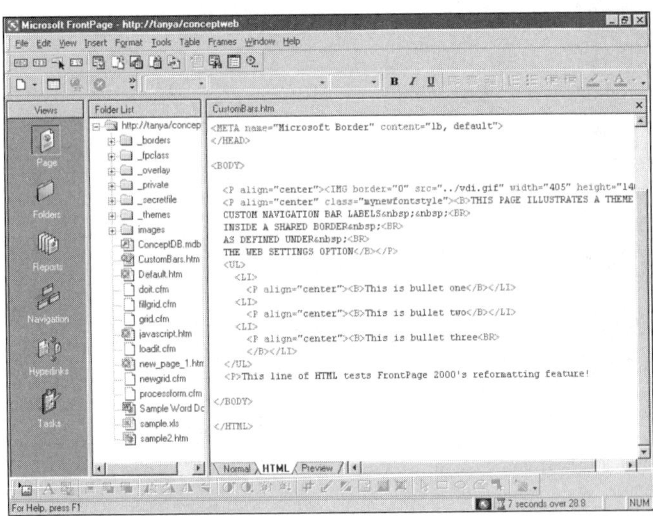

6.46

If you have a formatted HTML page open at the time that you make adjustments to the HTML Source formatting rules, you can select the Base on current page button to accept the HTML formatting defaults of the current active page.

Displaying HTML Tags in Page View

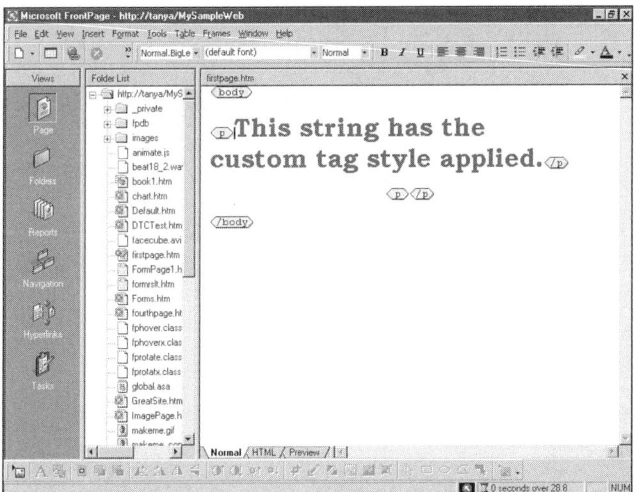

6.47

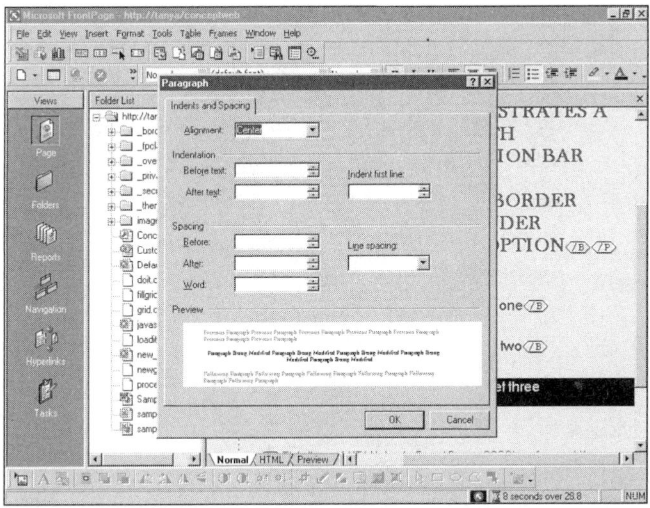

6.48

Another of the new features in FrontPage 2000 is the capability to view HTML tags in Page view as you work in the WYSIWYG editor. Using this feature is helpful if you've applied HTML code manually, and you want to perform a visual check to be sure that you've applied all required beginning and ending tags. This is also valuable in helping you learn HTML coding if you are not familiar with the common tags and properties.

1. Open a FrontPage 2000 Web in Page view.
2. Open a page containing page elements in the FrontPage 2000 Editing window.
3. Choose View→Reveal Tags to have HTML tags appear in the Editing window **(6.47)**.

Double-clicking a revealed HTML tag opens the dialog box associated with that tag (6.48).

You can hide HTML tags shown in the WYSIWYG editor by choosing View→Reveal Tags to deselect that option.

Editing HTML

Although FrontPage 2000 is designed to be a WYSIWYG HTML editor, the fact that it still makes HTML source code available is a plus. For example, you may want to apply tags to turn your static HTML into Active Server Page code or Cold Fusion code. You can use Find and Replace to do global edits on a page, to replace images or links. You can also use HTML view to troubleshoot problems found in the Normal WYSIWYG view, such as bad links, picture properties, extra spaces, and so on.

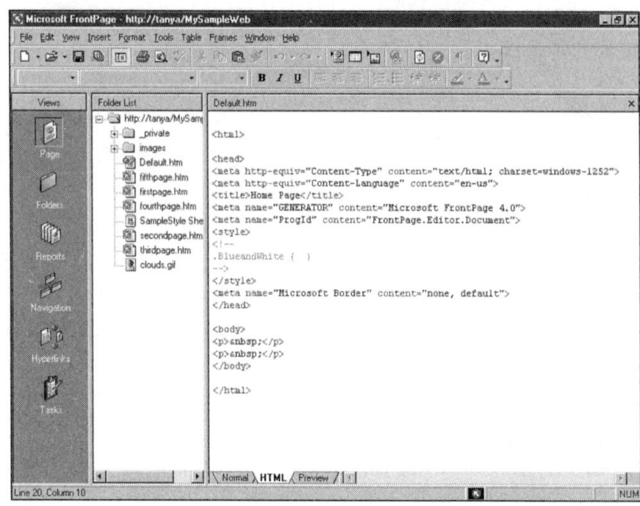

6.49

1. Open a FrontPage 2000 Web in Page view, and then from the Folder List, double-click the page whose HTML you want to edit.
2. Choose the HTML tab in the FrontPage 2000 Editing window to view and modify the displayed HTML source code **(6.49)**.

NOTE

You can list and view the contents of a site using the Folder view. Folder view is accessible by choosing View→Folders or by clicking the Folders icon from the View bar.

Folder view lists the contents of a Web by Name, Size, Type, Modified Date, Modified By, and Comments. The presented list may be sorted by clicking the button of a named column in the Folder view contents pane.

Applying a Background Color or Picture

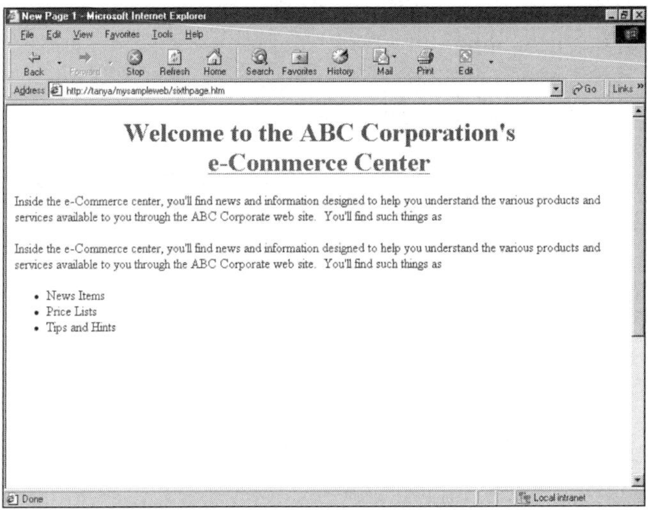

6.50

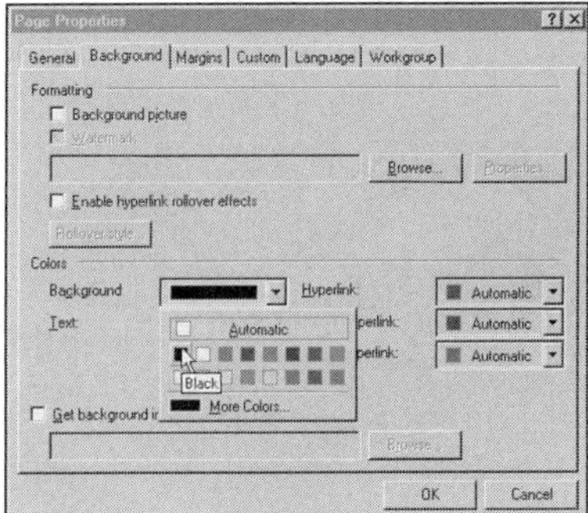

6.51

Although it may seem that white or gray are background color defaults for many Web pages, this need not be the case. FrontPage 2000 lets you change a default gray or white background to any color you choose. In addition, you can select an image to use as your background giving you additional control over the design of your Web.

1. Open a FrontPage 2000 Web in Page view, and then from the Folder List, double-click the page to which you want to add a background color.
2. Right-click inside the FrontPage 2000 Editing window, and then choose Page Properties from the shortcut menu to open the Page Properties dialog box **(6.50)**.
3. Select the Background tab on the Page Properties dialog box **(6.51)**.
4. Under the Colors section, click the Background drop-down menu, select a color, and then click the OK button to close the dialog box and apply the color to your page.

continues

If the page you select contains a theme, you cannot apply a background color to the page.

Applying a Background Color or Picture continued

5. You can also add an image to your background by selecting the Background picture check box in the Formatting section of the Background tab and entering the name of an image file in the field directly beneath the Watermark check box **(6.52)**.

6. Click the OK button to close the Page Properties dialog box and apply the selected image to the page's background **(6.53)**.

Watermarks are an image effect that allows text to scroll up and down a page while the background image remains stationary. Select the Watermark check box, if you want to invoke the watermark effect. Keep in mind that this effect is not compatible with all browsers.

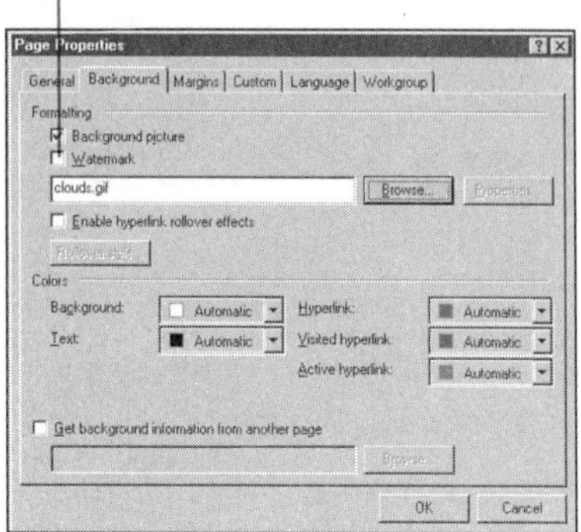

6.52

NOTE

Background picture tiling is automatic; however, you can limit the amount of tiling that occurs by limiting the page size. Unfortunately, the screen resolution of other machines is out of your hands. So, unless your background picture is designed to be tiled, as with wallpaper images, try to use a picture that appears approximately the same in both 800×600 and 640×480. You can attempt to prevent tiling by using Watermark (although this feature is not compatible with all browsers), or you can place background colors and images in tables and cells). Picture size is also an issue. As a rule of thumb, use a .jpg or .gif with the most compression and highest quality available, while maintaining a small file size, and then test the results in a 640×480 display at 256 colors over a 28.8K modem (the FrontPage 2000 status bar provides you with an estimated download time).

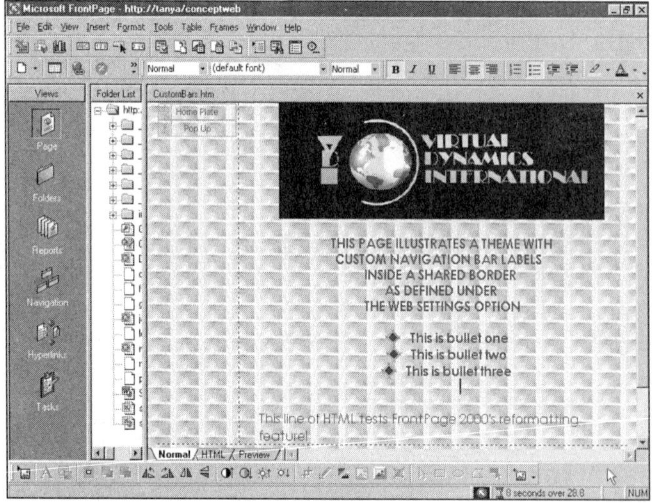

6.53

Applying Comments

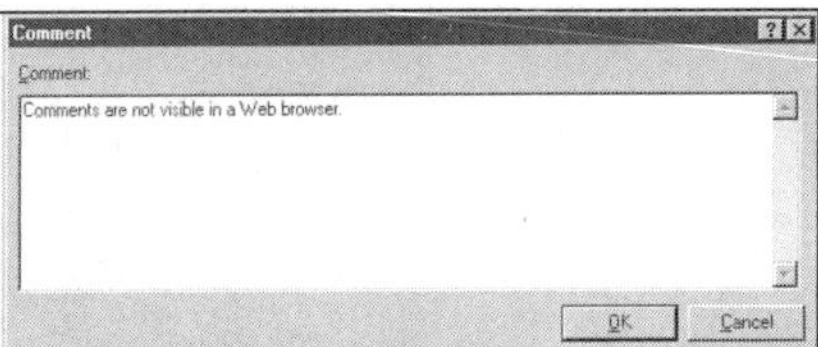

6.54

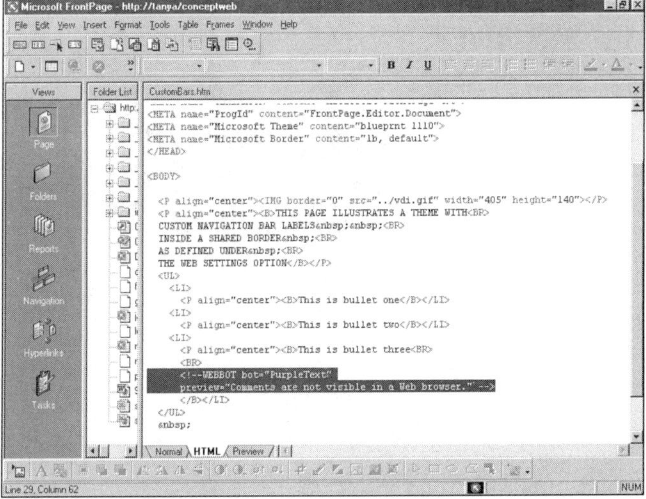

6.55

Comments are annotations that you make to Web pages that are not visible in a Web browser, but are visible in HTML. For example, you might add information about yourself, the date that the page was created, and any special tags or effects associated with the page. This kind of information is helpful when it comes to maintaining your site content. Commenting source code is a standard practice in the programming community.

1. Open a FrontPage 2000 Web in Page view, and then from the Folder List, double-click the page to which you want add a comment.
2. Choose Insert→Comment to open the Comment dialog box **(6.54)**.
3. Enter a comment of your choice, and then click the OK button to close the dialog box and add the comment to the editing window and background HTML **(6.55)**.

I P

By default, comments appear in FrontPage 2000's Page view in the color assigned to visited hyperlinks.

Previewing a Web Page

Although FrontPage 2000's WYSI-WYG editor gives you a real-time look at how your Web page will appear, certain page nuances may not appear correctly until they're viewed in a browser.

1. Open a FrontPage 2000 Web in Page view, and then from the Folder List, select the page you want to preview.
2. Choose File→Preview in Browser to open the Preview in Browser dialog box **(6.56)**.
3. Choose the Preview button to open the selected page in your Web browser **(6.57)**, **(6.58)**.

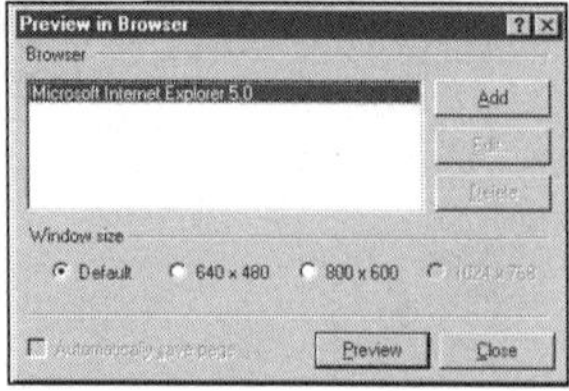

6.56

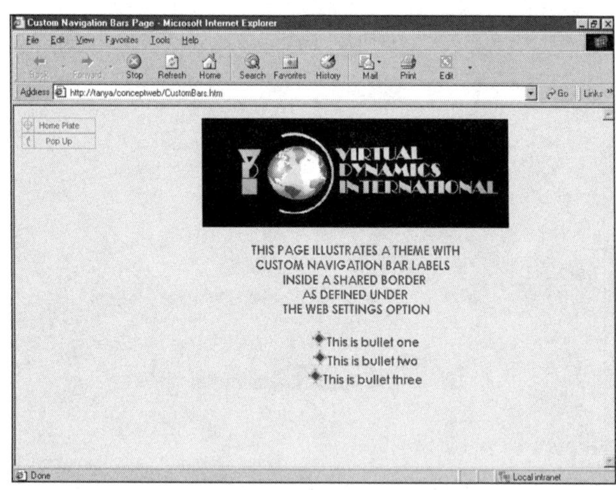

6.57

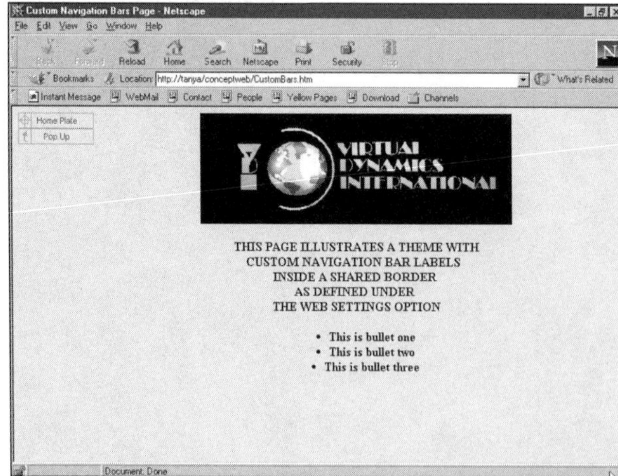

6.58

If you have more than one browser installed on your machine, you can add additional browsers for previewing pages by selecting the Add button on the Preview in Browser window.

The Preview tab on the FrontPage 2000 Editor, which also presents a browser view of a Web page, will not appear if Microsoft Internet Explorer 3.0 or higher is not installed.

CHAPTER 7

In this chapter you will learn how to...

- Apply Text Manually
- Apply Text Using a FrontPage Component
- Position Text
- Create Lists
- Make Collapsing Lists
- Apply Paragraph Formats and Styles
- Apply Font Type, Style, and Size
- Change Font Color and Convert Text to a Table
- Perform a Cross-Web Spell Check

Static Web pages are effectively plain old text-based documents formatted using HTML tags. Integrating HTML with standard text allows Web browsers to interpret and display documents with HTML-defined headers, footers, paragraphs, and lists. For this reason, when you're ready to work with text in FrontPage 2000, you'll be undertaking the task of adding text to a document, and then applying the appropriate HTML formatting options

WORKING WITH TEXT

to define the document's look and feel. Because of FrontPage 2000's close integration with Microsoft Office 2000, you can now copy text from any Office 2000 application, such as Word, Excel, or PowerPoint, and then paste the text with all HTML-compatible formatting in tact directly into your FrontPage 2000 Web page.

Text for your Web page can come from a variety of sources. Your organization might consider creating an E-company newsletter containing things like company announcements, job openings, current stock prices, and community news. Some companies even transfer their employee policies and procedures to the Web. Product information and frequently asked questions also provide rich sources for text-based content.

Applying Text Manually

Applying text to a page using FrontPage 2000 is identical to entering text into a Word or PowerPoint document. In other words, you can enter text directly or copy and paste text from another application (7.1).

You can manually add text to a Web page by opening a FrontPage 2000 Web in Page view, and then either type in the editing window or paste in the text if you've copied it from another application.

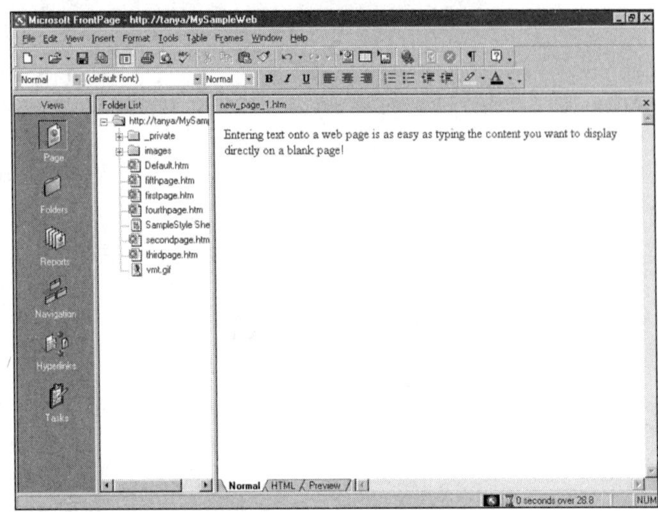

7.1

 **I P**

Should you find yourself at a loss for words, FrontPage 2000 provides a thesaurus to assist you with finding alternate meanings for selected words. In an open FrontPage 2000 Web, on a page containing text, select a word and then choose Tools→Thesaurus from the FrontPage 2000 menu bar to open the Thesaurus dialog box.

 **O T E**

Pages applied using the Include component must be in HTML format, and reside within the current FrontPage 2000 Web. Also, if you attempt to include a Frames page using an Include component, you get the following message:

[When you insert a frames page using the Include Page component, FrontPage cannot display it. To edit the frames page, right-click this message, and then choose the Open command.]

Applying Text Using a FrontPage Component

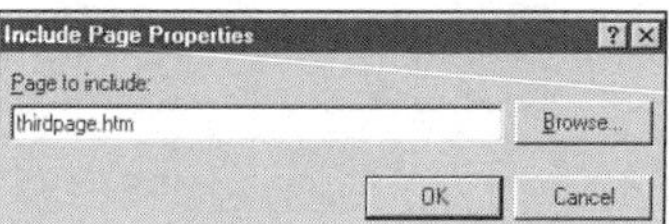

7.2

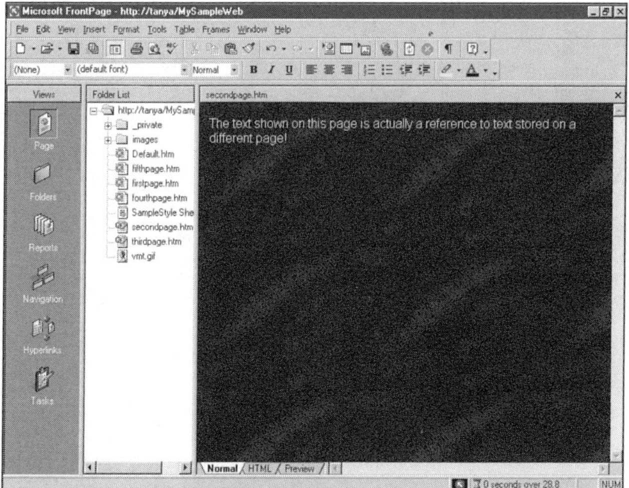

7.3

One of the more unique features of FrontPage is its capability to automate the application of text on a page. This is accomplished by using a FrontPage component called an *include* page. Include pages let you automatically apply text to other pages by referencing the URL of the page where the text you want to apply already exists.

1. Open a FrontPage 2000 Web in Page view.
2. With the blinking cursor in the editing window, choose Insert→Component→Include Page to open the Include Page Properties dialog box **(7.2)**.
3. In the Page to include field, enter the filename or URL of the page that contains the text you want to apply, and then click the OK button to see your result **(7.3)**.

A good place to store the files that you want to apply using the Include component is the _private folder. FrontPage 2000 creates this folder each time you create a new Web, and any content placed in this folder is not accessible to the public.

Positioning Text

Another capability introduced with FrontPage 2000 is positioning. With positioning, you can control, with some measure of precision, how and where a page element is placed on a page, and how other page elements sharing the page are displayed in relation to the positioned element.

1. Select the text string or block of text that you want to position **(7.4)**.
2. Choose Format→Position to open the Position dialog box **(7.5)**.

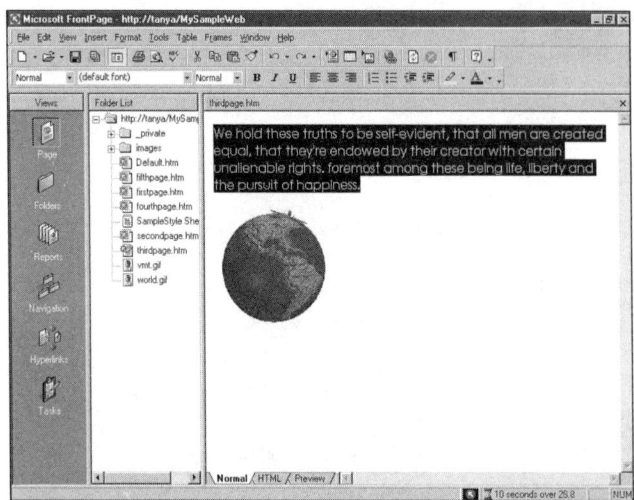

7.4

The Wrapping style section lets you set properties for how text in a position box will wrap.

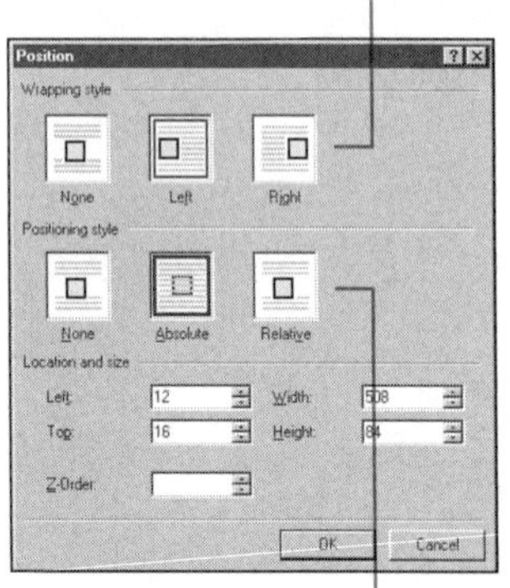

7.5 The Positioning style section lets you specify how to adjust the placement of a position box.

(N) O T E

One of the new features in FrontPage 2000 is the ability to overlap page elements. This is possible as a result of the z-index property. The z-index property is a numeric value that dictates the top to bottom order of layered page elements. For this reason, FrontPage 2000 gives you the option of making z-index property adjustments using the Z-order spinner on the Positioning dialog box. When you select the last item in a layered group of page elements, and you adjust its Z-order value, assigning the element a relative value of 1 places it in front of the page element preceding it.

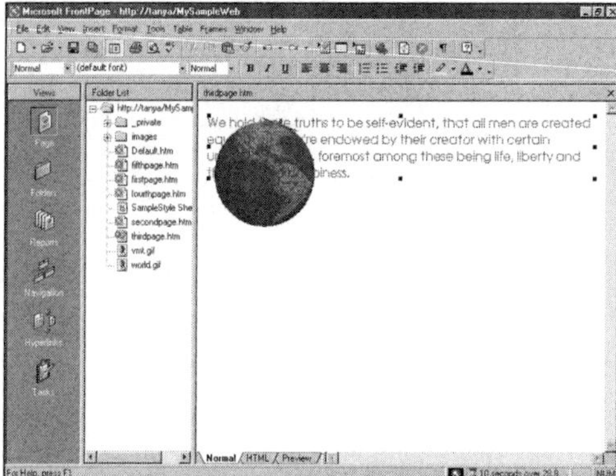

7.6

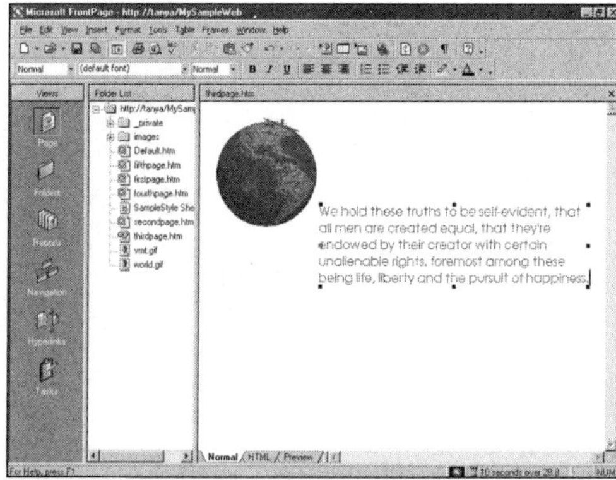

7.7

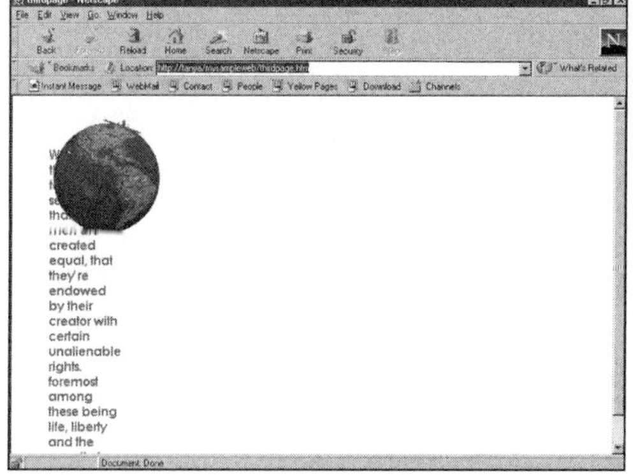

7.8

3. Select a wrapping style and a position placement option, and then click the OK button to apply the selected properties to the text inside the position box (7.6).

4. Use the position box handles to adjust the size of the box to see how the wrap property is applied, and then, if you've selected the Absolute positioning option, you can drag the position box to any location in the editing window (7.7).

TIP

You can also make positioning adjustments using the Positioning toolbar. You can access the Positioning toolbar by choosing View→Toolbars→Positioning on the FrontPage 2000 menu bar.

Although absolute positioning of page elements in IE5 works without incident, be aware of how browser compatibility might affect positioned elements. Netscape doesn't translate the absolute positioning of page elements in the same way that IE5 does (7.8).

Creating Lists

FrontPage 2000 supports a variety of stylized bulleted and numbered lists. This means that when you add text to a page that requires formatting as a list, you'll be able to quickly achieve the desired result.

1. Select the text that you want to format as a list.
2. Choose Format→Bullets and Numbering to open the Bullets and Numbering dialog box revealing the Picture Bullets tab **(7.9)**. Click OK if you want your list to be formatted with bullets that appear like the image bullets for the theme assigned to the page. You can also browse the current Web for another image to use as a bullet by selecting the Specify picture option.
3. Select an option from the Plain Bullets tab **(7.10)** or the Numbers tab **(7.11)** to apply a custom bullet style to your selected text. Click the OK button to see your results.

You can substitute the bullets in your list with images by selecting options on the Picture Bullets tab of the List Properties dialog box.

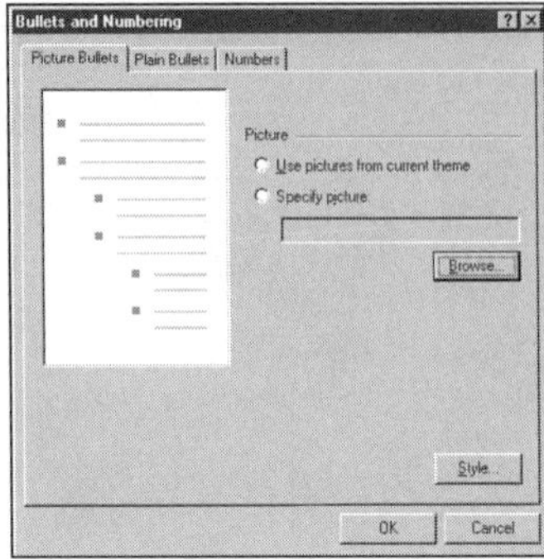

7.9

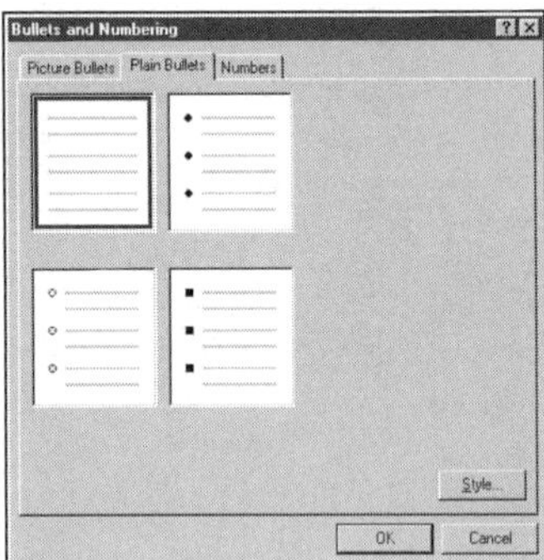

7.10

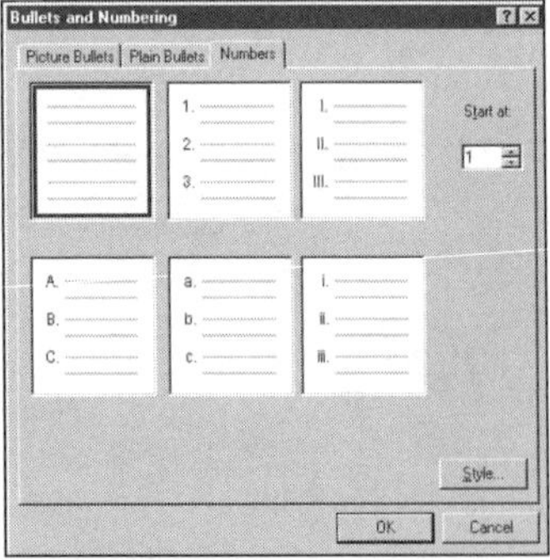

7.11

Making Collapsing Lists

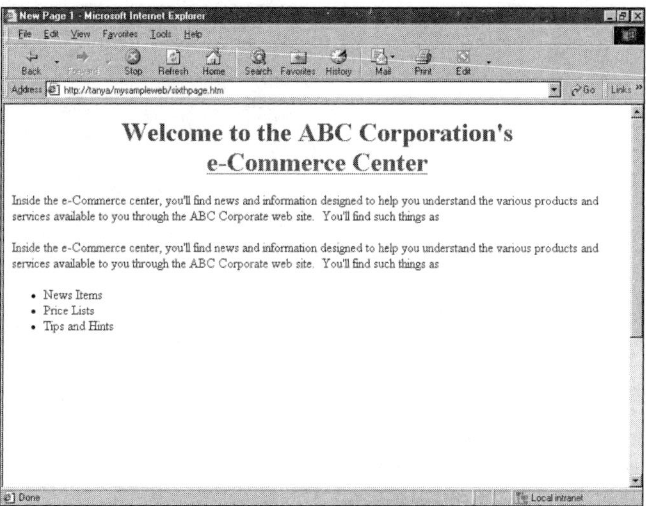

7.12

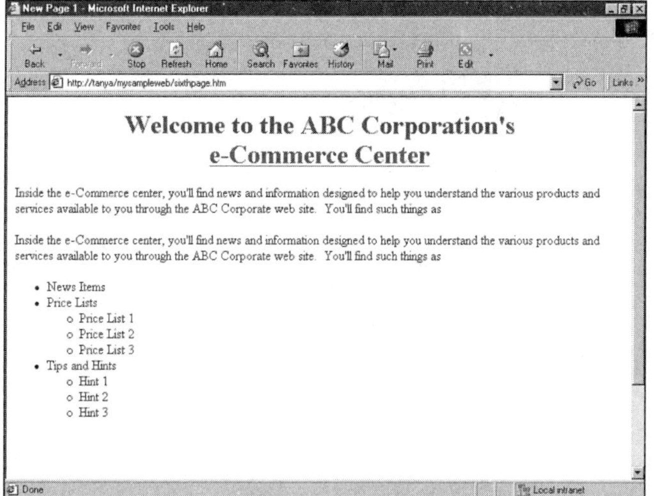

7.13

Creating collapsible lists shows the practical application of Dynamic HTML, as it allows you to let your site visitors drill down into a bulleted or numbered list for additional information about a list item. Think of collapsible lists as a text-based hierarchy that can expand and collapse just like the folder tree in Windows Explorer. Using collapsible lists also facilitate efficient page design, by allowing you to hide line item details that might otherwise consume valuable page space.

1. Make a list of items.
2. Select and indent those items that are to be subordinate to the main item, by clicking the Indent icon twice.
3. Right-click the main item, and then select List Properties from the shortcut menu.
4. Click both the Enable Collapsible Outlines check box and the Initially Collapsed check box, and then click the OK button.
5. Select the Preview tab or File→Preview In Browser and then click the main list item that you made collapsible (7.12), to see the subordinate list items (7.13).

Applying Paragraph Formats and Styles

FrontPage 2000 offers a number of paragraph formatting and style options that are accessible from both the Format menu and the Format toolbar. For example, the Normal style is usually the default style for text entry, while the Heading styles 1 (the largest) through 6 (the smallest) are typically used for page titles and subtitles within a paragraph's body. Paragraphs are generally characterized as text blocks ending with a hard return, so applying a paragraph style will affect the display of the entire paragraph.

1. Select the text block that you want to format.
2. Choose Format→Paragraph to open the Paragraph dialog box **(7.14)** to make adjustments to paragraph indenting and spacing, and then click OK to close the dialog box.
3. To change the style of the paragraph, choose the style option of your choice from the Change Style drop-down list on the Formatting toolbar **(7.15)**.

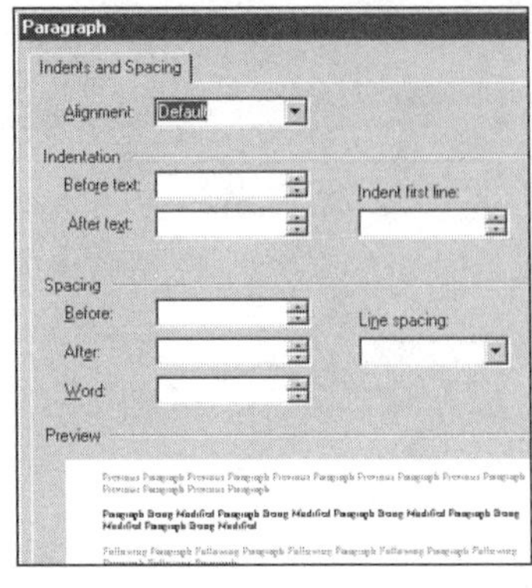

7.14

The Change Style drop-down list contains 15 styles that can be applied to your paragraphs.

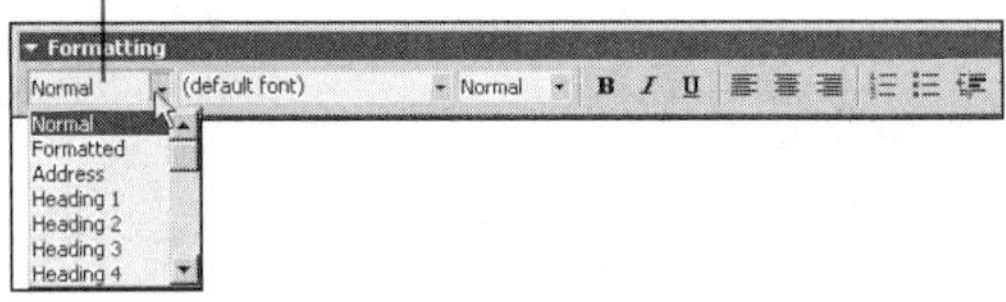

7.15

Align paragraphs by choosing Format→Paragraph and then choosing an alignment type from the drop-down list.

Applying Font Type, Style, and Size

You can make precise font spacing adjustments by setting values on the Character Spacing tab in the Font dialog box.

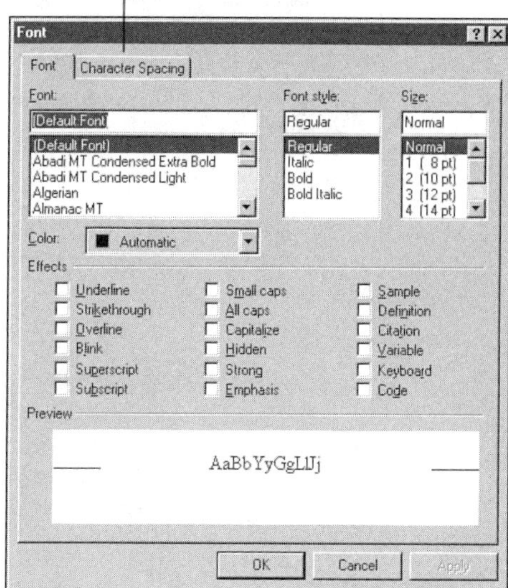

7.16

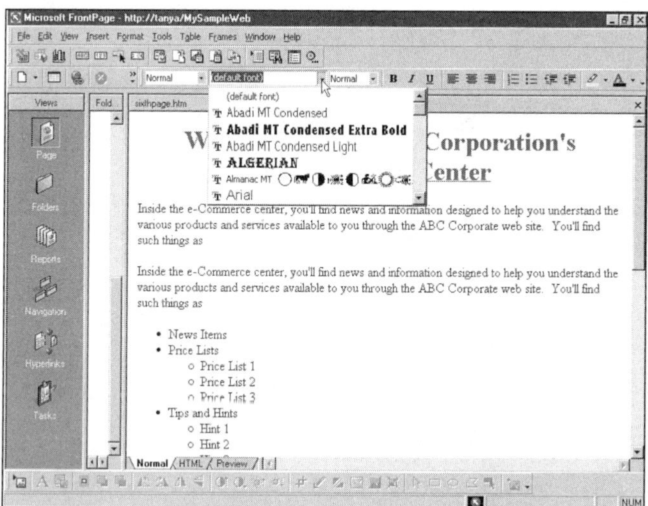

7.17

Because of its tight integration with Microsoft Office 2000, the capability to apply changes to font type and size has always been fairly standard across all Office applications, and FrontPage 2000 is no exception. However, it's still important to remember that you're formatting an HTML document and not a text document. Consequently, you'll find that there are slight differences in the way that type size is handled from Word to FrontPage 2000. Also, if you've used previous versions of FrontPage, you'll find that your font size selections range from 8pt to 36pt, and that the toolbar icons for increasing and decreasing font size are no longer available.

1. Select the text to which the font type and size change will be applied.
2. Choose Format→Font to open the Font dialog box **(7.16)**.
3. Make selections from the Font, Font style, and Size list boxes and click the OK button.

You can change a font style from the Style drop-down menu (7.17) or the Font Properties dialog box. Any new style selection overrides the existing one. The net effect, however, is the same regardless of the method used to apply the style.

Changing Font Color and Converting Text to a Table

Font colors are typically represented with a hexadecimal value in RGB color settings format #rrggbb. The "R" representing red, the "G" representing green, and the "B" representing blue. Each hexadecimal value combination is a composite of the colors red, green, and blue. After changing your font color in the FrontPage 2000 Editing window, select the HTML tab to see how FrontPage 2000 interprets your color choice as HTML.

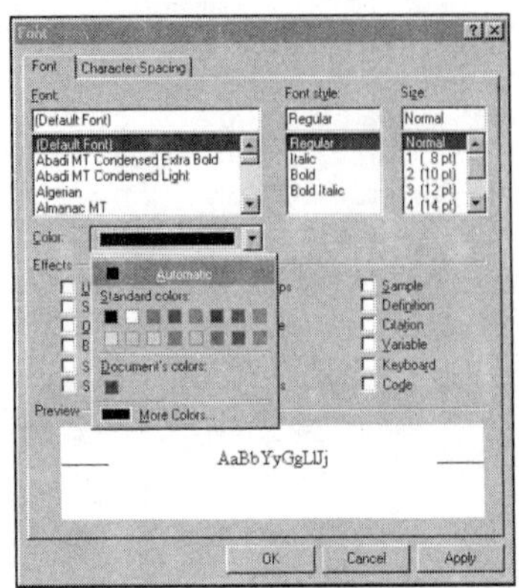

7.18

1. Select the text to which the font change will be applied.
2. Choose Format→Font to open the Font dialog box, and make a color selection from the Color drop-down list (7.18). Click OK.

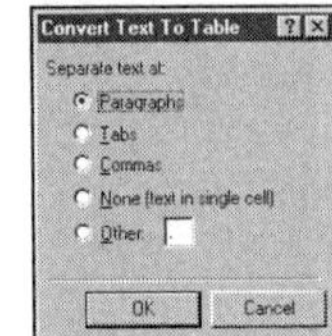

7.19

Converting text to a table can be beneficial when you want to add some symmetry to the appearance of text on your Web pages. You can easily have your text appear in table cells using the method outlined here:

1. Select the text that you want to convert.
2. Choose Table→Convert→Text To Table to open the Convert Text To Table dialog box (7.19).
3. Select an option for how the selected text is to be separated into table cells, and then click the OK button.

Performing a Cross-Web Spell Check

7.20

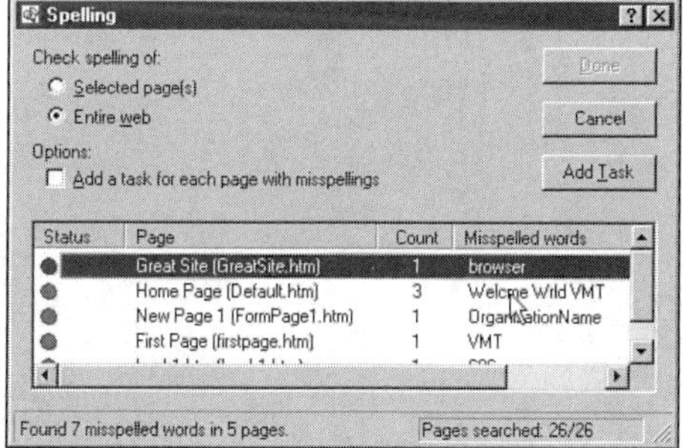

7.21

Spelling errors on your Web pages can have a significant impact on the impression your Web site makes on its visitors. FrontPage 2000 lets you automatically spell check all the pages in your Web site using its spelling tools.

1. Open the Web that you want to spell check.
2. Choose the Folders view button on the Views bar.
3. Choose Tools→Spelling to open the Spelling dialog box (7.20).
4. Select the Entire web option, and then click the Start button to expand the Spelling dialog box (7.21). This allows you to see the status of the spell check, the page where the misspelled words are found, the number of words found, and the misspelling.
5. Click the Done or Cancel button to close the Spelling dialog box.

I P

Double-click a page that appears in the list of pages with spelling errors on the FrontPage 2000 Spelling dialog box. This action opens the Office Spelling dialog box which allows you to instantly correct spelling errors on the selected page.

CHAPTER 8

In this chapter you will learn how to...

Create Hyperlinks to External Pages

Create Bookmarks

Link with Image Hotspots

Display Hyperlinks

Fix Broken Hyperlinks

Define Hyperlink Colors

Hyperlinks are references to files that are either internal or external to a Web site. Triggered by a mouse click, hyperlinks can be either color-coded text or hotspots that overlay an image. As you begin to work with hyperlinks, you'll discover that there are actually two types. One type is called a relative hyperlink. Relative hyperlinks send visitors to a page within the current Web or to a location on the current Web page. Relative hyperlinks

WORKING WITH HYPERLINKS

that point to a page within the current Web may be referenced by the name of the target file alone. In other words, you don't need to enter an absolute path containing http://www...and so on. On the other hand, relative hyperlinks that resolve to a location on the same page as the hyperlink itself reference the name of a bookmark. As you'll discover, bookmarks can add value to your pages as navigation tools that reference specific page areas, as well as specific strings or blocks of text.

The second type of hyperlink is called a fixed file hyperlink. This type of hyperlink sends visitors to a page that is not in your Web site, but rather is on the World Wide Web. Fixed file hyperlinks are generally characterized by a full pathname starting with the familiar `http://`. You can also create hyperlinks using pictures. When you do this, the hyperlinks that you create are called hotspots. This is because you specify a clickable area or spot on the picture, which sends the user to a target destination. In this chapter, you'll discover how to use FrontPage 2000 to create and use hyperlinks in your FrontPage 2000 Web.

Creating Hyperlinks to External Pages

The hyperlinks that you'll encounter most often are those text-based references to locations that are different from the page on which the hyperlink itself resides.

1. Select the text that you want to become a hyperlink.
2. Choose Insert→Hyperlink to open the Create Hyperlink dialog box (8.1).
3. Click the Look In drop-down list to select a location containing the Web pages to which you want to link.
4. Double-click a page in the scrolling list box to have that page appear in the URL field of the dialog box, or enter the URL of the page to which you want to hyperlink.
5. Click the OK button to complete the hyperlink creation process and close the Create Hyperlink dialog box.

Hyperlinks view gives you a graphic depiction of the links flowing out of your site, as well as the links flowing into it (8.2). Hyperlinks view is accessible by performing either of the following steps:

- *Choose View→Hyperlinks from the FrontPage 2000 menu bar.*
- *Choose the Hyperlinks icon from the View bar.*

The Globe, Folder, Envelope, and Page icons let you create different hyperlink types. The Globe icon lets you use your Web browser to retrieve a hyperlink destination external to the current Web. The Folder icon lets you establish a link to a file on your local drive. The Envelope icon lets you create a link that launches an email client, and the Page icon creates a link to a new page.

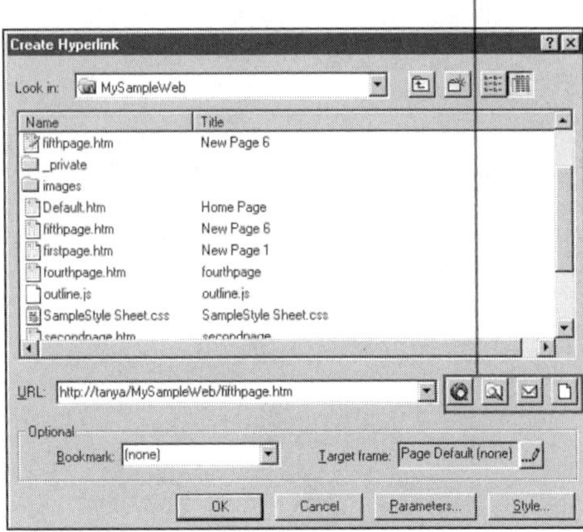

8.1

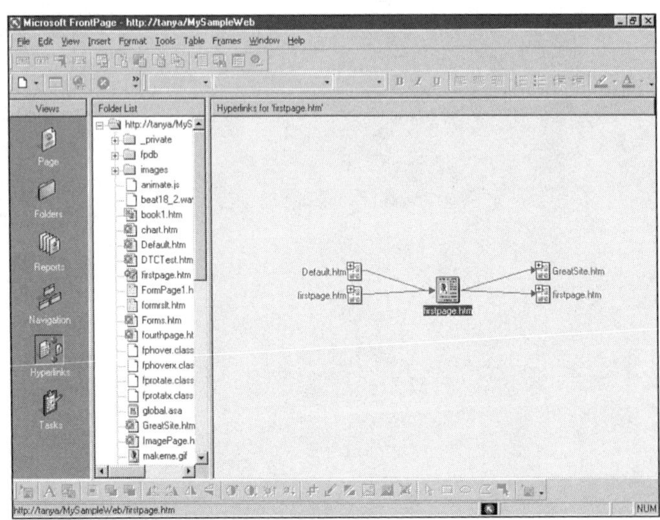

8.2

Creating Bookmarks

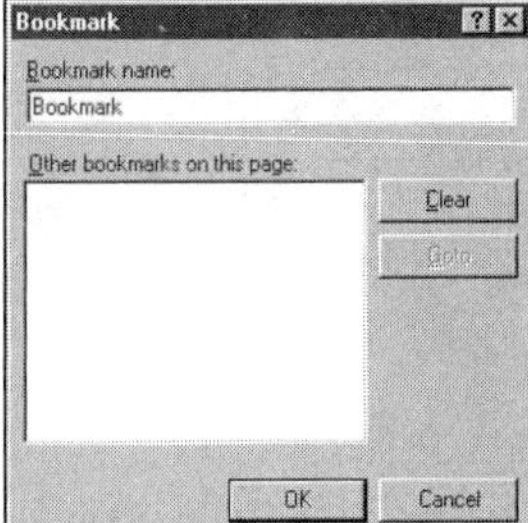

8.3

Now is the time for all good men to come to the aid of their country!

Normal HTML Preview

8.4

Now is the time for all good men to come to the aid of their country!

Normal HTML Preview

8.5

Bookmarks, also called internal hyperlinks, target destinations that reference locations on the same page as the hyperlink itself. For example, you may use bookmarks to allow your site visitors to avoid scrolling an entire page to find a specific reference. You might also use bookmarks if you want to avoid creating separate pages with individually referenced hyperlinks. In this case, you would place the content of many pages on a single page and use bookmarks as the content navigation device.

1. Select the text that you want to make a bookmark.
2. Choose Insert→Bookmark to open the Bookmark dialog box **(8.3)**.

continues

 I P

One way to keep your bookmark names short and easy to remember is to use a keyword approach. In other words, identify a unique term in the referenced content, and then use it as the hyperlink name.

  T E

Bookmarks are identified with small blue flags when referencing a page location (8.4), however, if the bookmark is a text string, the text appears with a blue-dotted underline (8.5).

Creating Bookmarks continued

3. Enter a name for the bookmark in the Bookmark name field.
4. Click the OK button to establish the selected text as a bookmark.
5. Create a hyperlink to your bookmark by selecting the text that will be the hyperlink trigger, and then choosing Insert→Hyperlink.
6. In the Create Hyperlink dialog box, select your bookmark from the Bookmark drop-down list **(8.6)**, and then click the OK button.

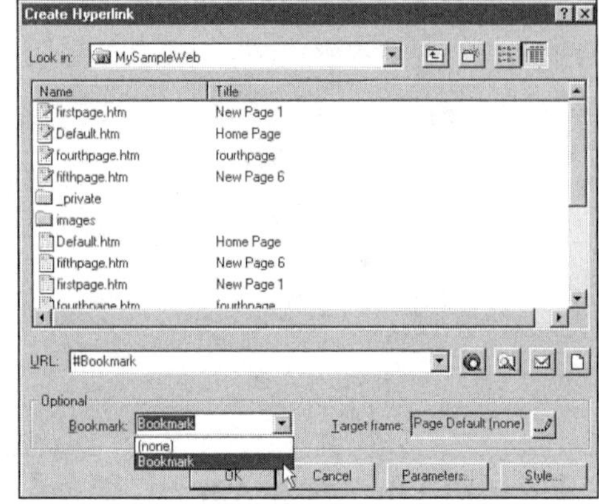

8.6

In HTML source code, a pound sign precedes bookmarks.

You can test a hyperlink while working in the FrontPage 2000 Editing window, by right-clicking the hyperlink and selecting Follow Hyperlink from the shortcut menu.

Linking with Image Hotspots

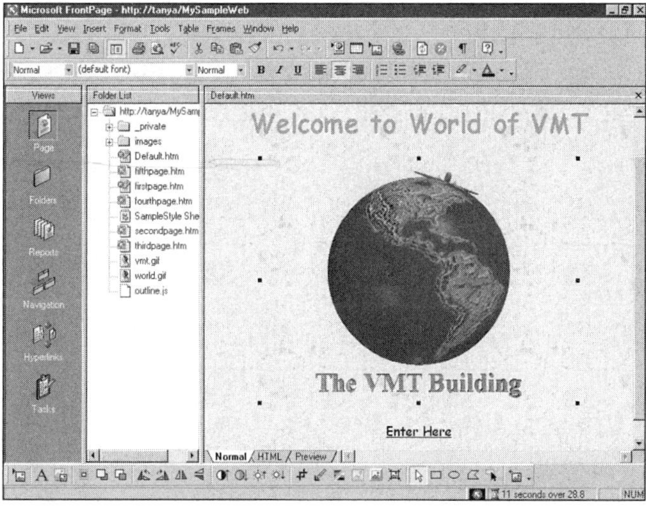

8.7

When creating hotspots, be careful to avoid overlapping your area definition shapes. Doing so could cause your visitors to hyperlink to an incorrect location.

8.8

Image maps are Web page graphics that contain hyperlinks known as hotspots. Hotspots define the coordinates for the area of an image capable of initiating a hyperlink to another page or URL.

1. Open a Web page containing an image to which you want to add hotspots.
2. Select the image so that sizing handles appear around it **(8.7)**.
3. Select the Rectangular, Circular, or Polygonal hotspot tool on the FrontPage 2000 Image toolbar **(8.8)**.
4. Hold down the left mouse button and drag the hotspot shape over an area of the image, and then release the mouse button to open the Create Hyperlink dialog box.
5. Click the Look In drop-down list to select a location containing the Web pages to which you want to link.
6. Double-click a page in the scrolling list box to have that page appear in the URL field of the dialog box, or enter the URL of the page to which you want to hyperlink.
7. Click the OK button to complete the hyperlink creation process and close the Create Hyperlink dialog box.

Displaying Hyperlinks

As you're developing your Web, it's likely that at some point you'll want to take a birds-eye view of the status of your Web's hyperlinks. FrontPage 2000 makes displaying your hyperlinks easy.

1. Select the Hyperlinks icon on the FrontPage 2000 Views bar.
2. Select a page in the Folder List pane to display the hyperlinks associated with that page in the Hyperlinks window (8.9).

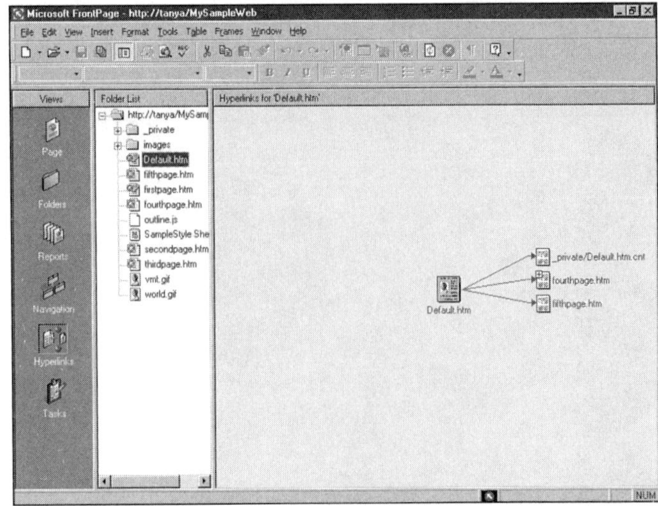

8.9

You can validate the hyperlink destinations defined in your Web by selecting the Reports icon under the Views bar, right-clicking in the Reports window, and then selecting Verify Hyperlinks from the shortcut menu (8.10) (you can also click the Verify Hyperlinks icon on the Reporting toolbar to open the Verify Hyperlinks dialog box). Click the Start button to begin the verification process.

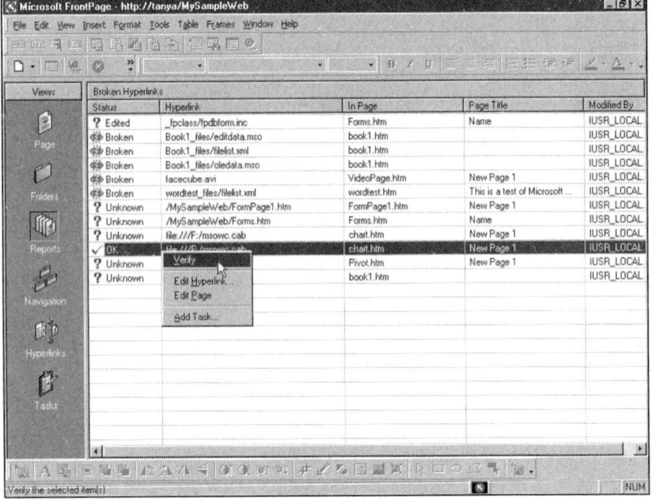

8.10

You can delete a hyperlink completely by selecting the hyperlink in Page view, and then pressing the Delete key.

Fixing Broken Hyperlinks

A broken line indicates a damaged link.

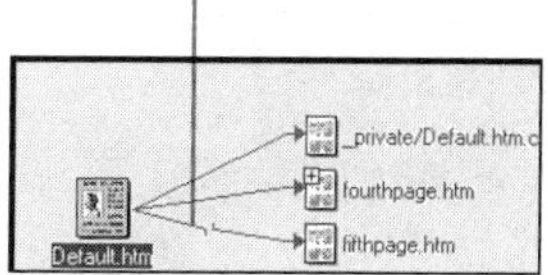

8.11

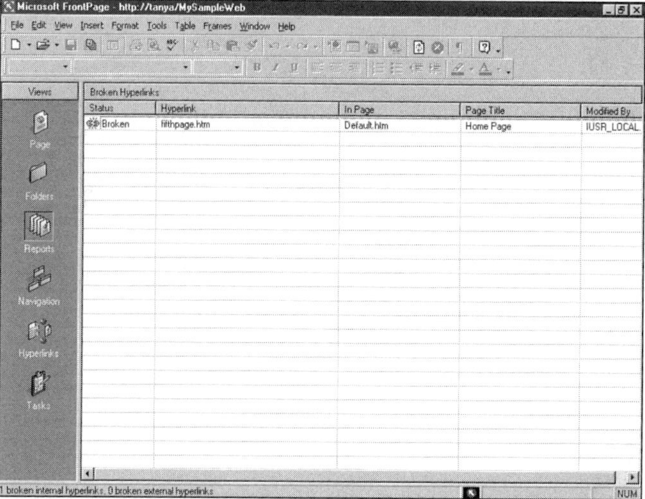

8.12

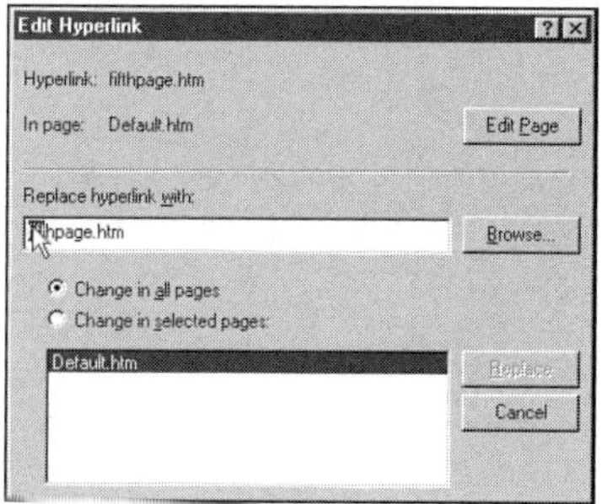

8.13

During the course of your Web development activities, you'll encounter "gotchas"—like a power outage, or a Web page deletion. These are events that can cause breaks in defined hyperlinks. When this occurs, you can fix these breaks by using one of the reports available in FrontPage 2000.

1. Select the Hyperlinks icon on the FrontPage 2000 Views bar to see what hyperlinks are damaged (8.11).
2. Choose View→Reports→Broken Hyperlinks to see a detailed list of broken hyperlinks in your Web (8.12).
3. Double-click the line item for the broken hyperlink you want to fix to open the Edit Hyperlink dialog box (8.13).
4. Enter a page to replace the broken hyperlink in the Replace hyperlink with field, select the Change in all pages option, and then click the Replace button to close the dialog box and execute the change.
5. Choose Tools→Recalculate Hyperlinks to have all references to broken links removed from your Web server.

Defining Hyperlink Colors

New hyperlinks are typically displayed in blue, while active and selected hyperlinks are displayed in red and purple respectively. However, if you find these default colors unsuitable for your Web site design, you can define new hyperlink color properties on the Background tab of the Page Properties dialog box.

1. In Page view, choose File→Properties to open the Page Properties dialog box.
2. Select the Background tab, and then make new color selections for new, Visited, and Active hyperlinks in the Colors section (8.14).
3. Click the OK button to close the dialog box and execute the change.

You will not be able to alter hyperlink color properties from the Page Properties dialog box if a theme is applied to your Web pages.

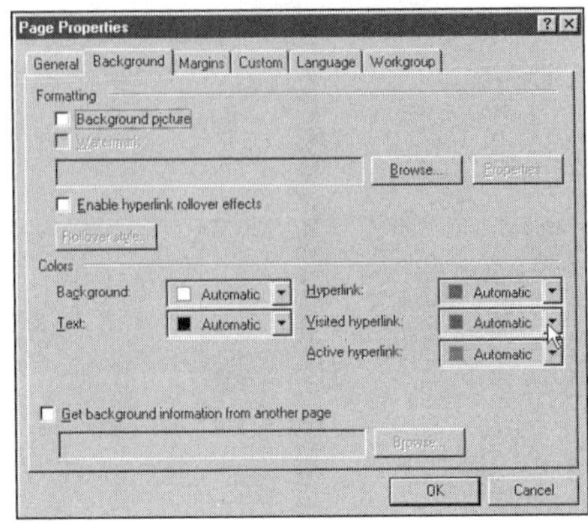

8.14

NOTE

Hover buttons as a hyperlink device have a number of optional color effects. The Color Fill effect causes the entire button to change to the effect color when the cursor passes over it. The Color Average effect causes the button to change to a color that is a mix between the Button color and the Effect color. The Glow effect changes the center of the hover button to the Effect color with the button color fading at the edges. The Reverse Glow effect calls for the button color to remain the same in the center but fade to the Effect color at the button edges. The Light Glow effect is a softer version of the Glow effect.

CHAPTER 9

In this chapter you will learn how to...

Create a Table

Add and Delete Table Cells

Merge and Split Cells

Create Table Captions

Modify a Table Layout

Add a Table Background

Change Table Border Colors

Add a Cell Background

Change Cell Border Colors

Modify Cell Layout and Width

As applied to FrontPage 2000, you can use tables to frame images, segment the display of data retrieved from a database, or enhance the appearance of a text label. You should be aware, however, that with FrontPage 2000 some of the page layout capabilities—once possible only with tables—are now available using positioning. For this reason, using a table as a page layout device is more an alternative than a default.

BUILDING TABLES

They are still a useful strategy, however, and the only strategy when developing for a mixed-browser Internet environment. Tables provide design control—the only way to control the size (width and length) of a presentation is to exploit the structure provided by tables. Absolute positioning is not absolute; nonetheless, you also can combine features and absolute position tables for even greater control of layouts. Border size, cell spacing, and padding enable creative and controlled spacing of text and graphics.

If you're familiar with creating tables in other Microsoft Office applications, such as Microsoft Word, your learning curve for table creation with FrontPage 2000 is significantly reduced. As you begin to create and enhance tables in FrontPage 2000, notice how the difference in the look and feel of the FrontPage 2000 interface and other Office 2000 applications is now transparent.

In this chapter, you'll discover how to create and modify table structures, as well as how to fine-tune some of the attributes of those structures.

Creating a Table

Tables organize Web page content into rows and columns. This is particularly useful if your site design seeks to structure the presentation of data or pictures. For instance, you can use tables as an alignment device. This allows you to left, right, or center justify text and pictures giving pages more of a publishing layout look. In fact, if you want to get creative, you can increase table border size and give your Web pages a 3D look by creating the effect of window panes.

1. In Page view, (if the Tables toolbar is not visible), choose Table→Draw Table to change the mouse pointer into a drawing cursor and to display the Tables toolbar **(9.1)**.

2. Hold down the left mouse button where you want the table to begin; drag the mouse down and to the right to form the table; and then release the mouse button to complete the process **(9.2)**.

Change the drawing cursor back to normal by selecting the Draw Table icon on the Tables toolbar.

9.1

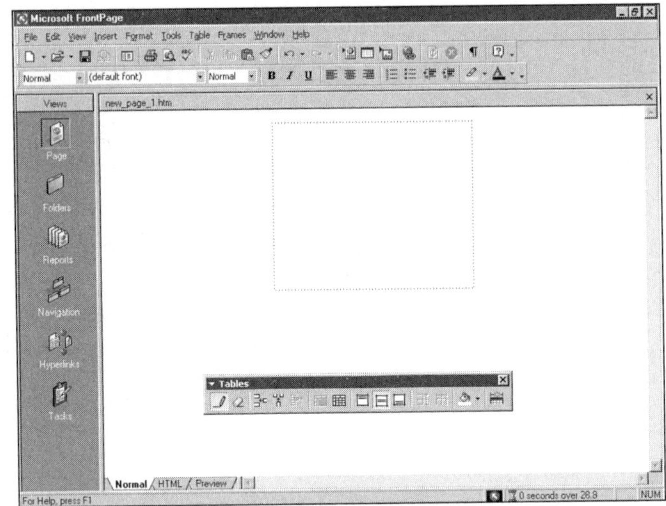

9.2

An alternate method for creating tables involves selecting the Draw Table icon, clicking the left mouse button, and then dragging and releasing the mouse button when your table is the size of your choice. You can also convert existing text to a table.

Adding and Deleting Table Cells

You can resize a table by dragging the table border left, right, up, or down.

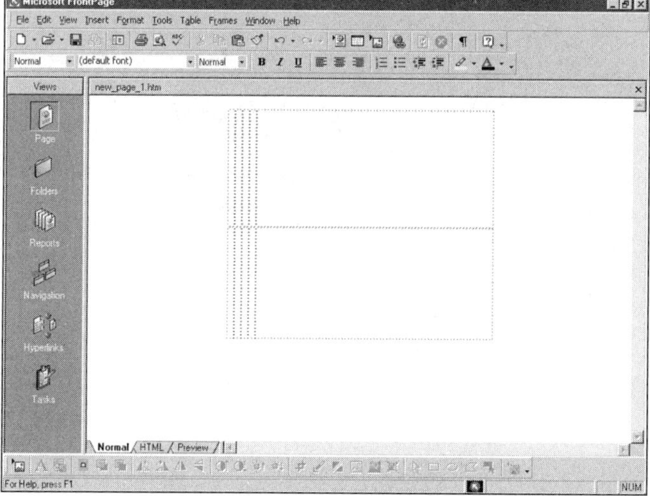

9.3

When you draw a new table, by default the result is a one-row, one-column table. This one-dimensional table represents a single table cell. However, if your intent is to use the table for something more than a framing device, it's likely you'll want to add a few more cells. Of course, you can also delete as many table cells as you add.

1. With the cursor inside a table cell, choose Table→Insert→ Cell to add a new table cell to the current cell **(9.3)**.
2. Delete this newly created cell by placing the blinking cursor inside the new cell.
3. Choose Table→Select→Cell to select the cell for deletion.
4. Choose Table→Delete Cells to complete the cell deletion process.

Dotted line table borders indicate that the table borders will not be visible on your Web page.

You can also delete a table cell by right-clicking the selected cell and choosing Delete Cells from the shortcut menu.

Merging and Splitting Cells

Perhaps you're working with a two-cell table that contains an oversized image in one cell and a small text description in the other **(9.4)**. In this case, it may be beneficial to add another cell to the text description area of the table to make another point about the figure. You might even decide to combine the text and the image into a single cell, or vice versa. This type of table modification is called merging and splitting.

1. With the blinking cursor inside a table cell, choose Table→Split Cells to open the Split Cells dialog box **(9.5)**.
2. In the Split Cells dialog box, choose either the Split into columns or Split into rows option button to split the selected cell into columns or rows, and then enter the number of columns or rows to split into as appropriate.
3. Click the OK button to complete the cell splitting process.

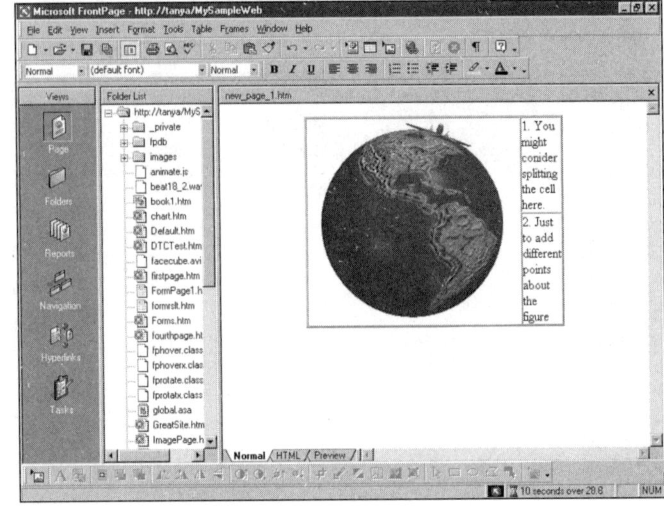

9.4

You can also open this dialog box by right-clicking inside a cell and choosing Split Cells from the shortcut menu.

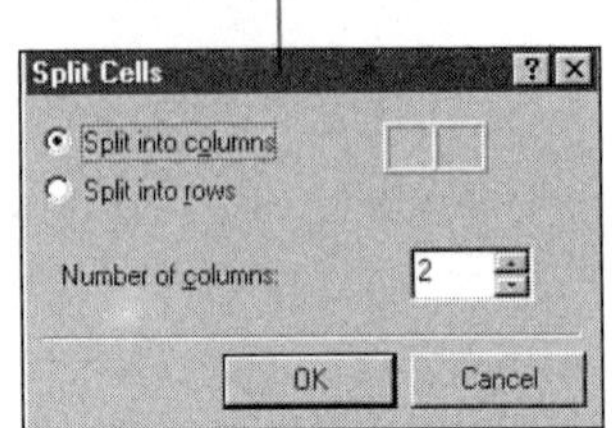

9.5

The sum of cell widths in a given row should not exceed 100 percent; otherwise, your table may appear differently when previewed in a browser than it does in Page view.

Creating Table Captions

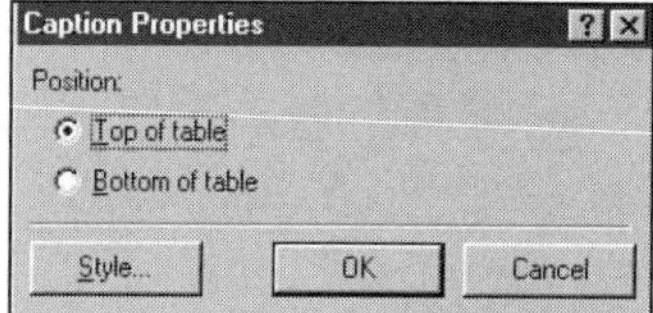

9.6

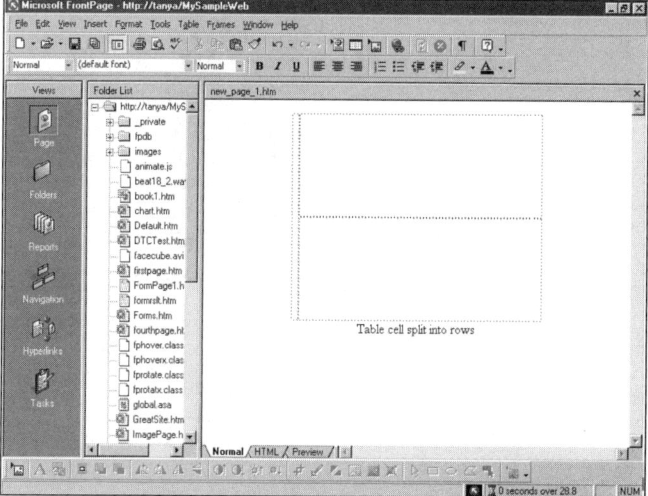

9.7

Table captions enable you to give your tables an identity. In other words, they establish a viewer context for the data displayed in the table by providing a brief description about table data or by identifying a table by name. Technically, table captions let you place an object directly above or below a table without a line space between.

1. Choose Table→Select→Table to select the desired table.
2. With the table selected, choose Table→Insert→Caption.
3. Enter the caption text of your choice.
4. If you prefer the caption to appear at the bottom of the table rather than the top, which is the default, right-click the caption, and then choose Caption Properties from the shortcut menu to open the Caption Properties dialog box **(9.6)**.
5. Select the Bottom of table option button and then click OK to see the result **(9.7)**.

Be aware that when you format table caption text, the way that the caption text actually displays can be unpredictable because the display itself is browser-related.

Modifying a Table Layout

Table layout is often determined by the overall design of your Web page. For example, if you're using tables to organize data on the page, you may choose to have a table set up in equal columns and rows to display the content. For a more design-oriented layout, you might have it set up in just a few precisely sized cells to display the images and text that comprise your page.

Moreover, depending on the effect you want to create, you may want to have text flow around the table in a specific way, increase the space and distance between a cell's content and its borders, or even make adjustments to the table's overall height and width.

1. Choose Table→Properties→Table to open the Table Properties dialog box (9.8).

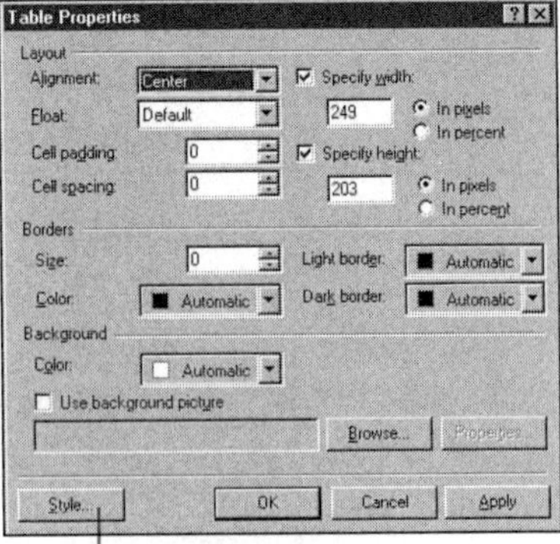

9.8 You can also access the Properties dialog box by right-clicking your table and choosing Table Properties from the shortcut menu.

Using FrontPage 2000's absolute positioning feature, you can position cell contents outside of a table border, or reposition an entire table. You can also position and layer tables over each other. You'll find a discussion of absolute positioning in Chapter 8.

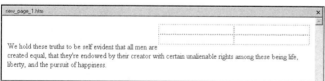

9.9

9.10

9.11

9.12

2. If your table is center-aligned when you create it, you can adjust the alignment left **(9.9)**, which is the default, or right **(9.10)** by choosing an option from the Alignment drop-down menu on the Table Properties dialog box, and then clicking the OK button.

3. If your table's Float property is set to Default when you create it, this means that text will not wrap around the table. You can adjust the Float property so that the table will left justify and the text will wrap to the right by selecting Float to Left from the Float drop-down menu **(9.11)**. Select Float to Right so that text will wrap to the left **(9.12)**. Click the OK button to finish.

continues

A good rule of thumb is to make sure that a blank line exists between each new table you create on a page, because FrontPage 2000 merges tables together when no blank line exists.

Modifying a Table Layout continued

4. Without cell padding or spacing, text placed in a table is displayed flush with the cell border **(9.13)**. Enter a numeric value (0–10) in the Cell Padding field, and then click the OK button to add space between the edges of the table and the text **(9.14)**.

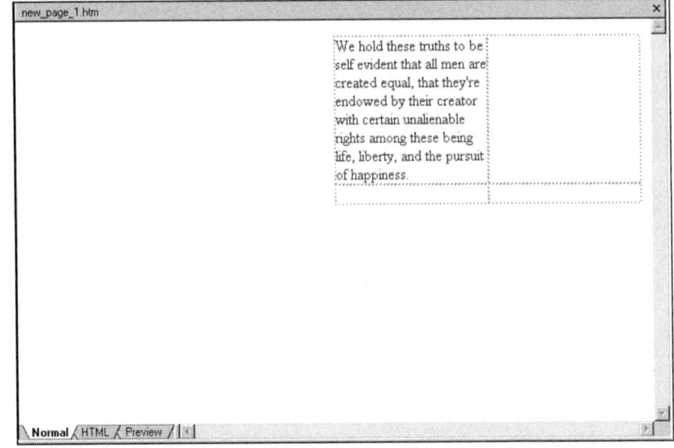

9.13

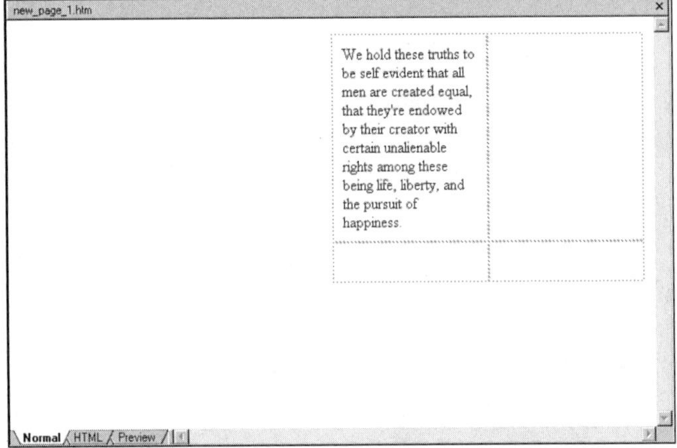

9.14

In HTML, all tables are bound with a <TABLE> ...</TABLE> *tag pair. The* <TR>... </TR> *tag pair marks the beginning and end of each table row, and the* <TD>...</TD> *tag pair marks the beginning and end of each data cell.*

Converting a table to text takes the content of each of your table cells and formats them as a sequence of paragraphs. This feature is useful when you require the data stored in a table, but don't want to take the time to copy and paste the content of each individual table cell into its own sentence or paragraph. This feature is also useful if you want to repurpose content found in a table for use in a narrative or on another page. Using a prepared table, choose Table→Convert→ Table To Text and review your results.

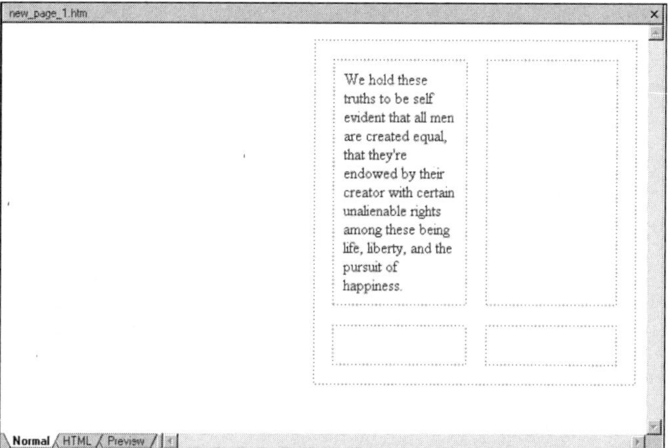

9.15

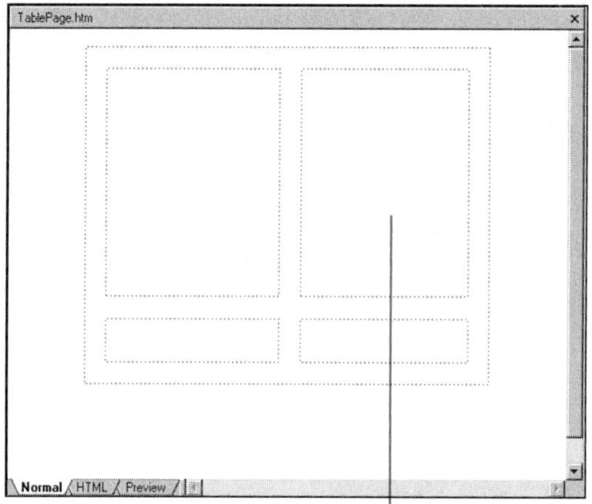

9.16 If you enter 75 as the value for each field and select the percent option, your cells appear as shown here in the top row.

5. To add space between the individual table cells **(9.15)**, enter a numeric value (0–20) in the Cell Spacing field, and then click the OK button.
6. To make height and width adjustments to a table, select the Specify Width or Specify Height check boxes. Set the adjustment unit as pixel or percent using the option buttons, enter a numeric value in the Specify Width field/Specify Height field, and click the OK button **(9.16)**.

When you use percentage-based table widths, the table changes dynamically based on the sizing of the browser window.

The amount of space that appears between table cell content and the sides of the table cell is called padding.

Adding a Table Background

Using FrontPage 2000, you can enhance the background of a table with a solid color or an image. As always, the choice you make is driven by your overall Web design. For example, you might want to create the effect of looking through a window out into space by making the table background black, and then placing an image filled with stars as a table cell background. You might also choose to highlight the text in a table cell by contrasting the font color against the table's background.

1. Using the Table Properties dialog box (Table→Propterties→Table), make a color selection from the Background section's Color drop-down menu **(9.17)**, and then click OK to see the result **(9.18)**.

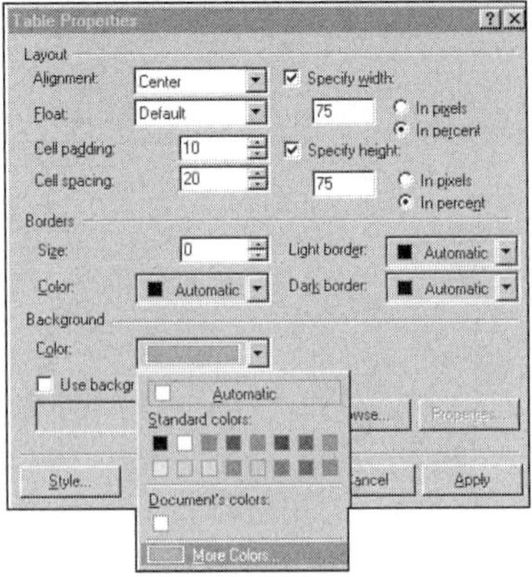

9.17

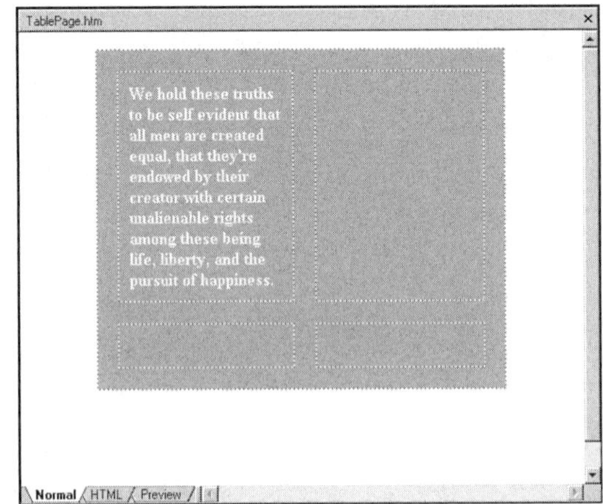

9.18

Selecting the More Colors option on the Color drop-down menu in the Background section of the Table Properties dialog box gives you the option to create custom table background colors.

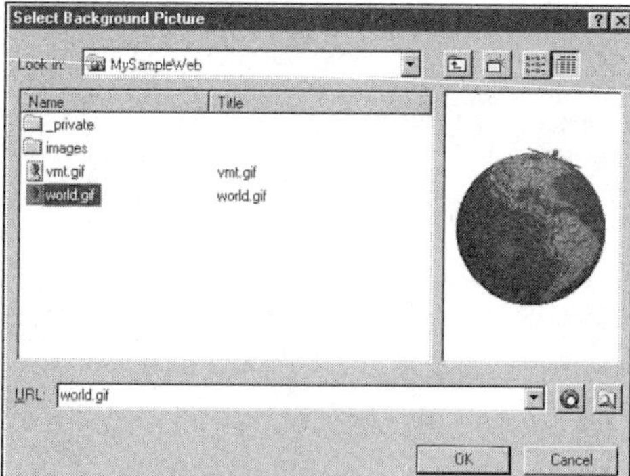

9.19

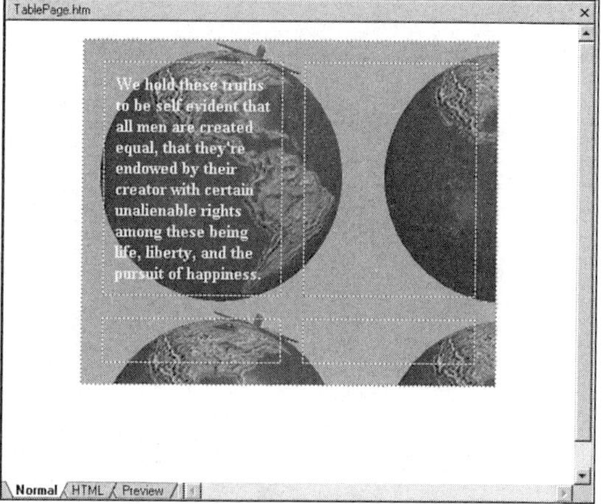

9.20

2. To choose an image as the background instead, select the Use Background Picture check box under the Background section of the dialog box, and then enter an image filename or select the Browse button to open the Select Background Picture dialog box **(9.19)**.
3. Select a file from disk and then click OK to close the dialog box.
4. Click OK to close the Table Properties dialog box, and to view the result of your background choice(s) **(9.20)**.

You can select multiple table cells in different columns and rows by holding down the CTRL key while clicking the cells of your choice.

If you're feeling creative, try splitting a cell and placing an image in one half and a solid background color in the other. You could then use a different font color to add some jazz to your image description.

Changing Table Border Colors

When made visible, borders can add an eye-catching symmetry to the appearance of your tables. For example, by increasing the size of your table borders, and then adding a splash of color, you can create the effect of a raised frame for your page content. Spend some time manipulating your border sizes and colors, you'll be surprised at how adding the appearance of depth to your tables enhances the presentation of your content.

1. From the Table Properties dialog box (Table→Properties→Table), make a color selection from the Color drop-down menu in the Borders section **(9.21)**, and then click OK to see the result **(9.22)**.

To ensure display in Netscape when using borders, place a non-breaking space in each cell.

Borders with a setting of one are provided by default and can be annoying or detract from your presentation. To prevent borders from being displayed in all browsers, set the border to zero. If you leave the setting blank, some browsers will still display borders. To create monochrome borders for IE, set all border colors the same. This does not work for Netscape, although it does produce an attractive raised border.

If you select colors from the Light border and Dark border drop-down menus, you add a shading effect to the border color.

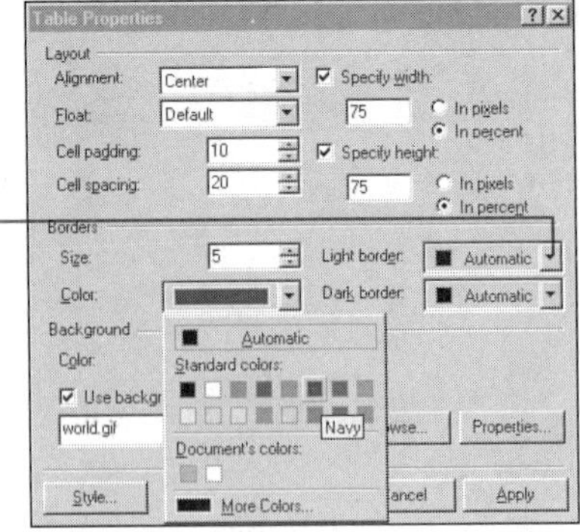

9.21

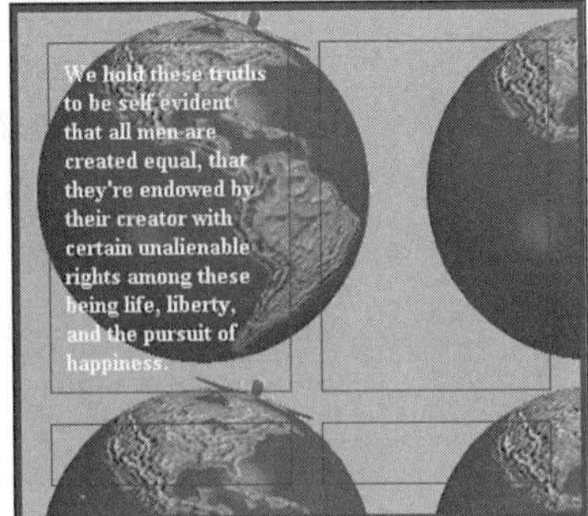

9.22 **You can remove table borders at any time by setting the Borders Size parameter to 0 in the Table Properties dialog box.**

Adding a Cell Background

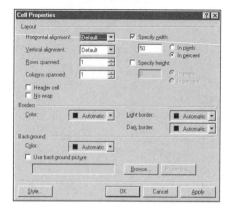

9.23

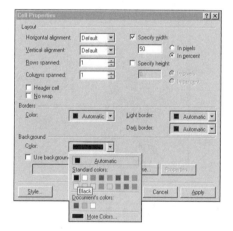

9.24

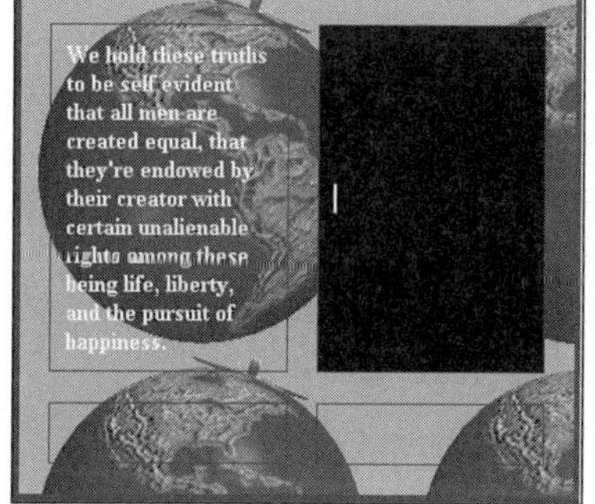

9.25

As table backgrounds can be enhanced with colors and images, so can table cell backgrounds. Being able to modify specific table cells is a great way to create a checkerboard effect for gaming purposes, create cool organizational charts for your company by filling table cells with employee pictures, or highlight specific pieces of content using colorized cells. Again, your use of tables and color is limited only by your imagination.

1. With the cursor in a table cell, choose Table→Properties→Cell to open the Cell Properties dialog box **(9.23)**.
2. Choose a color from the Color drop-down menu in the Background section **(9.24)**, and then click OK to see the result **(9.25)**.

continues

 I P

Table headers appear in bold by default.

 I P

You can also access Cell Properties by right-clicking a table cell and choosing Cell Properties from the shortcut menu.

Adding a Cell Background continued

3. To use an image as the cell background, select the Use Background Picture check box under the Background section in the dialog box, and then enter an image filename or select the Browse button to open the Cell Properties dialog box **(9.26)**.

4. Select a file from disk by double-clicking it or entering a filename in the URL field, and then click OK to close the dialog box.

5. Click OK to close the Cell Properties dialog box, and to view the result **(9.27)**.

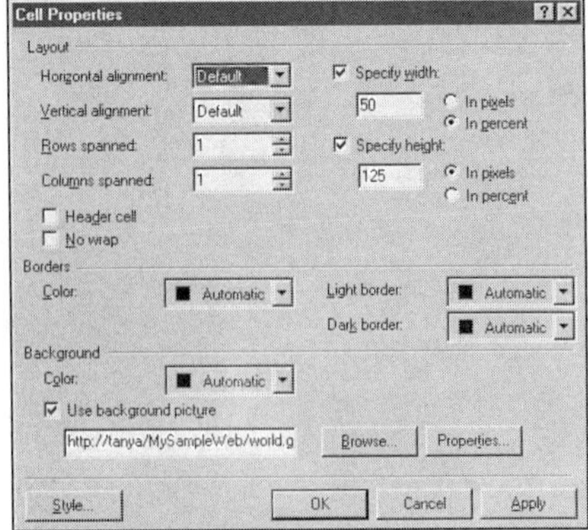

9.26

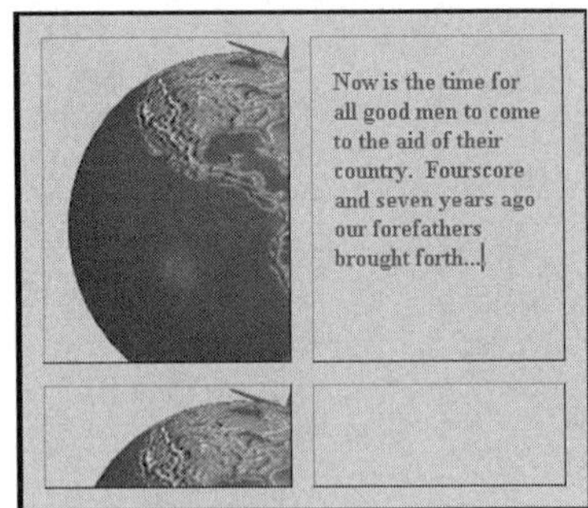

9.27

You can make several rows or columns the same width automatically by highlighting two or more rows, and then selecting Table→Distribute Rows Evenly on the FrontPage 2000 menu bar.

Changing Cell Border Colors

9.28

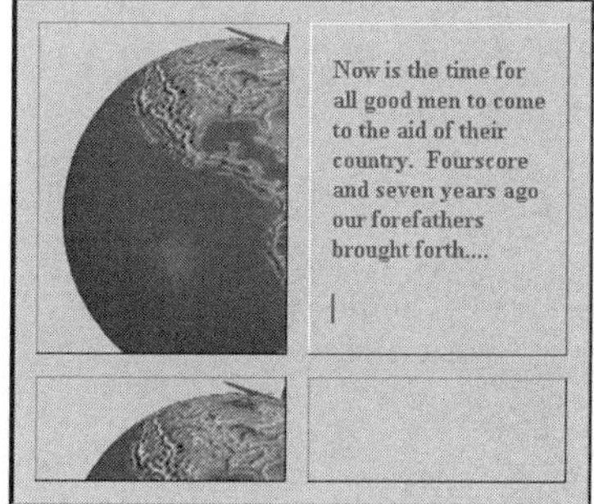

9.29

Cell borders are a variation on table borders and, as with table borders, give a splash of color that can make all the difference in how your table data is displayed. Imagine a coloring book without lines to bound the colors. Colorizing your cell borders is much the same. By adding colors to the borders of your table cells, you can emphasize text by using a contrasting font color and style, or enhance the appearance of a cell-framed image.

Open the Cell Properties dialog box (Table→Properties→Cell). Make a color selection from the Color drop-down menu in the Borders section **(9.28)**, and then click OK to see the result **(9.29)**.

If you select colors from the Light Border and Dark Border drop-down menus, selecting a color from the Color drop-down menu has no effect.

You can also access the Cell Properties dialog box by right-clicking a table cell, and then selecting Cell Properties from the short-cut menu.

Modifying Cell Layout and Width

Modifying cell layout is much the same as making adjustments to the overall table layout with just a few differences. One of the more notable differences has to do with the concept of cell span. When you apply values in the Rows Spanned or Columns Spanned field, you can manipulate the width and height of an individual table cell. This allows you to customize your tables with cells of varying sizes, thereby giving you added page design flexibility overall **(9.30)**.

1. With your cursor in a table cell, choose Table→Properties→Cell to open the Cell Properties dialog box.
2. To horizontally align the contents of a table cell, choose an option from the Horizontal Alignment drop-down menu **(9.31)**.

Whenever you manually size a table or cell, any height settings that were left open are automatically defined, and may need to be resized to eliminate space when you move or delete text or images from the cells.

When working with split columns, you should watch out for inserting images and URLs. They can override cell settings, which then override the table settings. This is where manually coding the width using the HTML tab comes in.

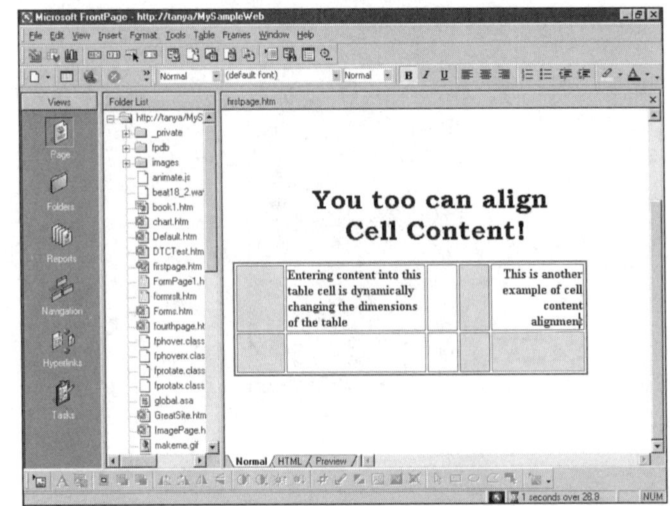

9.30

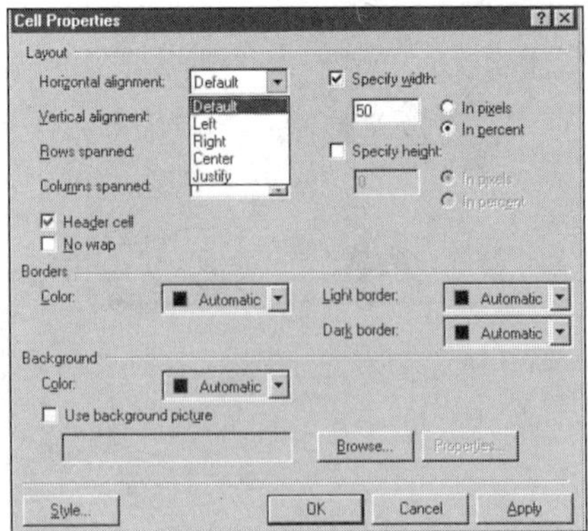

9.31

When you size a table cell in pixels, cell size remains constant, regardless of the size of the table in which it is displayed. However, when you size a table cell as a percentage of the table, its size changes depending on the size of the table.

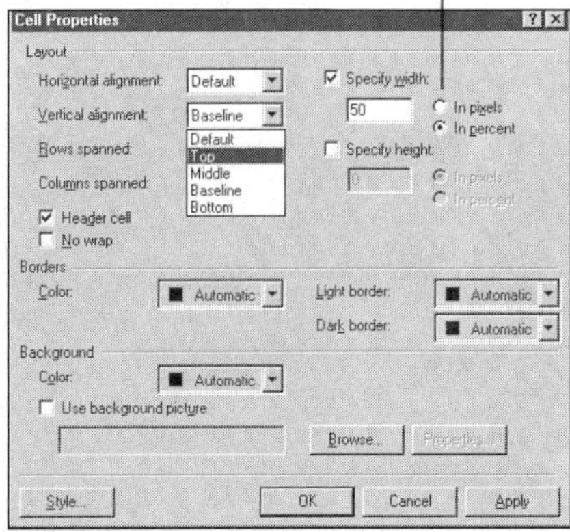

9.32

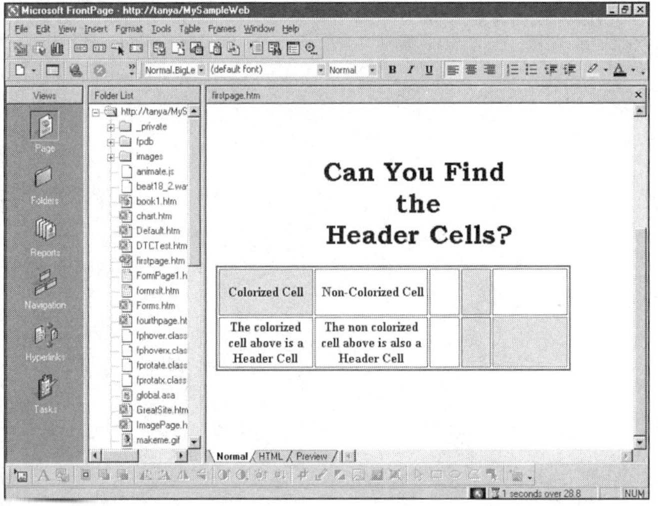

9.33

3. To vertically align the contents of a table cell, choose an option from the Vertical Alignment drop-down menu **(9.32)**.
4. Increase or decrease the row and column span for the contents of a table cell by entering a numeric value in either the Rows Spanned or Columns Spanned fields.
5. Select the Header Cell check box to designate the contents of a table cell to be bolded for emphasis as a table header **(9.33)**.
6. Prevent table cell text from wrapping inside the cell by selecting the No Wrap check box.
7. Click the OK button when you are finished with your layout modifications.

NOTE

You can make height or width adjustments to a table cell by selecting the Specify Width or Specify Height check boxes. After making a size property selection, select the option button to establish the adjustment unit as pixel or percent. Finally, enter a numeric value and then click OK.

CHAPTER 10

In this chapter you will learn how to...

- **Create and Save Page Frames**
- **Edit Page Frames**
- **Specify Target Frames**
- **Segment Frames**
- **Hide Frame Borders**

Frames are Web page design features that enable you to divide a single page into multiple viewing regions. Each of these regions is capable of displaying its own unique content, such as navigation controls or menu options, and arguably improves the visitors' interaction with your Web site. For this reason, frames are used to guide a visitor's navigation through your site, as well as to

WORKING WITH FRAMES

expose them to other sites without leaving their point of origin. Even though a frame might contain multiple pages, the frame itself is also an HTML page that's displayed in response to a browser request. When your site visitors request a frames page, the Web server delivers the page to the visitor's browser, and then follows with the individual documents specified to fill each section of the delivered frames page. Each frames page section is called a target frame, and as such is designated as the host for a specific page stored on your Web site or on a site external to your Web. In this chapter, you'll learn what is required to create and use frames in FrontPage 2000.

Creating and Saving Page Frames

FrontPage 2000 helps you expedite the frame creation process with just a few clicks. You can create a frames page by choosing from a variety of 10 templates.

1. In Page view, choose File→New to open the New dialog box. Select the Frames Pages tab **(10.1)**.
2. Select the frames pages template of your choice.
3. Click the OK button to generate the new frames page **(10.2)**.

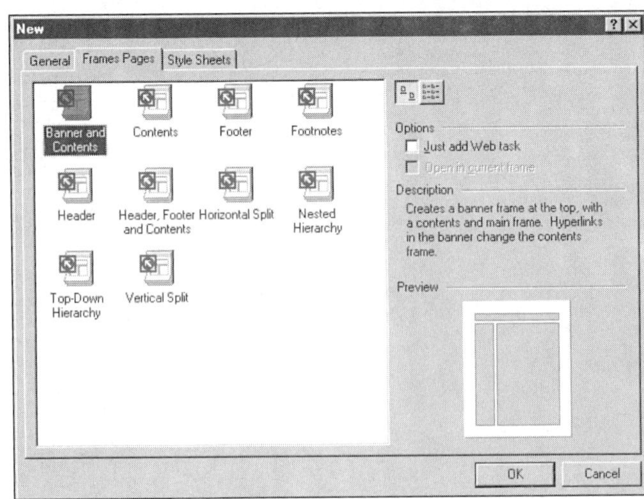

10.1

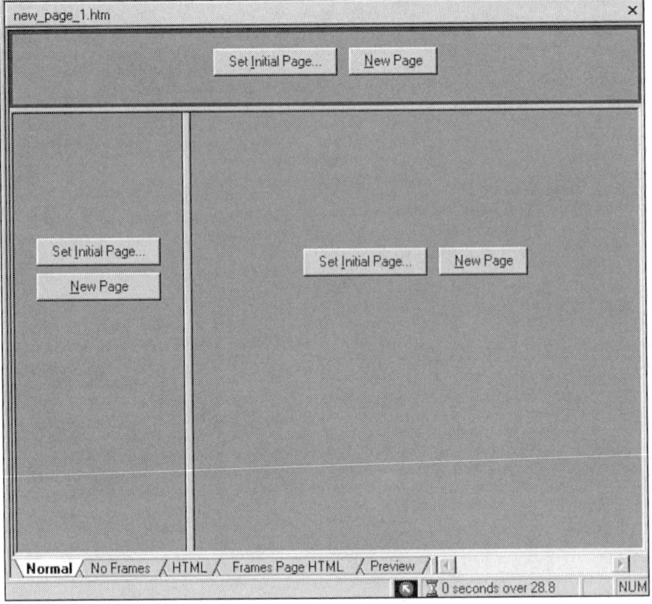

10.2

Frames pages are defined in HTML using the <FRAMESET></FRAMESET> tag pair, while the frames that compromise a frames page are defined with the <FRAME></FRAME> tag pair.

The Set Initial Page button in each frame opens the Create Hyperlink dialog box. From there you choose a preexisting page to display in the selected frame segment. The New Page button in each frame opens a blank page in the selected frame segment.

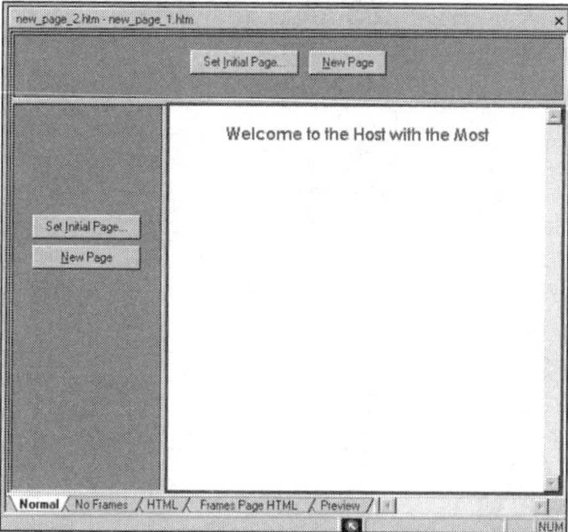

10.3

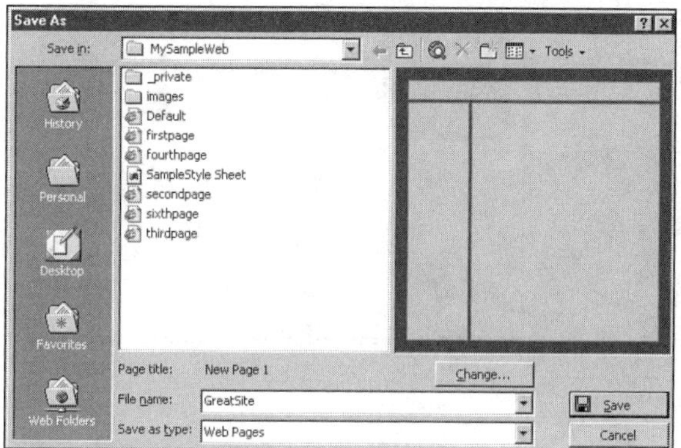

10.4

4. Use the buttons on the layout to provide the content for the frames **(10.3)**.
5. After you've added content to each frame pages segment and you're ready to save the whole thing, choose File→Save to open the Save As dialog box **(10.4)**.
6. Enter a name for the Frames Pages in the File name field, and then click Save. You are prompted to enter filenames for any frame segment pages that have not been previously saved.

 I P

You can also save an individual page in a frame segment in isolation by choosing File→Save on the FrontPage 2000 menu bar, entering a name for the page in the File name field, and then clicking the Save button.

 O T E

When you use frames, you'll notice that two additional tabs are added to the bottom of the editing window. The No Frames tab lets you edit the selected frame segment in full view, and the Frames HTML tab lets you view the HTML source code for the active Frames Pages.

Editing Page Frames

So, you've created a frames page and populated its individual segments with fabulous new content. However, you want to add a little fine-tuning to your new masterpiece. You can make adjustments to the frame, such as size and margin, using the Frame Properties dialog box.

1. In Page view, select the frames page segment that you want to edit.
2. Right-click inside the frames page segment and then choose Frame Properties from the shortcut menu to open the Frame Properties dialog box **(10.5)**.
3. Make adjustments to the overall Frame size and Margins. Decide whether the frame will be resizable when displayed in a Web browser and change the name of the file that appears in the segment (if desired).
4. Click the OK button to close the dialog box and allow the change to take effect. Notice that prior to editing, the frames page contained scrollbars **(10.6)**. After editing, the scrollbars no longer appear **(10.7)**.

For details on various style options available when the Style button is selected in the Frame Properties dialog box, see Chapter 6, "Developing Static Web Pages."

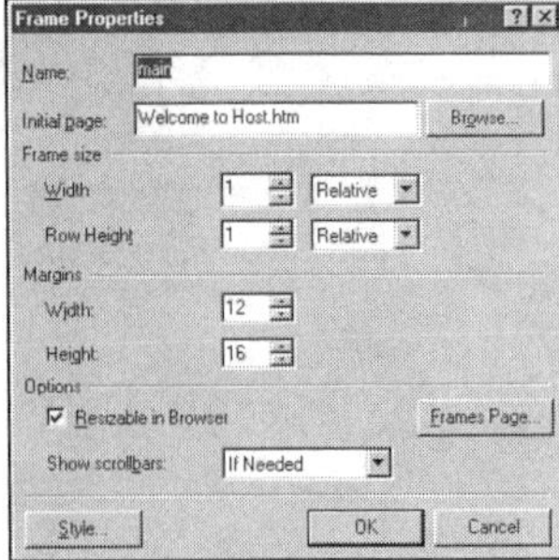

10.5

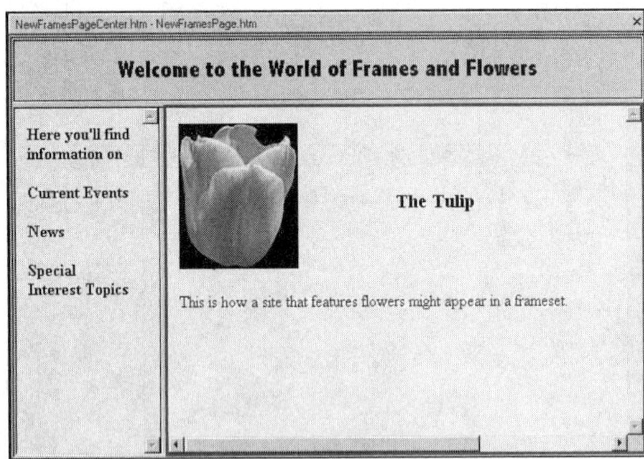

10.6

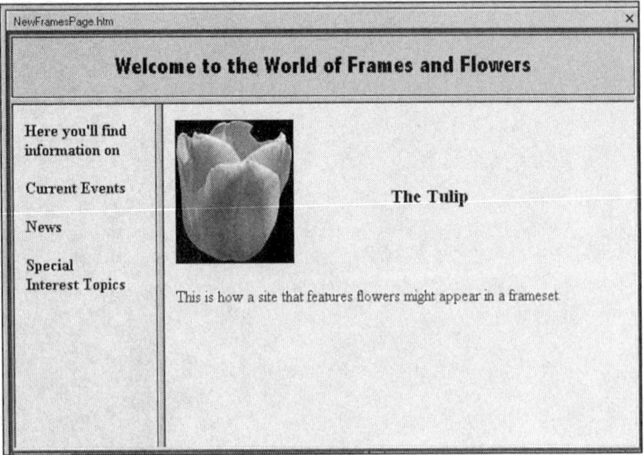

10.7

Specifying Target Frames

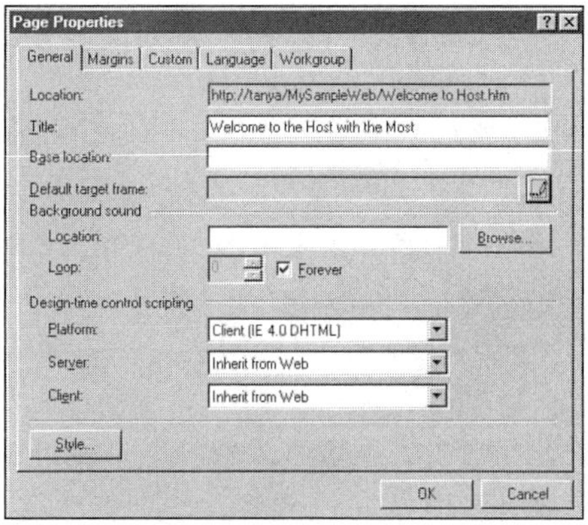

10.8

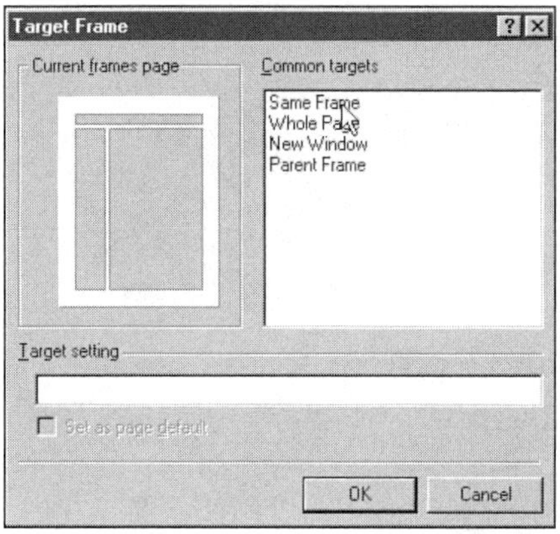

10.9

One of the advantages of using frames is that you can control what happens when a hyperlink is selected in one of the frame page segments. For example, you can determine if the referenced hyperlink appears in the current frame segment, in a different frame segment, or in a brand new browser window. These feats of magic require that you know how to specify the frame segment where a selected hyperlink will resolve its display.

1. In Page view, select a frames page segment for which you want to specify target behavior.

2. Right-click inside the frame page segment and then choose Page Properties from the shortcut menu to open the Page Properties dialog box **(10.8)**.

3. On the General tab, click the Default target frame button to open the Target Frame dialog box **(10.9)**.

4. Select a target frame from the Common targets list box. Completing this action establishes where the hyperlink destination page will appear, when you select a hyperlink in one of your page frame segments. Next, click the OK button to close the Target Frame dialog box, and then click the OK button to close the Page Properties dialog box.

Segmenting Frames

Perhaps you'll encounter a situation when you'll want to have a frame within a frame, similar to splitting a table cell. However, this is not recommended because it can make your pages appear too busy and cumbersome. I discuss it here only to make you aware that it can be done.

1. In Page view, select a frames page segment that you want to segment further.
2. Choose Frames→Split Frame to open the Split Frame dialog box **(10.10)**, and then choose to either split the frame into columns or rows.
3. Click the OK button to create the new frame within a frame **(10.11)**.

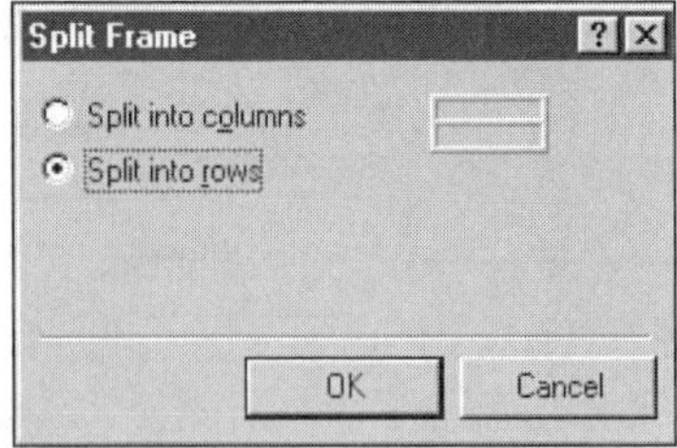

10.10

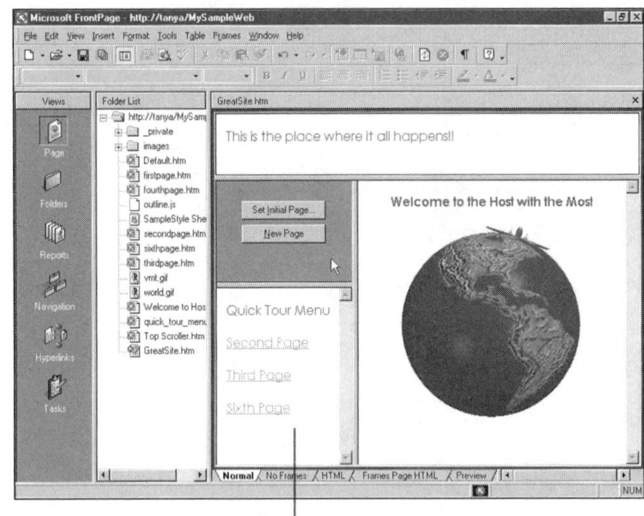

10.11

You can delete frame segments from a Frames page by choosing Frames→Delete Frame.

I P

You can also split a frame by placing the cursor on the border of the frame segment. When the mouse cursor changes into a double-headed arrow, press the Ctrl key while holding down the left mouse button. Drag the border down and then release the mouse button to create a new frame within a frame.

Hiding Frame Borders

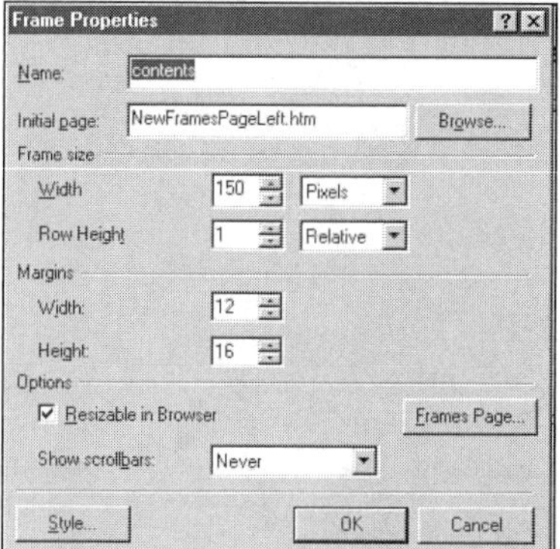

10.12

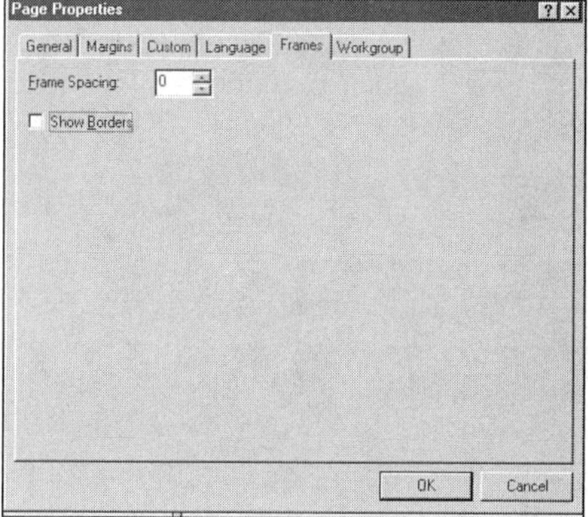

10.13

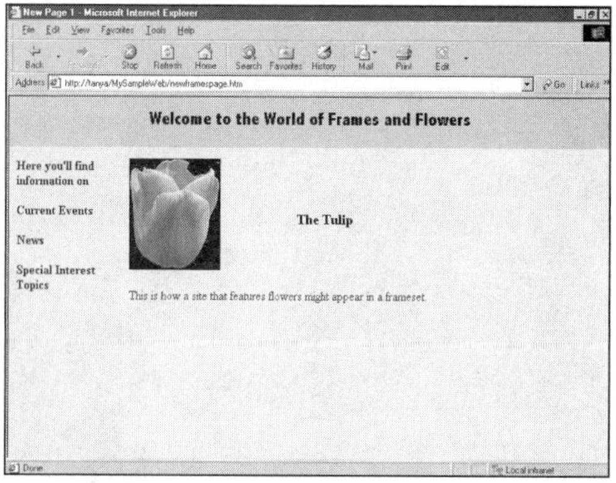

10.14

Just like borderless tables, borderless frames pages can be used to effect page layout enhancements that are user transparent. Using a borderless frames page lets you create and present the illusion of a standard Web page with multiple sections, rather than a frames page comprised of multiple pages.

1. Select a target frame in an active frames page, and then choose Frames→Frame Properties from the FrontPage 2000 menu bar to open the Frame Properties dialog box **(10.12)**.
2. Select the Frames Page button to open the Page Properties dialog box with the Frames tab displayed by default **(10.13)**.
3. Deselect the Show Borders check box on the Frames tab, and then click OK.
4. Click OK to close the Frame Properties dialog box.
5. Select File→Preview In Browser to see your results **(10.14)**.

CHAPTER 11

In this chapter you will learn how to...

Add a Form to a Page

Add a One-Line Text Box

Create a Scrolling Text Box

Add a Check Box and Radio Button

Create a Drop-Down Menu

Add a Push Button and Label Field

Add an Image Control

Save Form Results to a Database or Text File

Process Form Results Using Custom Form Handlers

View Form Results

Create a Custom Confirmation Form

Define Confirmation Form Parameters

Web pages have evolved from just static information displays to interfaces to online applications. These applications typically interact with a backend database and serve not only to collect data from a site visitor, but also to process that data and return some user-specific result. For this reason, online forms are now a standard mechanism for Web-based interaction. For example, Web-based forms are one of the

BUILDING FORMS

principal drivers of Internet information exchange. Search engines are form-based, online business account registrations; applications are form-based, as are many online customer support sites. FrontPage 2000 provides two methods for creating form pages. You can either use the Form Page Wizard or develop a form from scratch by adding form objects to a blank page.

As far as dealing with your form results, FrontPage 2000 continues to support features for sending data to a file, to an email address, or to a processing script. In addition, you'll also enjoy a new option that allows you to save form results to a database. Be advised, however, that if you want to take advantage of this new feature you'll need to have the FrontPage 2000 Server Extensions installed. In this chapter, you'll learn to use FrontPage 2000 to build and configure the elements of an online form using wizards, fields, and processes for data submission via email and into databases.

Adding a Form to a Page

All FrontPage forms that you develop support the same functional process on the user side. A user enters information in one or more form fields, or selects a form object, such as a check box or radio button. The user then clicks a Submit button to process the form data or clicks a Reset button to clear all form fields and start the data entry process from the beginning.

1. In Page view of an open FrontPage 2000 Web, choose File→New→Page to open the New dialog box **(11.1)**.
2. Select the Form Page Wizard from the page template options and then click the OK button.
3. Click the Next button on the Form Page Wizard panel to advance to the wizard's second panel **(11.2)**.
4. Click the Add button on the second Form Page Wizard panel to select the type of data you want to use the form to collect and to edit how the form prompts the user for information **(11.3)**.

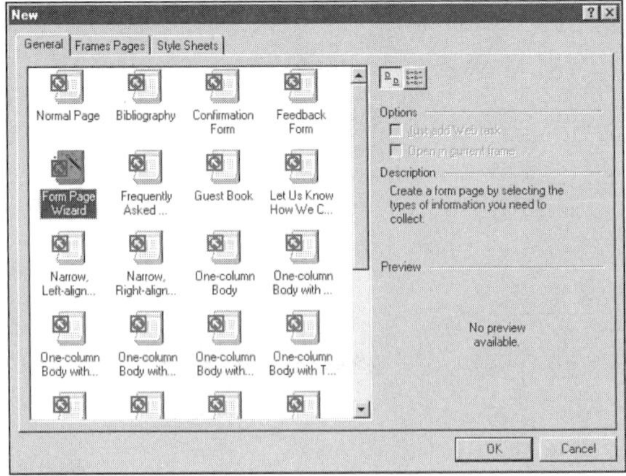

11.1

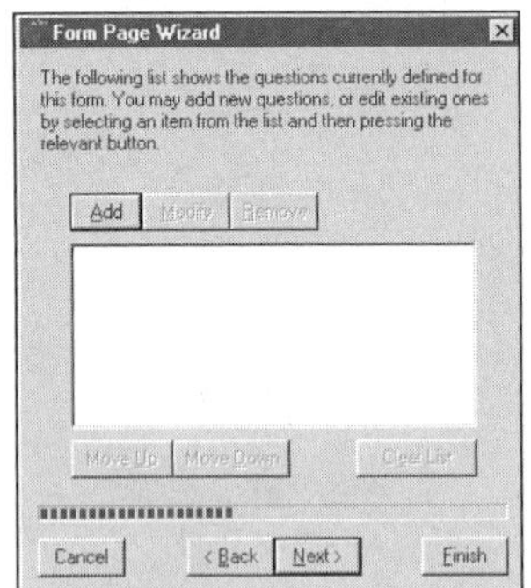

11.2

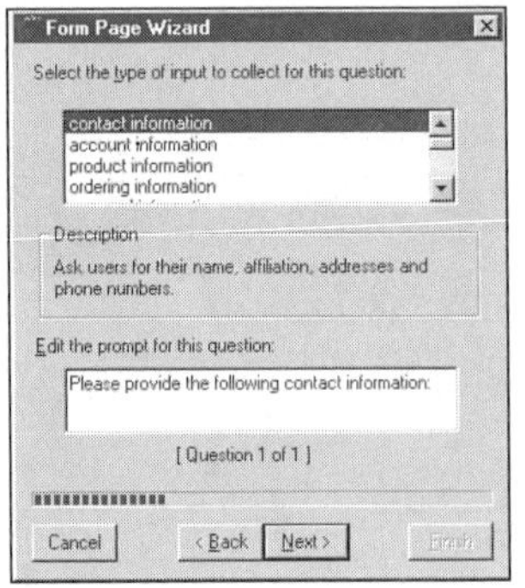

11.3

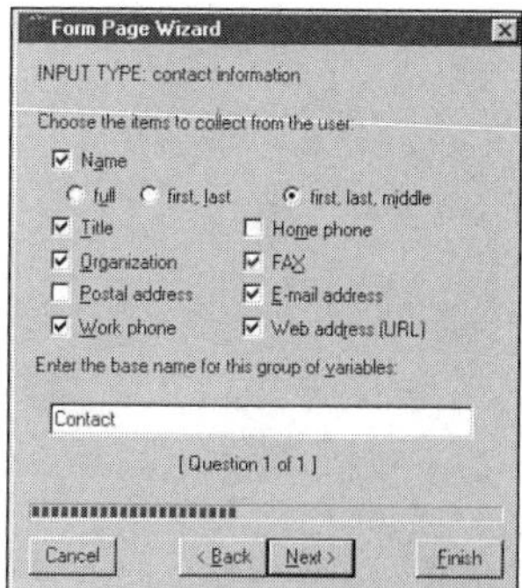

11.4

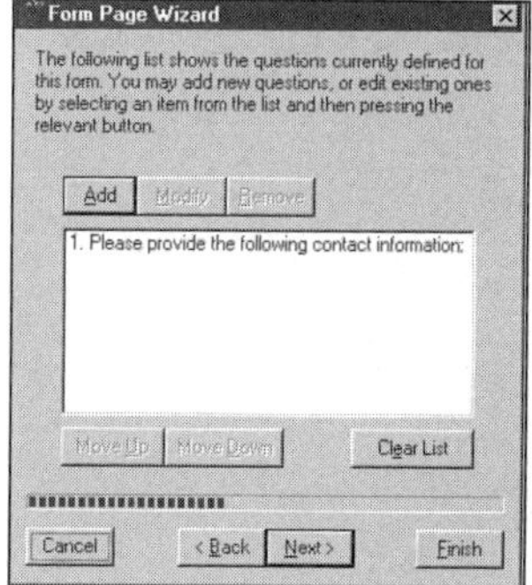

11.5

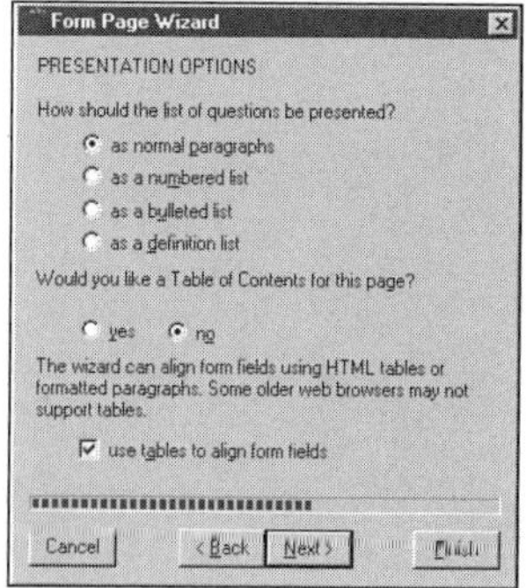

11.6

5. Click the Next button on the second Form Page Wizard panel to advance to the next panel **(11.4)**, select the options for the type of data you want to collect on the form, click the Next button on the current panel to see that a question has been added to the Add list box **(11.5)**, and then click the Next button.

6. On the Form Page Wizard's Presentation Options panel **(11.6)**, select the options for how the form elements will display, and then click the Next button to advance to the Output Options panel.

continues

The Save Results to a Web Page option saves form data to an HTML file. The Save Results to a Text File option saves form data to text files stored in the private folder. The Use Custom CGI Script option passes your form data for processing to a CGI script, ASP code, or other data processing mechanism.

The Use Custom CGI Script option usually provides the most benefit for processing form data, as you have more control over how the output data is parsed and used. For example, using the CGI Script option allows you to direct your form output to a database.

Adding a Form to a Page continued

7. On the Form Page Wizard's Output Options panel **(11.7)** select the options for how you want the collected form data to be handled when the Submit button is clicked. Enter a name for the file to which form results will be saved, and then click the Finish button to view the results **(11.8)**.

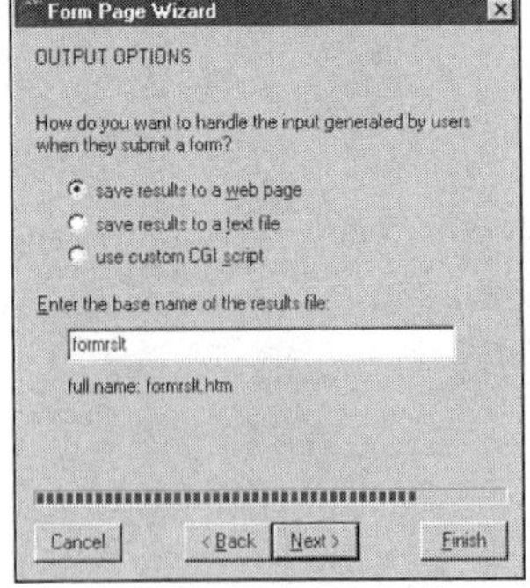

11.7

11.8

NOTE

If you've decided to add a form to your page from scratch, choose Insert→Form→Form from the FrontPage 2000 menu bar to add a form element with Submit and Reset buttons to your page.

Forms created using the Form Page Wizard can be customized to support your specific style requirements.

Adding a One-Line Text Box

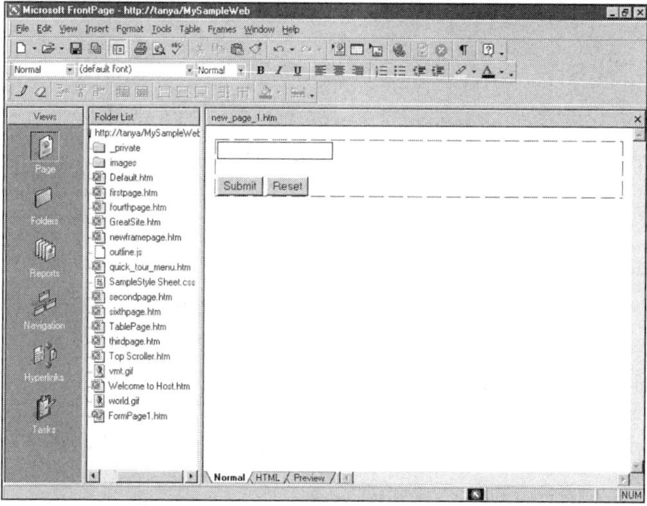

11.9

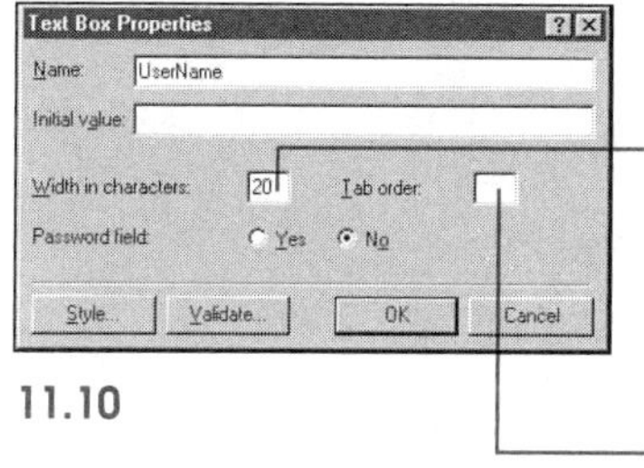

11.10

The Width In Characters field establishes the number of allowable characters that can be entered into the text box.

The Tab Order field requires a numeric value to establish the sequence in which the text box has focus when each form element is tabbed.

Collecting data with a Web-based form can be done in a variety of ways depending on what you're trying to accomplish. If you've used a search engine, you've entered data into a one-line text box. If you've ever completed an online guest book, you've encountered the one-line text box many times. Generally, you'll use the one-line text box to gather a single piece of data, for instance: First or Last Name, Email Address, or Job Title.

1. Within the dotted border of a form object, choose Insert→Form→One-Line Text Box to add the One-Line Text Box page element to the form **(11.9)**.
2. Right-click the One-Line Text Box, and then choose Form Field Properties from the shortcut menu to open the Text Box Properties dialog box **(11.10)**.
3. Enter or select values for the Text Box Name, Initial Value, Character Width, Tab Order, and whether the text box is to be a Password field.
4. Click the OK button to accept your selections.

Focus refers to the object that is ready to receive mouse or keyboard input.

Creating a Scrolling Text Box

Although online text boxes are used to collect bite-sized pieces of data such as Name, Address, or Zip Code, scrolling text boxes are larger and are used to collect paragraphs of data, such as visitor problem descriptions, book reviews, or general comments.

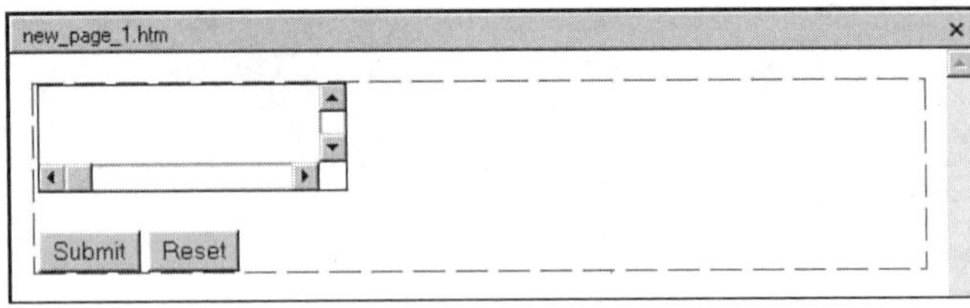

11.11

Scrolling Text Box Properties

Name: ReviewComments
Initial value:
Width in characters: 20
Tab order:
Number of lines: 2
Style... Validate... OK Cancel

11.12

1. Within the dotted border of a form object, choose Insert→Form→Scrolling Text Box to add the Scrolling Text Box page element to the form (11.11).
2. Right-click the Scrolling Text Box, and then choose Form Field Properties from the shortcut menu to open the Scrolling Text Box Properties dialog box (11.12).
3. Enter or select values for the Scrolling Text Box Name, Initial Value, Character Width, Tab Order, and the number of text box lines.
4. Click the OK button.

The Initial Value box is used to store and display any data that you want to appear in a form field by default. For example, you could enter an Initial Value of Enter a description here and have it displayed on the form by default to inform users about what kind of data should be entered as an actual field value.

Adding a Check Box

11.13

11.14

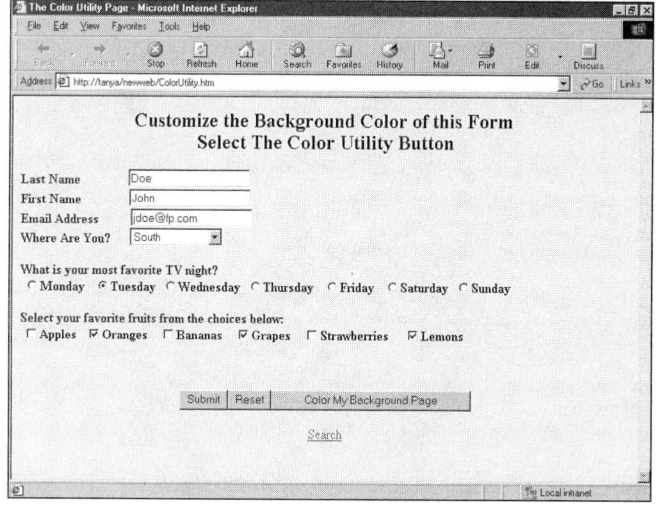

11.15

In FrontPage 2000, you add check boxes to your page or form to enable the site visitor to use a check mark to indicate one or more selections from a list of choices.

1. Within the dotted border of a form object, choose Insert→Form→Check Box to add the Check Box page element to the form **(11.13)**.
2. Right-click the check box and choose Form Field Properties from the shortcut menu to open the Check Box Properties dialog box **(11.14)**.
3. Enter or select values for the Name of the check box, the Value returned with form results, whether the check box is initially Checked, and Tab Order.
4. Click the OK button.

Use radio buttons on your form when you want the user to select one of multiple options. Use check boxes when you want the user to select more than one choice from multiple options (11.15).

Adding a Radio Button

Radio buttons, also known as option buttons, are used to represent a grouping of data items. For example, if you applied three radio buttons to a page, the buttons would have a group name of R1, with individual button names of V1, V2, and V3. With regard to application, you might use radio buttons on a form that identifies the desired salary range for a job seeker. For example, in an option group called Salary, $20K to $30K might be salaryoption1, $40K to $50K salaryoption2, and $50K and above salaryoption3. On the other hand, you might use check boxes if you want the job seeker to select more than one salary range.

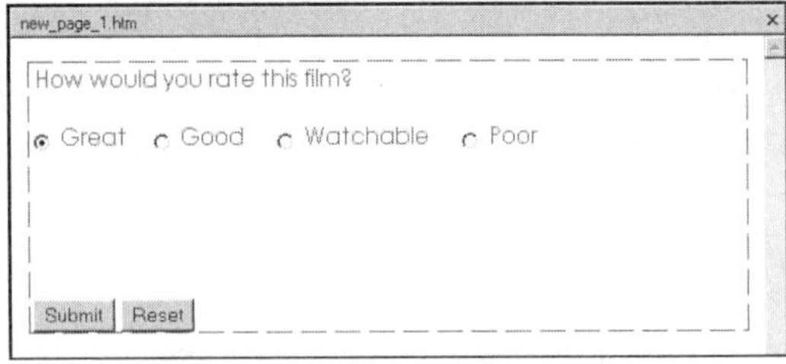

11.16

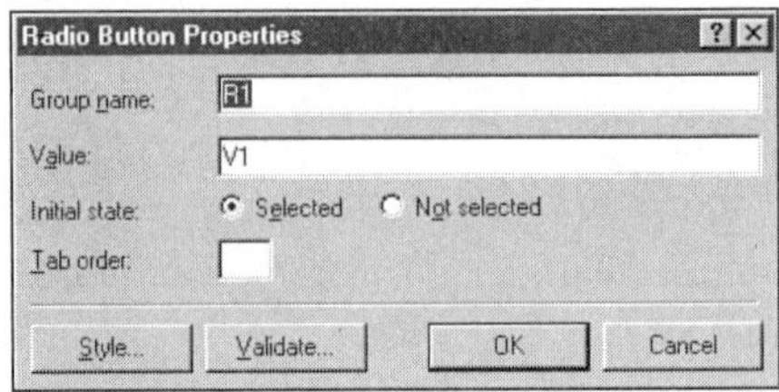

11.17

1. Within the dotted border of a form object, choose Insert→Form→ Radio Button to add the radio button page element to the form **(11.16)**.
2. Right-click the radio button, and then choose Form Field Properties from the shortcut menu to open the Radio Button Properties dialog box **(11.17)**.

Only one radio button may be selected in an option group by default. So, if you want to be able to select multiple radio buttons on the same form, you should create a different group name for each set of radio button options you want to make available.

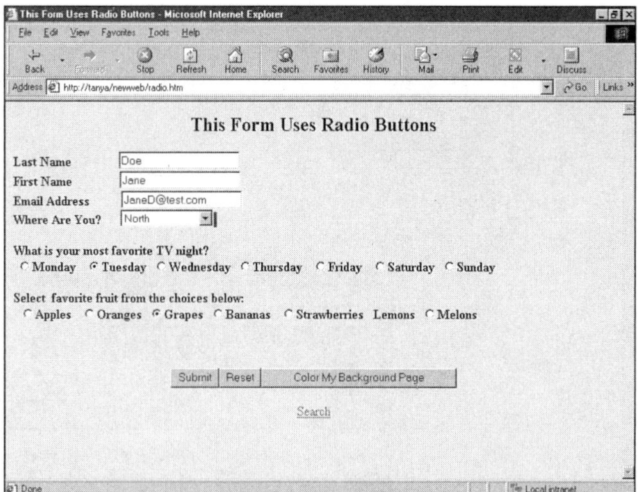

11.18

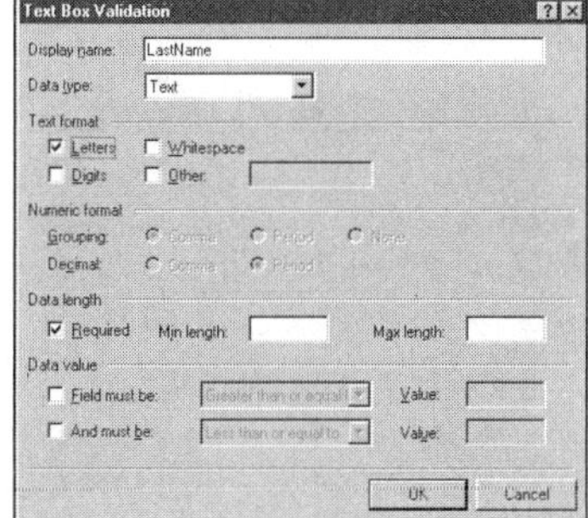

11.19

11.20

3. Enter a value that specifies the name of the option group to which the radio button belongs, the value returned with form results, whether the radio button is initially selected, and the tab order.
4. Click the OK button to accept your selections **(11.18)**.

Use FrontPage 2000's form field validation features to control what a user is able to type into a form field (11.19). For example, you can use form field validation to require that certain fields be completed, or to dictate that only certain character types such as numbers or commas can be entered.

You can make a radio button selection required, by right-clicking the radio button page element, and selecting Form Field Validation from the shortcut menu to open the appropriate Radio Button Validation dialog box (11.20).

Creating a Drop-Down Menu

Drop-down menus let users make one or more choices from a list of available selections. Consequently, they may be configured to work like radio buttons or check boxes. For example, you may have seen forms that request you to enter a state as part of contact information. Generally, rather than entering a state abbreviation, you point and click your selection from a drop-down menu of state abbreviations.

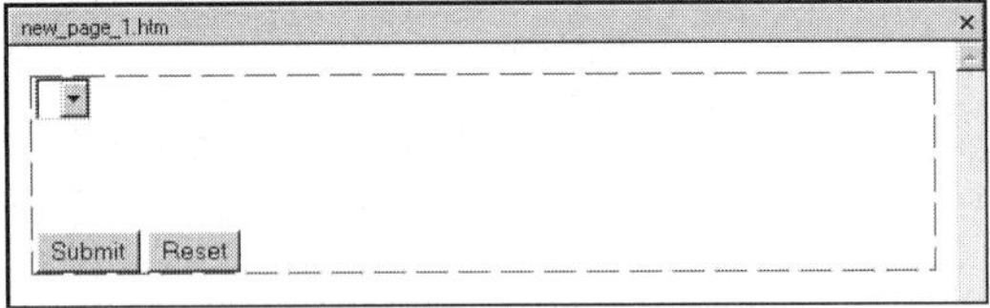

11.21

11.22

11.23

1. Within the dotted border of a form object, choose Insert→Form→Drop-Down Menu to add the drop-down menu page element to the form **(11.21)**.
2. Add items to the drop-down menu by right-clicking the drop-down menu page element. Then choose Form Field Properties from the shortcut menu to open the Drop-Down Menu Properties dialog box **(11.22)**.
3. Enter a value that specifies the drop-down menu name, and then click the Add button to open the Add Choice dialog box **(11.23)**.
4. In the Choice field, enter the value that you want to appear on the list of selectable menu choices. If you want to submit a value other than what appears on the list of menu choices when you click the

The Disallow First Choice option is selected when the first drop-down menu item is an instruction such as Please Specify or Choose One. When the Disallow option is selected, users are alerted that the first option is not a valid selection.

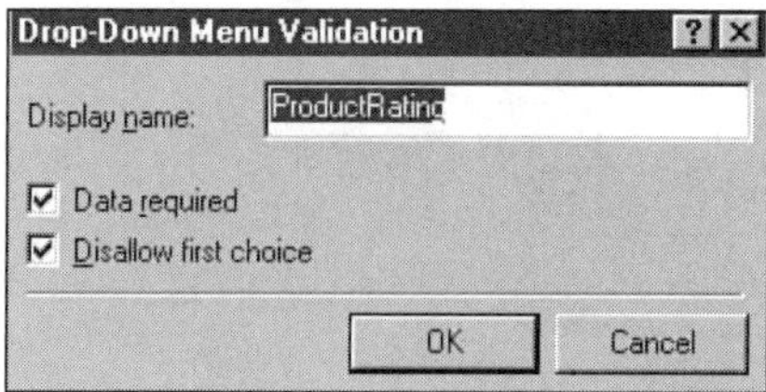

11.24

Submit button, make sure that you check the Specify Value check box, and enter the value that you want to actually appear in your form data submission.

5. Choose one of the Initial state radio buttons to determine if the menu choice will be initially displayed in the drop-down menu field.
6. Click the OK button and repeat the process for as many items as you want to appear on the list of available menu choices.
7. After entering your last selection item, enter and select values for the height of the drop-down menu in number of lines, whether or not to permit selection of multiple list options, and tab order from the Drop-Down Menu Properties dialog box.
8. Click the OK button to accept your selections.
9. You can also make choices from the drop-down menu required or disallow selection of the first menu item, by right-clicking the drop-down menu page element and selecting Form Field Validation from the shortcut menu. This will open the Drop-Down Menu Validation dialog box **(11.24)**, and enable you to make those selections. Click the OK button when finished.

continues

Creating a Drop-Down Menu continued

10. When you're done, select the Preview tab and click the arrowhead on the drop-down menu to see your result **(11.25)**.

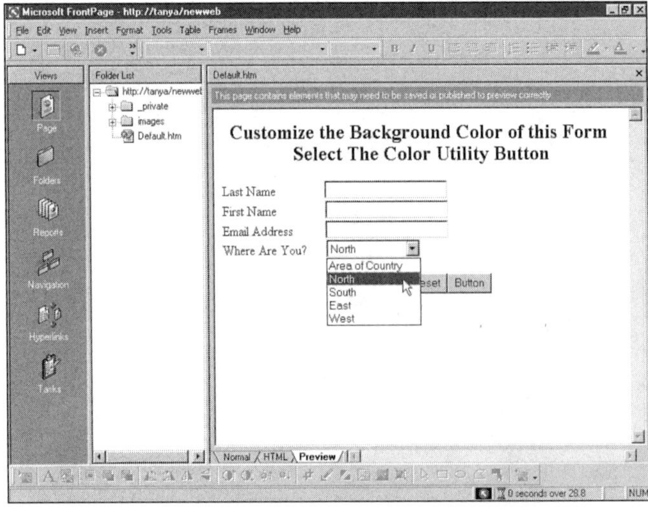

11.25

You can establish limiting parameters, such as Data Type, Text Format, Numeric Format, Data Length, and Data Value for text box page elements. To do so, right-click the text box page element and select Form Field Validation from the shortcut menu to open the appropriate Form Field Validation dialog box (11.26). Make your selections and then click the OK button.

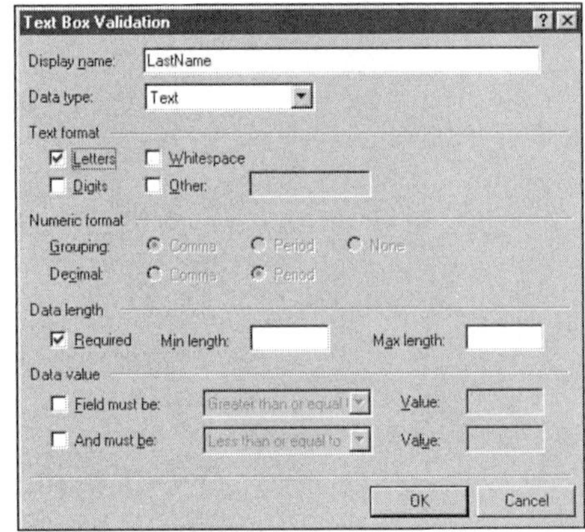

11.26

If you want to modify or remove a menu item, select either the Modify or Remove button on the Drop-Down Menu Properties dialog box. If you want to reorder the list of items on the drop-down menu, select the menu item on the Drop-Down Menu Properties list box, and then click either the Move Up or Move Down button to push the menu choice to the top or bottom of the list box.

Adding a Push Button

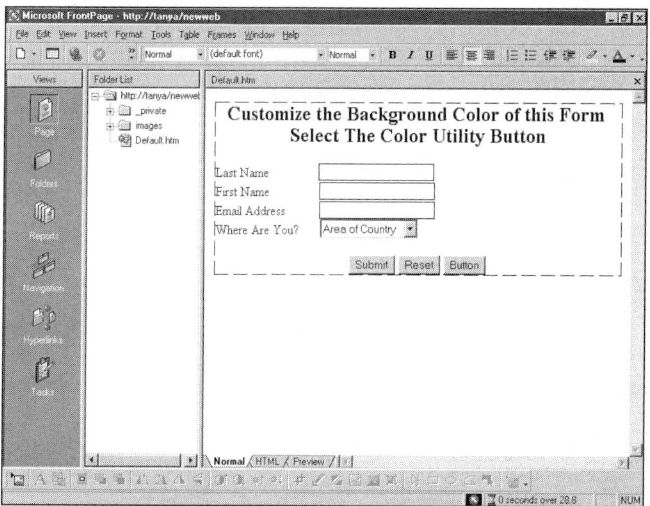

11.27

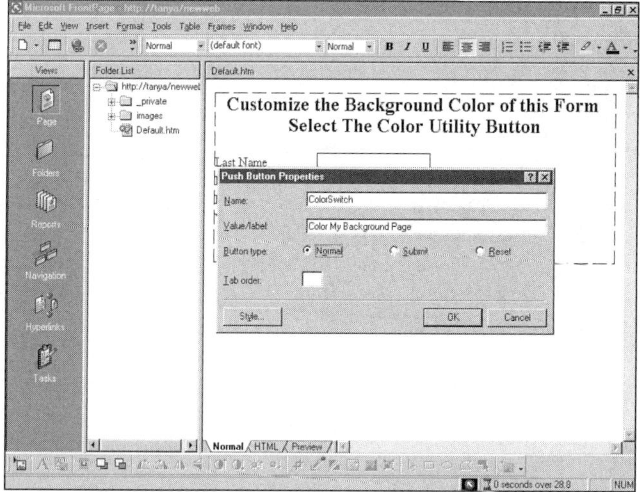

11.28

Form-based push buttons allow users to submit or clear the data that they've entered on a form. You may have noticed that push buttons were automatically applied when you added a form page element to a blank page. However, you can also apply push buttons manually.

1. Within the dotted border of a form object, choose Insert→Form→Push Button to add the push button page element to the form **(11.27)**.
2. Right-click the push button, and then choose Form Field Properties from the shortcut menu to open the Push Button Properties dialog box.
3. Enter and select values to name the button, change its label, specify its function as Normal for triggering a script, Submit to trigger submission of the form data, or Reset to clear all populated data fields, and the tab order **(11.28)**.

continues

The Display Name in the Drop-Down Menu Validation dialog box is the name you gave to the drop-down menu page element.

Adding a Push Button continued

4. Click the OK button to accept your selections. Click the button after reading the Note below to trigger the script (11.29).

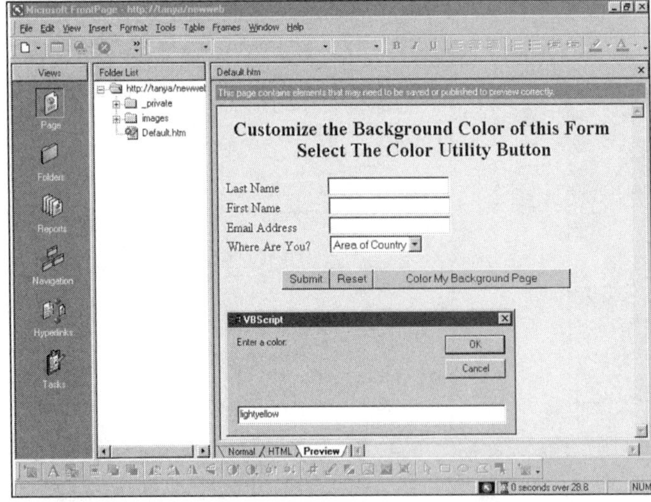

11.29

```
<input type="button" value="Color My Background Page"
name="ColorSwitch">
```

11.30

```
<SCRIPT LANGUAGE =VBScript>
Sub ColorSwitch_OnClick()
        Dim NewColor
    NewColor = InputBox("Enter a color:")
    Document.bgColor = NewColor
End Sub
</SCRIPT>
```

11.31

Use the Normal button type when you want to trigger a script embedded in your HTML code. Use the Submit button to send your form data to a Web server for processing, and use the Reset button to cause the Web browser to return the form's fields to their default state.

 O T E

When using the Normal button property to trigger a script, the HTML code will appear similar to that shown (11.30).

The name parameter for the button corresponds to the name of the Sub statement that comprises the button's script. Applying the following script to the button (created in the preceding example) allows you to change the form's background color (11.31).

Adding a Label Field

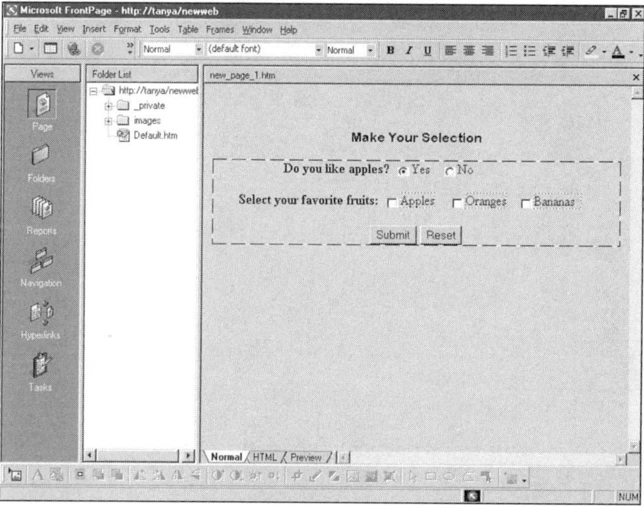

11.32

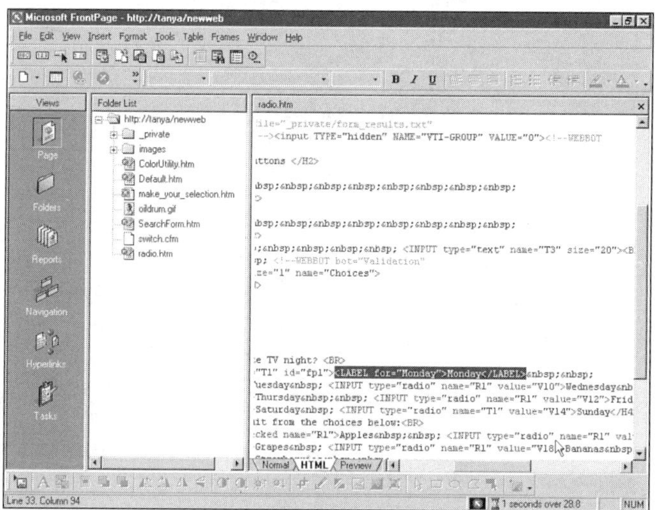

11.33

In FrontPage 2000, using label fields allows you to make a form field and its associated label a selectable page element. For example, if you apply a check box to a page and give it a plain text label, you must specifically click the check box to select it. Using a label field, you could click the check box or the label itself to select the check box.

1. Within the dotted border of a form object, choose Insert→Form and add a page element to the form.
2. Enter a text label for the page element, select both the page element and its label, and then choose Insert→Form→Label on the FrontPage 2000 menu bar **(11.32)**.

When you apply a label field to a form control, FrontPage 2000 adds a <LABEL>...</LABEL> tag pair to your HTML source code (11.33).

In the interest of user-friendly page design, using label fields means your site visitors don't need to be precise in their selection of a given form control.

Adding an Image Control

In FrontPage 2000, you can use an image as a substitute for a form's submit button. This might be useful if you were building an e-commerce application that allowed a user to complete an order form, and then click a picture of the ordered product to submit the order.

1. Within the dotted border of a form object, choose Insert→Form→Picture to open the Picture dialog box **(11.34)**.
2. Select an image file using the Look In drop-down menu, make a selection from the Picture dialog box list box, or enter the URL for the image file you want to use. Click OK.
3. Right-click the image added to the page, and then choose Form Field Properties from the shortcut menu to open the Picture Properties dialog box **(11.35)**.

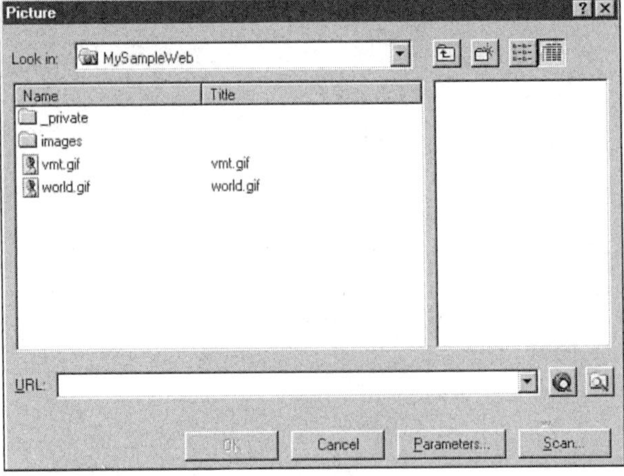

11.34

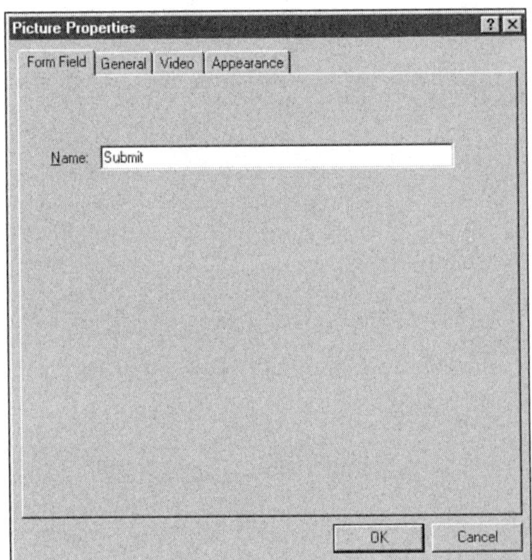

11.35

The fact that selecting the Form Field Properties menu option doesn't open the Picture Properties dialog box instead of the Form Field Properties dialog box when you apply an image control to a form is somewhat of a curiosity.

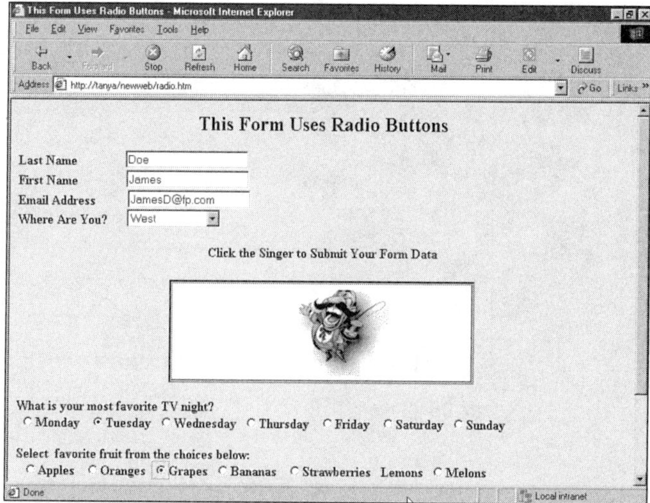

11.36

4. On the Form Field tab in the dialog box, type Submit in the Name field, and then click the OK button **(11.36)**.

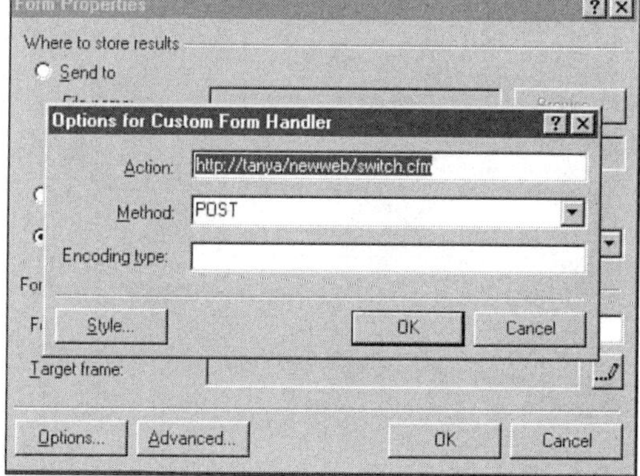

11.37

You can cause your form image to behave like a Submit button that sends form data to a custom script using the POST method. All you need to do is enter the URL of your custom script into the Action field of the Options for Custom Form Handler dialog box, and then click OK (11.37). Clicking your form image will then send the location of your button click to the server, which will respond by triggering the custom form handler.

Saving Form Results to a Database or Text File

Form results are processed using form handlers. Form handlers are scripts or programs that tell your Web server how to process the data collected by your form. In the case of saving results to a text file, email, or a database table, form handlers are a component of the FrontPage Server Extensions and thus run behind the scenes on the Web server.

1. Right-click inside the dotted border of a form object, and then choose Form Properties from the shortcut menu to open the Form Properties dialog box **(11.38)**.
2. In the Form Properties dialog box, enter the name of the file to which you want your form results saved or enter email address to which form data can be sent, and then click the OK button. Completing this action saves your submitted form data to the named text file and to the specified email address.
3. To send your results to a database instead, select the Send to Database option, and then click the OK button to open the Options for Saving Results to Database dialog box **(11.39)**.

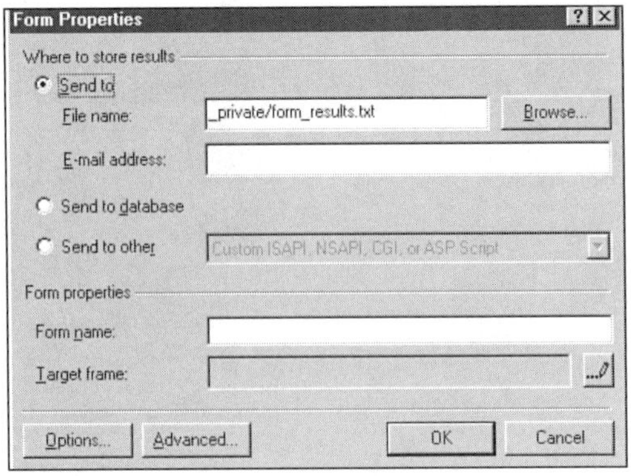

11.38

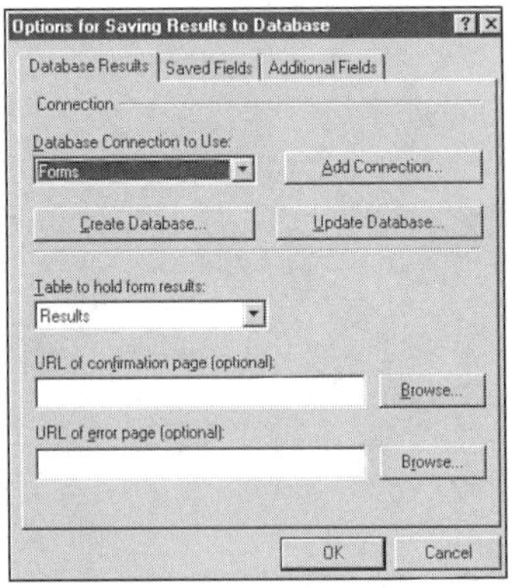

11.39

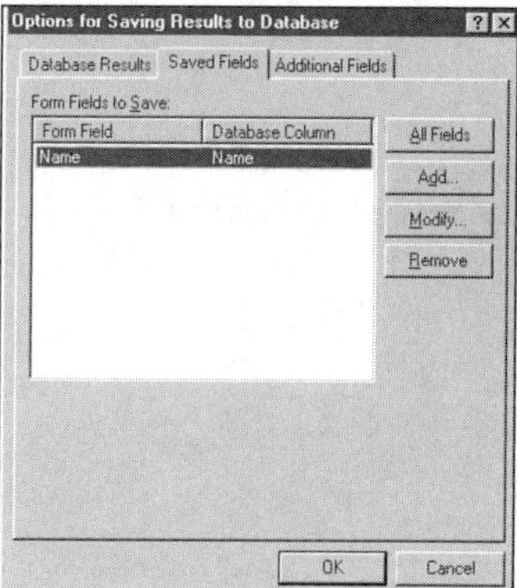

11.40

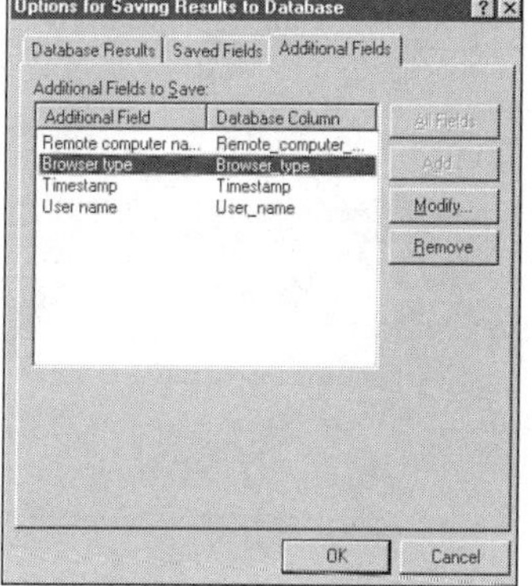

11.41

4. If the Database Connection to Use drop-down menu is blank, click the Create Database button to have FrontPage 2000 automatically create a Microsoft Access database and default table. A successful database creation adds the default table name to the Table to Hold Form Results drop-down menu with the name Results.

5. Select the Saved Fields tab to see the field names to which the form data will be saved **(11.40)**. You can select the Additional Fields tab **(11.41)** to see the additional fields that FrontPage 2000 created in the Results table.

6. Click the OK button to have your submitted form results saved to the newly created database.

Although most ISPs today support the use of FrontPage Server Extensions, there are still those who don't. Suffice it to say that if your ISP doesn't support the FrontPage Server Extensions, the capabilities provided by FrontPage 2000 become limited to basic WYSIWYG editing.

Processing Form Results Using Custom Form Handlers

In the Web's infancy, custom form handlers were typically CGI scripts written in PERL. CGI or Common Gateway Interface is a standard for how to pass data from a Web server to an external program for processing. CGI form handlers can be written in any language that is compatible with your Web server. Today, FrontPage supports not only CGI form handlers, but custom form handlers written in VBScript as with Active Server Page files, JavaScript, Cold Fusion Markup Language, and Visual Basic just to name a few.

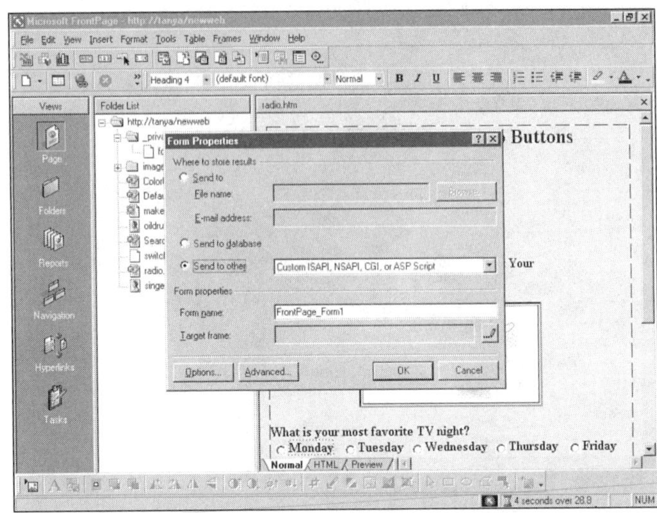

11.42

1. Right-click inside the dotted border of a form object, and then choose Form Properties from the shortcut menu to open the Form Properties dialog box **(11.42)**.
2. Select the Send to Other option to have your form results saved to a custom form handler such as a CGI script or Cold Fusion template.
3. Select the Options button on the dialog box to open the Options for Custom Form Handler dialog box **(11.43)** to designate the action path for the custom form handler.

Options for Custom Form Handler
Action: http://www.test.com/data.cfm
Method: POST
Encoding type:
Style...
OK
Cancel

11.43

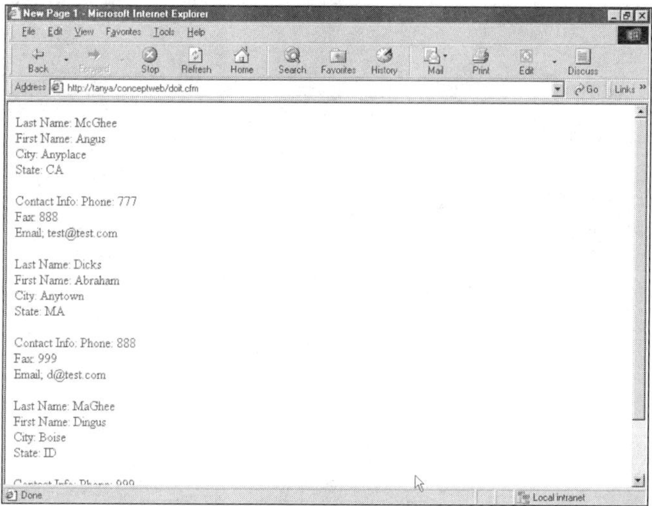

11.44

4. Click the OK button to close the Options for Custom Form Handler dialog box, and then click the OK button to close the Form Properties dialog box. Your submitted form data can now be saved to the specified custom form handler for processing **(11.44)**.

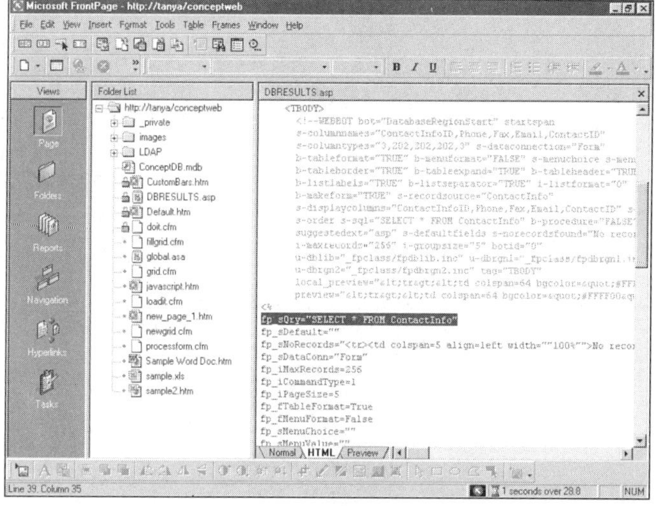

11.45

TIP

If your form data is saved to a backend database, your results will be retrieved for display using Structured Query Language (SQL). If you're using Active Server Pages, SQL statements can be embedded into your HTML source code (11.45).

NOTE

Be aware that while viable, using CGI scripts as a form handler can be problematic because of the resource drain that they place on the Web server. For this reason, some ISPs prefer that you use a method other than CGI to process form data.

Viewing Form Results

The most immediate method of viewing form results is the confirmation form that FP 2000 returns by default when your form is previewed and data is submitted via your Web browser **(11.46)**. As noted in the previous section, you can view your form results by accessing the Save Results file on your Web server, or retrieving an email confirmation message. In addition, if you've used a custom form handler like a CGI script or Active Server Page to send your data to a database, you can see your form results by opening the database table referenced in your custom form handler.

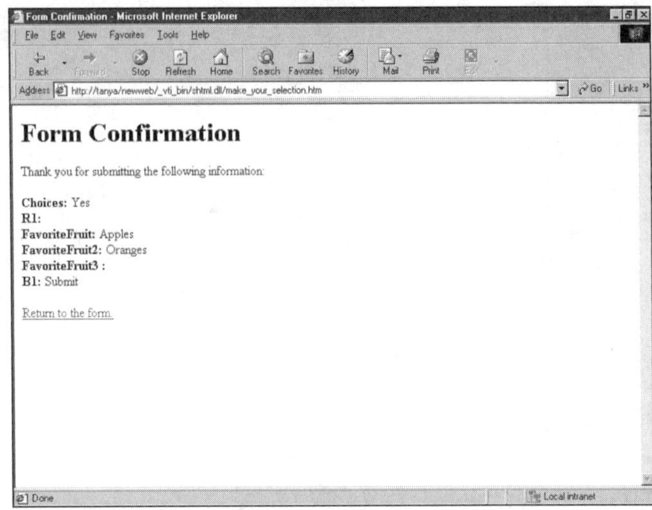

11.46

1. If you've accepted the send to file defaults for your form results, in the Folder List pane of Page view, double-click the _private folder **(11.47)**.

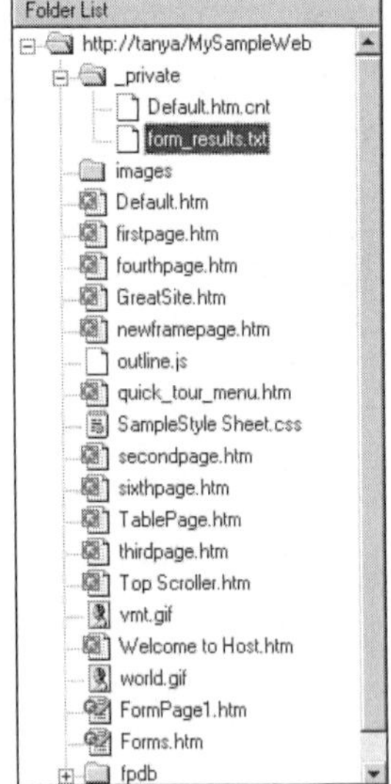

11.47

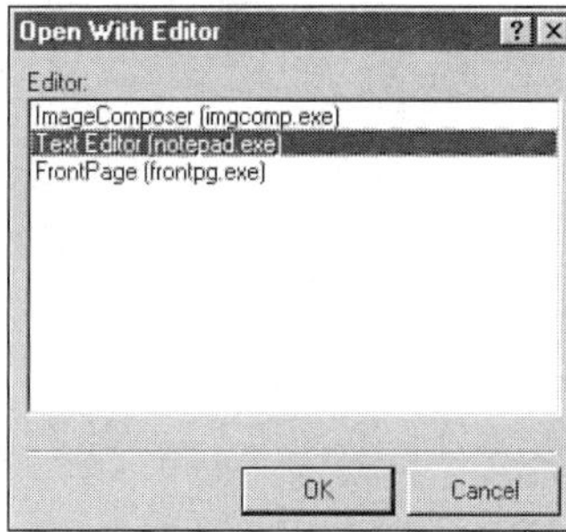

11.48

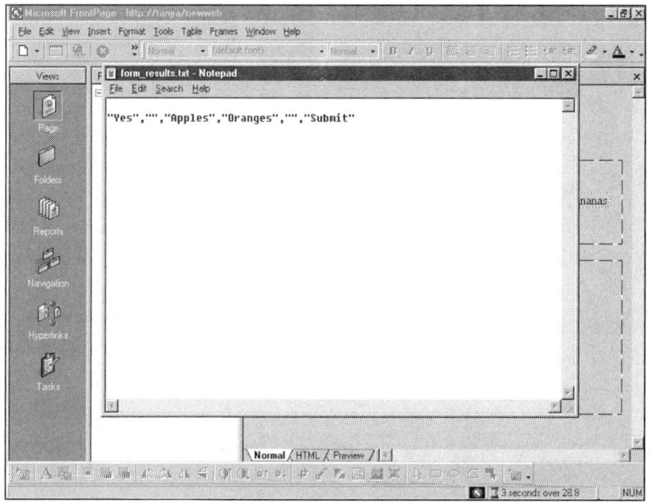

11.49

2. Right-click the file form_results.txt, and choose Open With from the shortcut menu to open the Open With Editor dialog box **(11.48)**.

3. Select Text Editor from the Open With Editor dialog box, and then click the OK button to view the form_results.txt file **(11.49)**.

4. If you've sent your results to yourself via email, use an email client like Microsoft Outlook to view the results message.

5. If you sent your result to a FrontPage generated database, use Microsoft Access to open the database Forms to View the Results table where your form results are stored.

If your form data has been written to a file on a remote Web host, you may use FTP to download your form results.

Although the Confirmation Page tab on the Options for Saving Results of Form dialog box calls for an optional URL as a pointer to the location of your custom confirmation page, you can also point to a file on your local machine by entering a full directory path.

Creating a Custom Confirmation Form

Sometimes the default confirmation form generated by FrontPage 2000 doesn't do the job. This is especially true when you're trying to maintain a consistent design throughout your Web. In this case, you'll want to create a custom confirmation form.

1. In Page view of an open FrontPage 2000 Web, choose File→New→Page to open the New dialog box.
2. Select the Confirmation Form from the page template options, and then click the OK button.
3. Edit the confirmation form text to meet your requirements.
4. Right-click each form field embedded in the form, and then choose Confirmation Field Properties to open the Confirmation Field Properties dialog box **(11.50)**.
5. Enter a form field name that corresponds to a form field in the form it will be associated with, and then click the OK button **(11.51)**.

When submitted, the data collected on your form will be placed in accordance with your custom confirmation form design (11.52).

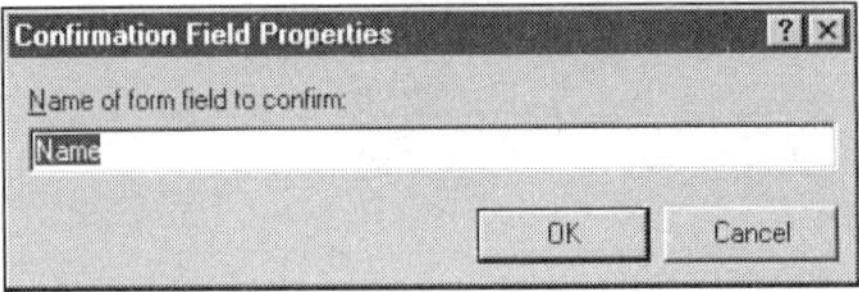

11.50

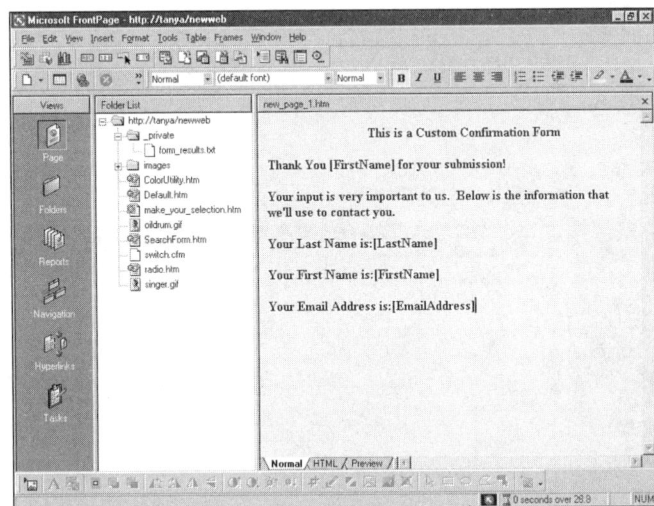

11.51

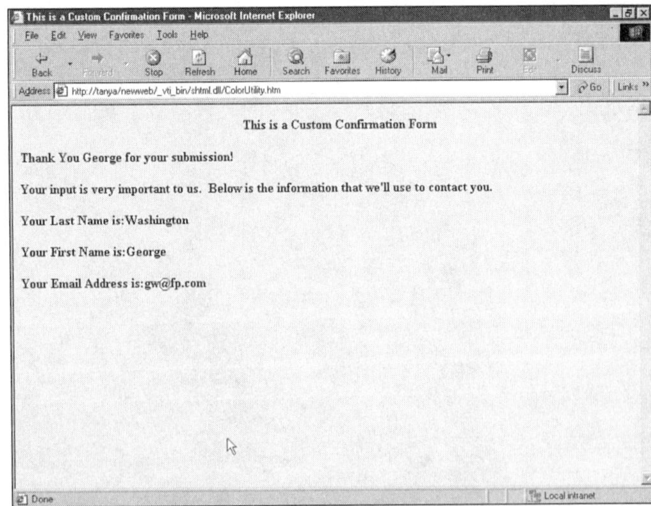

11.52

Defining Confirmation Form Parameters

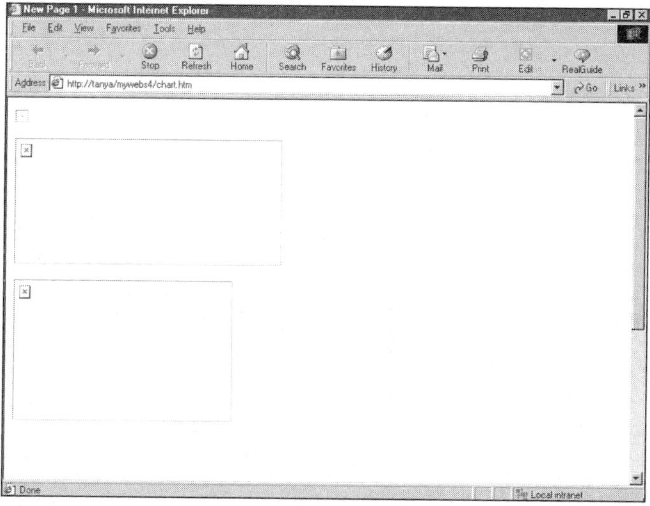

11.53

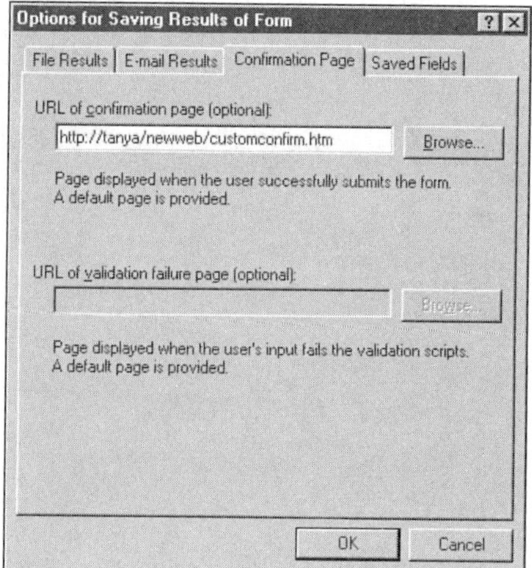

11.54

When you've saved your custom confirmation form and want to make sure that it's returned when a user submits form data, you need to once again access the Options for Saving Results of Form dialog box in order to specify the location of the form to be sent.

1. Right-click inside the dotted outline of your form **(11.53)**, and then choose Form Properties from the shortcut menu.
2. Click the Options button on the Form Properties dialog box to open the Options for Saving Results of Form dialog box.
3. In the Options for Saving Results of Form dialog box, select the Confirmation Page tab **(11.54)** and enter the URL of your custom confirmation page.
4. Click the OK button to close the Options for Saving Results of Form dialog box, and then click OK to close the Form Properties dialog box.

You can disable default form field behavior by selecting ToolsfiPage Options and then clearing the Automatically Enclose Form fields within a form check box on the dialog box's General tab.

CHAPTER 12

In this chapter you will learn how to...

- Add a Microsoft Office Spreadsheet and Pivot Table
- Connect an Excel File to a Pivot Table
- Populate a Pivot Table with Spreadsheet Data
- Implement a Microsoft Office Chart
- Add a Hit Counter and a Table of Contents
- Create a Hover Button and a Marquee
- Implement the Banner Ad Manager
- Apply a Confirmation Field
- Add and Schedule an Include Page
- Set Up a Scheduled Picture
- Apply a Substitution Component
- Create a Search Page and Correct Errors
- Apply a COM Component

APPLYING FRONTPAGE COMPONENTS

FrontPage components are self-contained automation objects that let you apply functionality to your Web, typically associated with PERL-based CGI scripting. FrontPage 2000 makes this possible through interaction with the FrontPage Server Extensions, which are a set of server-side programs that must be installed on your Web server to interpret FrontPage component code. Consequently, applying and using FrontPage components gives you the ability to turn a static Web into an interactive Internet experience. For example, you can use FrontPage components to automatically date and time stamp your Web pages, direct the disposition of results submitted using an online form, display the number of visitors to your site, scroll text across your page, and even embed Microsoft Office objects. Unlike FrontPage components, which are dependent on the FrontPage Server Extensions for their functionality, Office 2000 Web components—like spreadsheets, pivot tables, and charts—are ActiveX controls that can be embedded into a Web page without FrontPage Server Extension dependency (see Chapter 16, "Extending Web Page Functionality," for more on ActiveX controls). In this chapter, you'll discover how to apply FrontPage components to take advantage of a variety of robust capabilities with point and click simplicity.

Adding a Microsoft Office Spreadsheet

If visitors to your site have the Office 2000 installed, you can take advantage of FrontPage 2000's close integration with Office 2000 components such as spreadsheets, pivot tables, and charts. This is especially useful when working with an intranet site where you can be assured that all site visitors will have the needed components installed.

1. In Page view of an open FrontPage 2000 Web, choose Insert→Component→Office Spreadsheet to apply an Office Spreadsheet component on the open page **(12.1)**.
2. Select the spreadsheet component and then drag it by its sizing handles to make it compatible with the page size **(12.2)**.

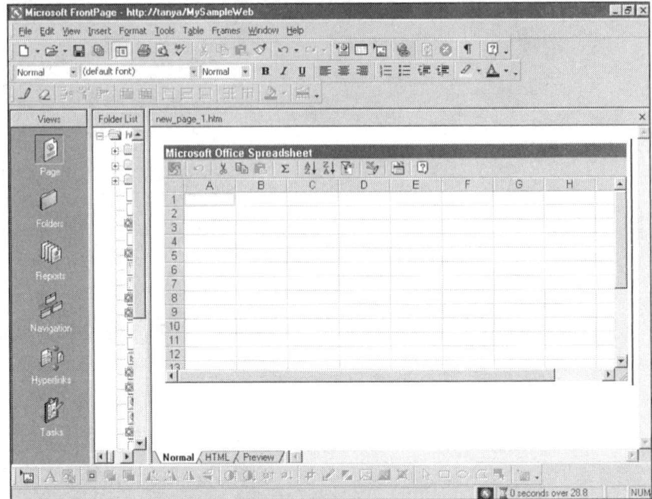

12.1

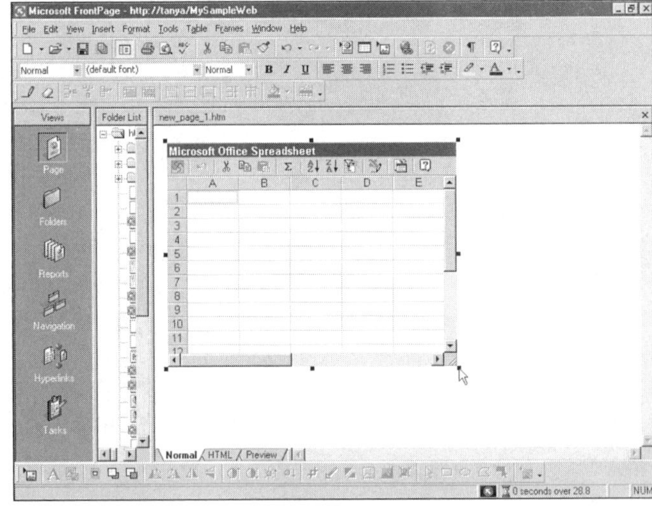

12.2

Office 2000 components, such as spreadsheets, charts, and pivot tables are implemented as ActiveX controls. You can consider ActiveX controls the Microsoft version of Java applets.

Entering a value in the Name field provides a data source reference for using the Chart component.

Use the Style button to apply inline styles to the component.

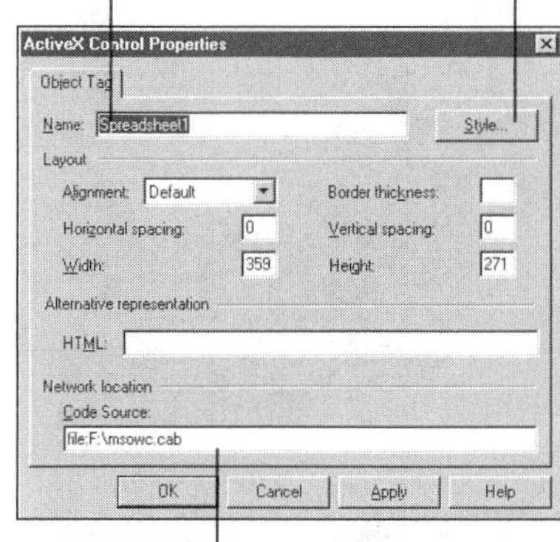

12.3 **The Code Source field contains the path to the Office installation server that installs the Office components from your local machine or from the Web.**

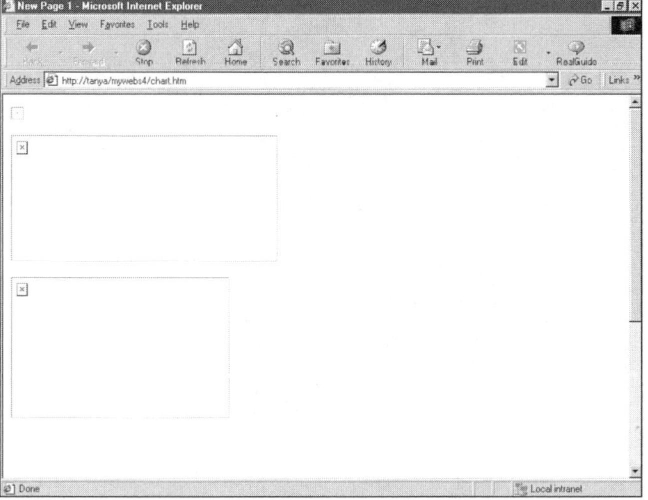

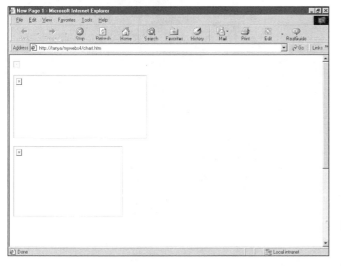

12.4

3. Right-click the spreadsheet component, and then select ActiveX Control Properties from the shortcut menu to open the ActiveX Control Properties dialog box **(12.3)**.

4. Define the layout settings for the spreadsheet under the Layout section of the ActiveX Control Properties dialog box.

5. Enter a URL to redirect visitors to another location, if their browser doesn't support the spreadsheet component. The value of the URL is entered under the Alternative Representation section's HTML field in the ActiveX Control Properties dialog box.

6. Click OK to close the dialog box and apply the defined properties.

continues

If your site visitors access a page containing an Office 2000 Web component object and they don't have the Office Web components software installed, they will see a watermark where the control has been placed (12.4).

Adding a Microsoft Office Spreadsheet continued

7. Define properties for one or more spreadsheet cells by selecting a cell or group of cells, right-clicking your selection, and then choosing Property Toolbox from the shortcut menu to open the Spreadsheet Property Toolbox (12.5).
8. Close the Spreadsheet Property Toolbox by clicking the Close button on the Toolbox window.

Advanced lets you define spreadsheet properties such as scrollbars and maximum spreadsheet width and height.

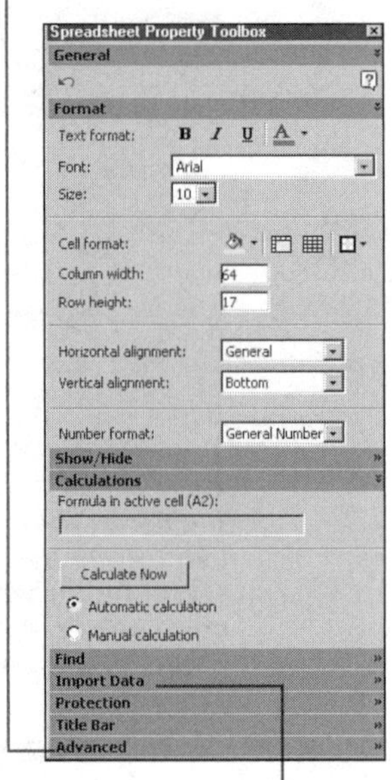

12.5

Import Data lets you import spreadsheet data from another Web site.

Office 2000 Web Components must be installed on your development machine for the Office Spreadsheet, Office PivotTable, and Office Chart components to appear as FrontPage 2000 menu items. Visitors to your site must also have Office 2000 Web Components installed on their machine to view any of the Microsoft Office 2000 components.

Applying a Microsoft Office Pivot Table

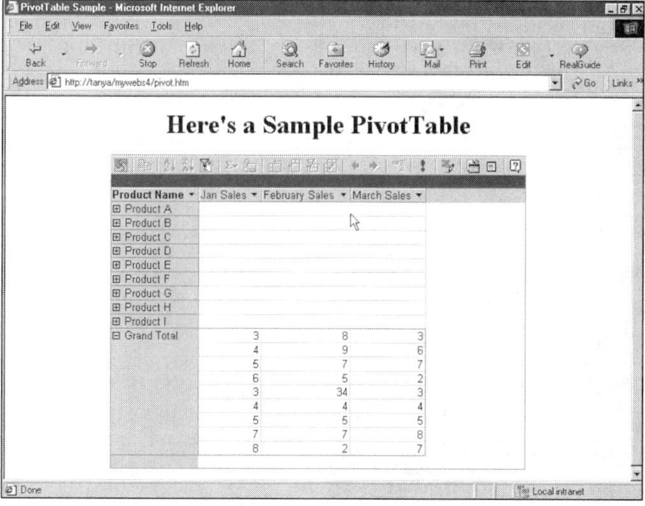

12.6

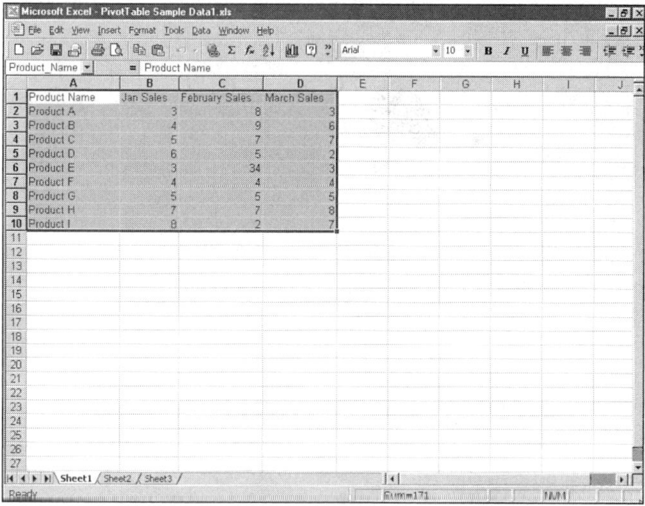

12.7

Using a pivot table **(12.6)** on your Web page lets your visitors sort, filter, and display different aggregate views of detailed data stored in an Excel spreadsheet or an Access database, even if these source applications are not installed on the visitor's computer. This feature effectively enables you or your site visitors to perform real-time data analysis on your Web page. Consequently, this means you'll need a data source from which to pull relevant data, and a little patience, as working with pivot tables can be a bit daunting.

Before you can use a pivot table for online data analysis, you'll need to create some source data. For this example, your source data will consist of a named block of cells stored in an Excel spreadsheet.

1. Open an Excel workbook containing the information to be summarized in your pivot table.
2. Select a block of cells in the spreadsheet **(12.7)**, and then choose Insert→Name→Define from the Excel menu bar to open the Define Name dialog box.
3. Click the Add button, and then click the OK button to establish the name for the data block you selected.

continues

Applying a Microsoft Office Pivot Table continued

4. Save your Excel file, remember the name defined for your data block, and then return to FrontPage 2000.
5. In Page view of an open FrontPage 2000 Web, choose Insert→Component→Office PivotTable to apply an Office pivot table component to the page **(12.8)**.

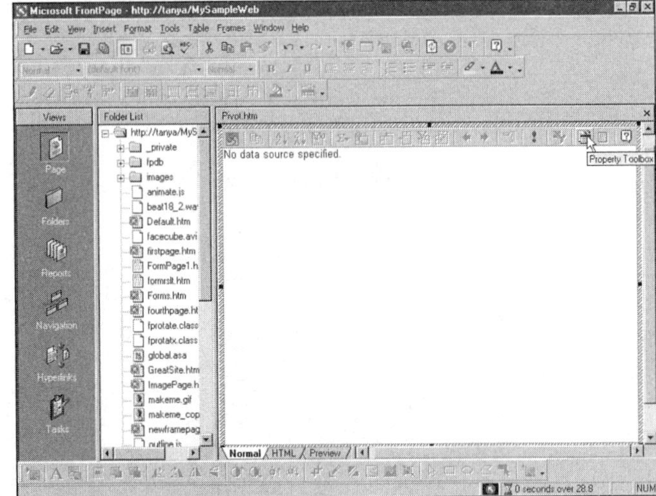

12.8

You can edit and set properties for an Office pivot table component in Page view, even if you don't have Microsoft Excel installed.

The default file path for the pivot table component is located in the Code Source field of the ActiveX Control Properties dialog box.

Connecting an Excel File to a Pivot Table

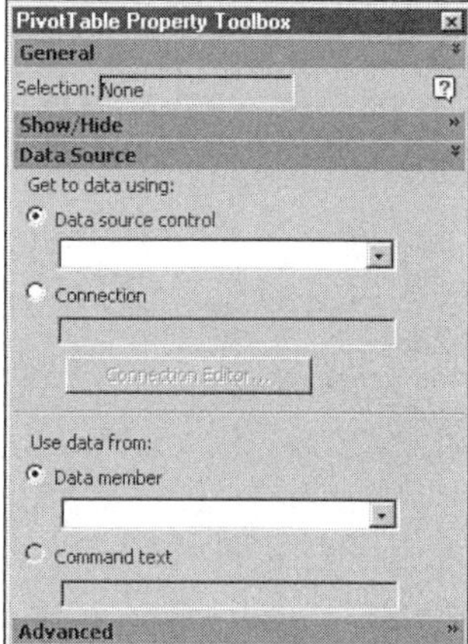

12.9

12.10

After you've defined your data and applied a pivot table to your Web page, you need to make the data accessible to the empty pivot table component. You'll do this by creating an Open Database Connectivity (ODBC) connection between the data source and the pivot table.

1. Select the Property Toolbox icon on the component toolbar (shown previously in Figure 12.5) to open the PivotTable Property Toolbox, and then select the Data Source option to expose the Data Source Selection panel **(12.9)**.
2. Select the Connection option, and then click the Connection Editor button to open the Data Link Properties dialog box **(12.10)**.
3. Select the Provider tab, choose Microsoft OLE DB Provider for ODBC Drivers from the list box, and then choose Next to expose the Connection tab.

continues

I P

Pivot tables allow you to perform online data analysis by summarizing and sorting data into various categories.

Connecting an Excel File to a Pivot Table continued

4. Select the Use connection string option, click the Build button to open the Select Data Source dialog box, and then select the Machine Data Source tab **(12.11)**.
5. Select the New button to open the first panel of the Create New Data Source Wizard **(12.12)**.
6. Select the User Data Source option, and then click Next to advance to panel 2 of the Create New Data Source Wizard **(12.13)**.

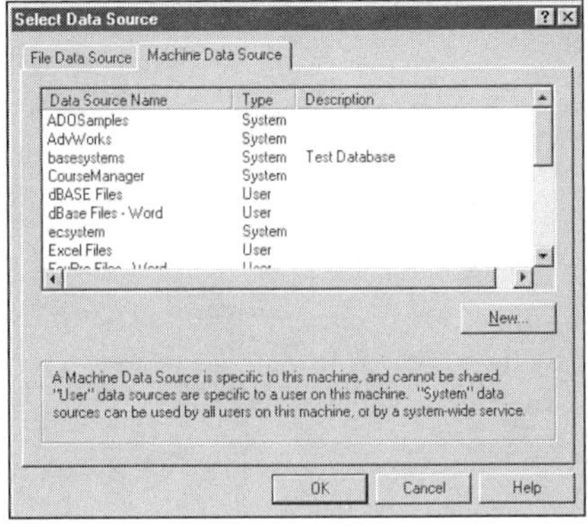

12.11

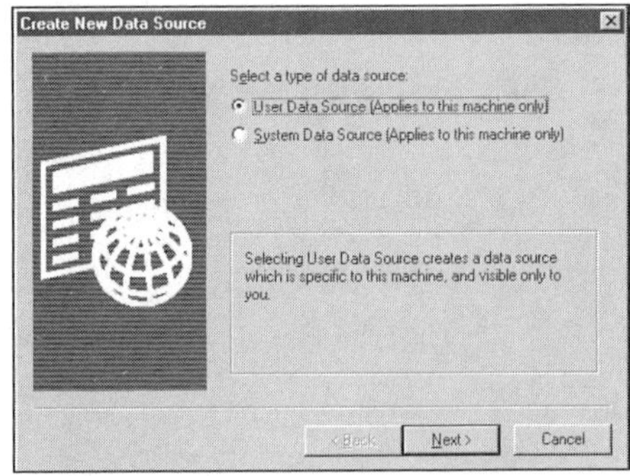

12.12

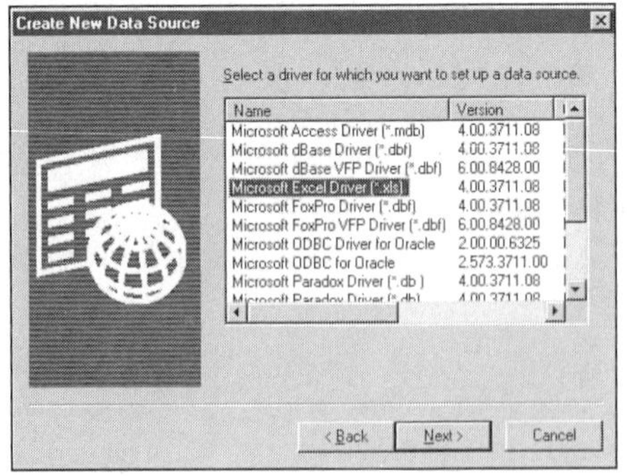

12.13

Data Source Names store information about how to connect to an ODBC-compliant database. In case you didn't know, ODBC stands for Open Database Connectivity, which is a protocol for accessing database engines.

There are typically two types of Data Source Names (DSN)—the File DSN, which is machine independent, and the Machine DSN, which stores connection data in the Windows Registry of a specific computer.

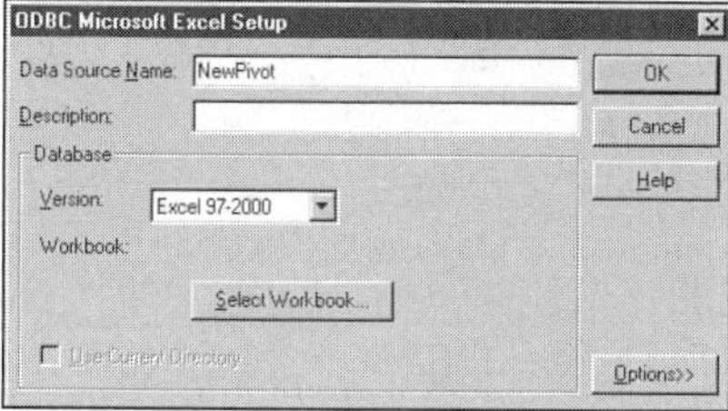
12.14

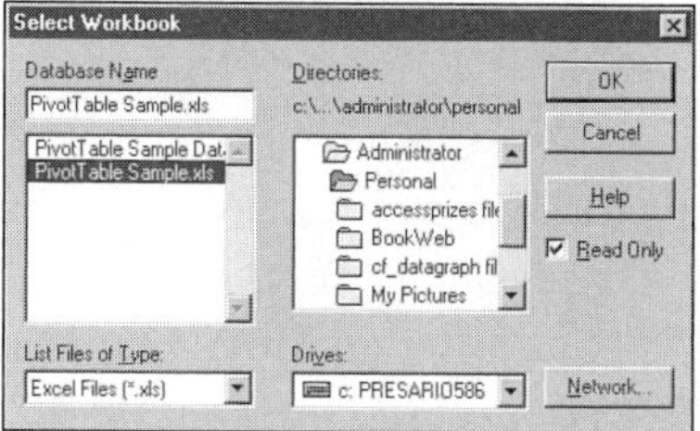
12.15

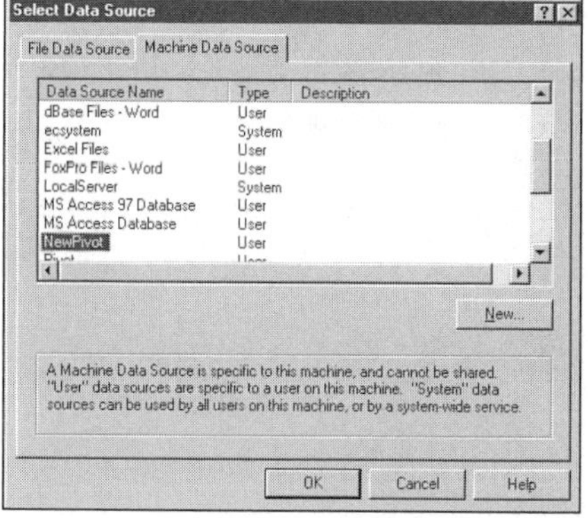
12.16

7. Select the Microsoft Excel Driver from the list box, click Next, and then click Finish to open the ODBC Microsoft Excel Setup dialog box **(12.14)**.

8. Enter the name of your choice in the Data Source Name field, and then click the Select Workbook button to open the Select Workbook dialog box **(12.15)**.

9. Browse your machine to locate and select the Excel file that you saved earlier, and then click OK.

10. Click OK to close the dialog box, click OK to close the ODBC Microsoft Excel Setup dialog box, and then click OK to close the Select Data Source dialog box when your new data source appears on the Machine Data Source tab list box **(12.16)**.

11. If the Select Workbook dialog box is not closed, select your data source file, and click OK to have a connection string added to the connection string field of the Data Link Properties dialog box. If the Select Workbook dialog box is closed, proceed to the Data Link Properties dialog box.

continues

Connecting an Excel File to a Pivot Table continued

12. On the Data Link Properties dialog box, select the Use Data Source Name option, click the Refresh button, select your data source name from the drop-down menu **(12.17)**, and then click OK. This action establishes the connection between your pivot table and the Excel file data source.

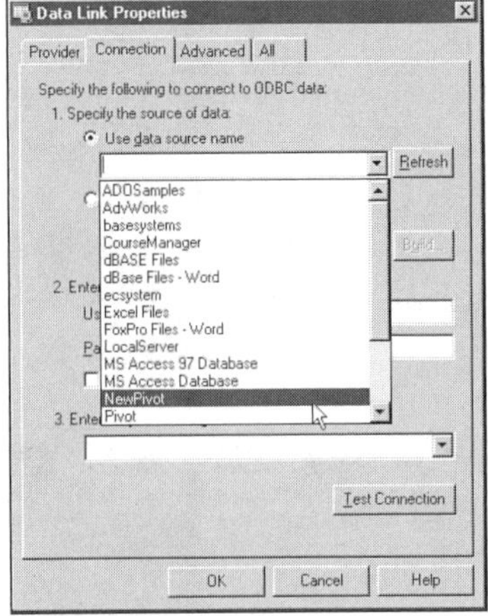

12.17

13. On the PivotTable Property Toolbox, select the Command Text option, enter `select * from YourDataBlockName`, press the Enter key, and then close the PivotTable Property Toolbox. This action overlays your blank PivotTable with data placement grids **(12.18)**.

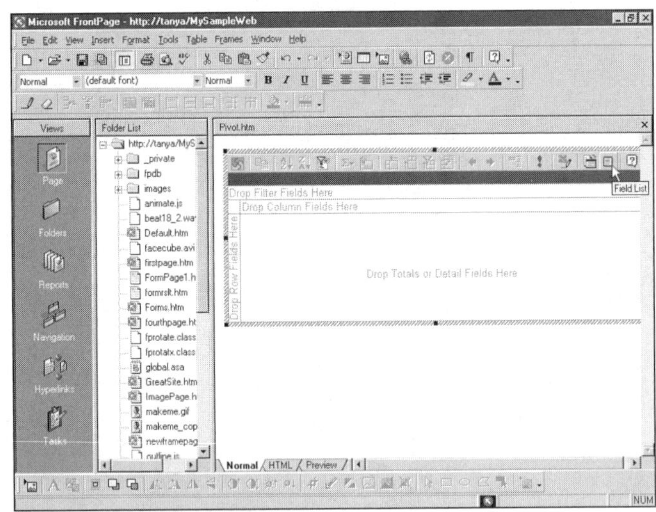

12.18

YourDataBlockName is the name you defined for the block of cells you selected in the Excel file.

Creating a new data source connection is not always necessary. If you previously created a data source name to a file that would support the analysis you want to perform, you can select it from the Data Source Name drop-down menu and use it instead.

Populating a Pivot Table with Spreadsheet Data

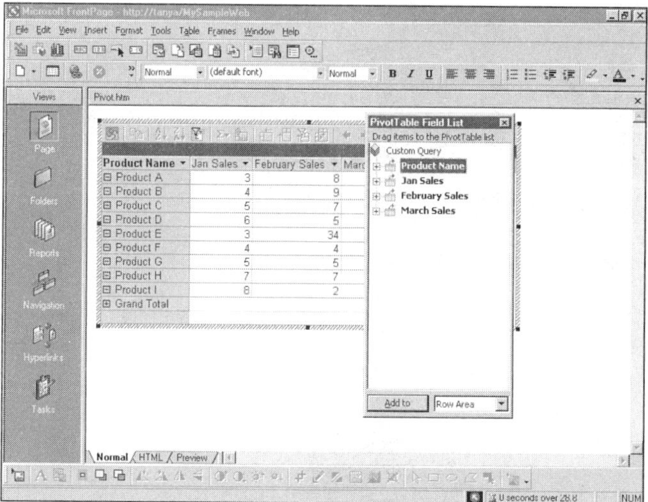

12.19

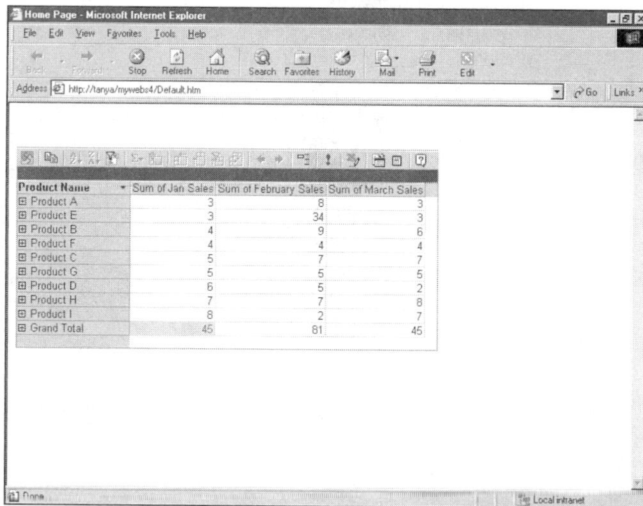

Product Name	Sum of Jan Sales	Sum of February Sales	Sum of March Sales
Product A	3	8	3
Product E	3	34	3
Product B	4	9	6
Product F	4	4	4
Product C	5	7	7
Product G	5	5	5
Product D	6	5	2
Product H	7	7	8
Product I	8	2	7
Grand Total	45	81	45

12.20

After your data is linked to your pivot table component, you'll need to apply the data to the pivot table itself, before you're ready to offer your online data analysis tool to your visitors.

1. Select the Field List icon on the PivotTable toolbar to open the Field List dialog box **(12.19)**.
2. Drag and drop field names to their applicable column, row, and detail grid location on the pivot table.
3. Sum your field data by right-clicking a detail field and then choosing Autosum→Sum to achieve the desired result **(12.20)**.

Generally, you'll find that pivot tables are useful when you want to compare related spreadsheet totals, or when you want to summarize a long list of figures while comparing facts about each figure. Because pivot table functionality is derived from Microsoft Excel, you can sort, subtotal, and total, as well as change your view of the data to see more details.

Implementing a Microsoft Office Chart

Not only are spreadsheets a good source of data for pivot tables, but you can also use them to generate charts and graphs to support your Web-based data analysis activities. FrontPage 2000 lets you build custom charts and graphs from spreadsheet components embedded in your Web pages. This is another great example of FrontPage 2000's integration with Office 2000 productivity tools. By using Office spreadsheet and chart components on your Web site, you can tailor your pages to facilitate dynamic what-if analysis. Visitors could enter or change data values in the spreadsheet component and see it charted or graphed in real-time. You might consider offering a service that allows your customers Web-based data analysis tools.

1. In Page view of an open FrontPage 2000 Web, choose Insert→Component→Office Spreadsheet to apply a spreadsheet component.
2. Fill the spreadsheet with data (12.21).
3. Choose Insert→Component→Office Chart to apply a blank Chart component and open the Microsoft Office Chart Wizard (12.22).

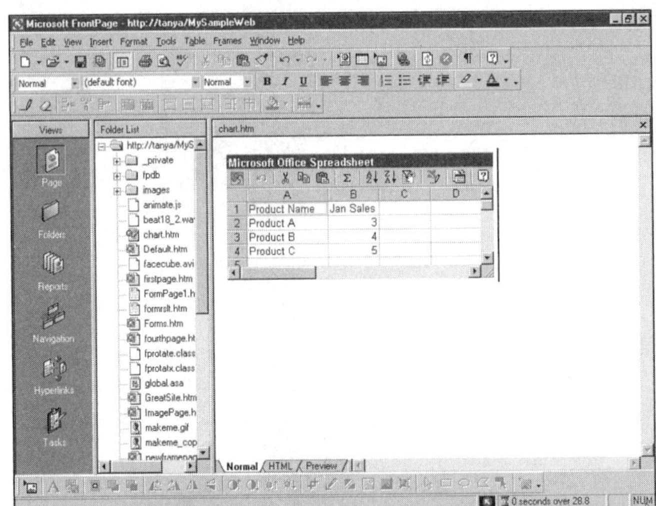

12.21 **You can rotate or flip an embedded chart by right-clicking on the chart, selecting Property Toolbox, selecting Plot Area on the Chart Properties Toolbox, and then selecting a rotation or flip option.**

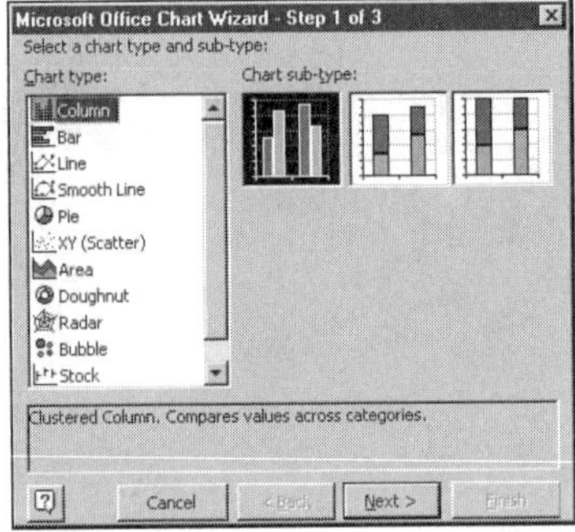

12.22

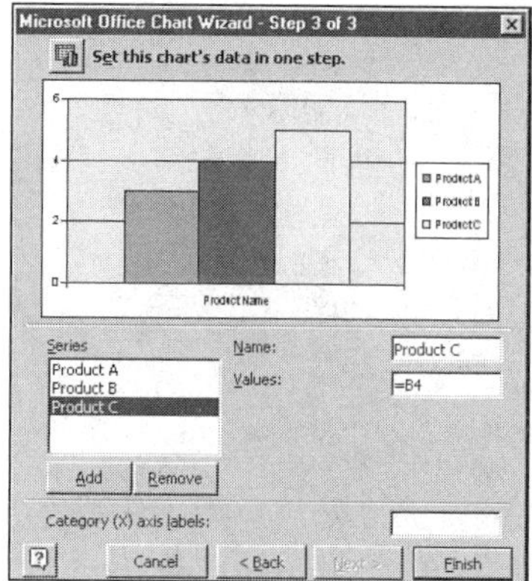

12.23

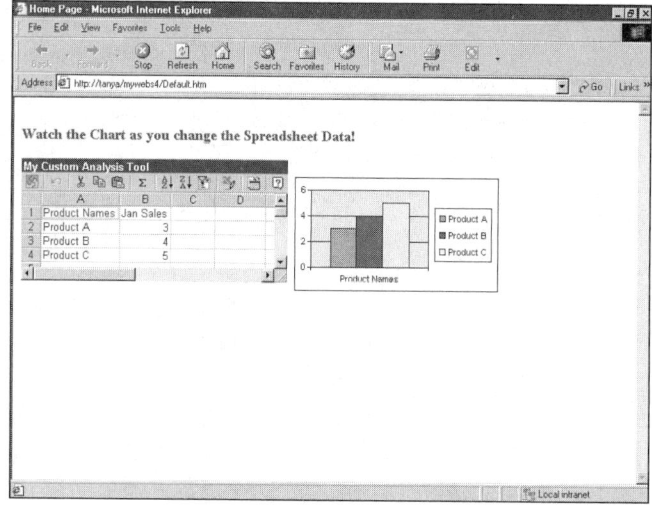

12.24

4. Select the Chart type you want to create and then click Next.
5. Select the spreadsheet name to use as a data source, and then click Next.
6. Enter a Name and a Value based on the Excel row and column for each data point to see your chart take shape **(12.23)**, and then click Finish to apply your chart to the Web page **(12.24)**.

Data source files can be stored on your Web server and updated as necessary to support your requirements.

When you click the Finish button, the chart is placed at the last cursor position in Page view. However, you can use FrontPage 2000's absolute positioning feature to place the completed chart on the page at any location.

Adding a Hit Counter

Hit counters are often applied to a Web site because they are thought to show the number of visitors that have viewed a given page. FrontPage 2000 provides a hit counter as a FrontPage component that is easily applied with a few mouse clicks. Remember that components such as the hit counter require that the FrontPage Server Extensions be installed on the host Web server.

1. In Page view of an open FrontPage 2000 Web, with the cursor positioned where you want the Hit Counter to appear, choose Insert→Component→Hit Counter to open the Hit Counter Properties dialog box **(12.25)**.

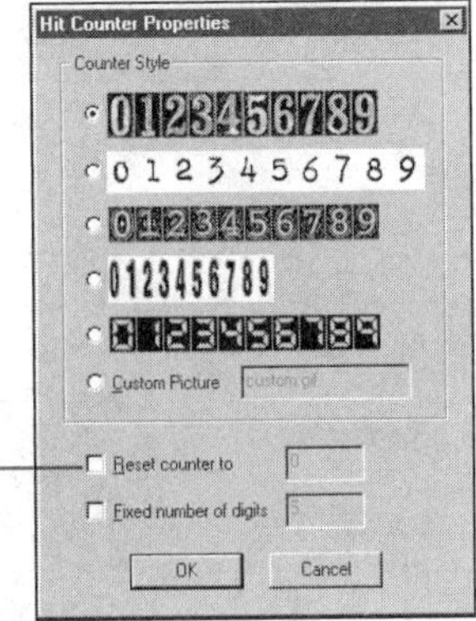

The Custom Picture option lets you base your hit counter style on your own custom graphic. Your custom graphic should contain the numbers 0–9 like the other hit counter styles. The FrontPage Server Extensions parse the graphic to increment the counter as needed.

12.25

TIP

Hit counters can be misleading. This is because hit counters actually increment based on the number of times a page is accessed. This means that the numbers shown by a hit counter reflect only the number of times a page has been viewed by someone, not necessarily the number of times it has been viewed by different people. For example, when a visitor accesses your home page, it counts as a hit. If the same visitor were to hit the Refresh button on their browser, the hit counter would register a second hit.

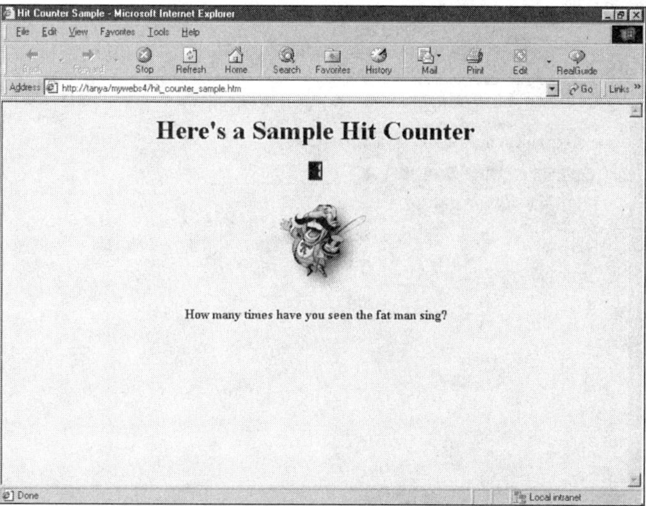

12.26

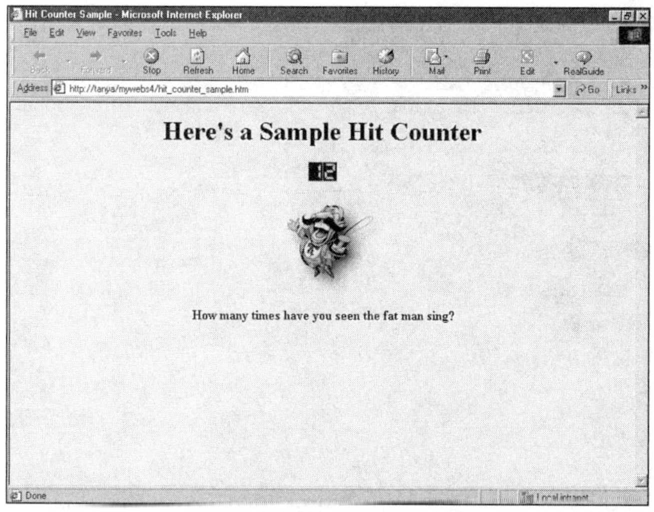

12.27

2. Select the Hit Counter design of your choice by selecting a specific radio button, and then click the OK button.
3. Select File→Preview in Browser to see your hit counter **(12.26)**.
4. Check your hit counter by clicking the Refresh button on your browser. Notice that the counter increments with each refresh **(12.27)**.
5. Close the browser and right-click the hit counter in FrontPage 2000.
6. Choose FrontPage Component Properties from the shortcut menu to re-open the Hit Counter Properties dialog box as shown previously in Figure 12.25.
7. Select the Reset Counter to check box and then enter a value. The counter clears any previous values entered and resets the counter to the value you entered on the dialog box. Although you can reset the hit counter to 0, the counter is incremented by 1 as soon as you access the page where the counter resides.

continues

The indicator [Hit Counter] is shown in Page view as a placeholder for the hit counter component applied to your Web page.

Adding a Hit Counter continued

8. Select the Fixed Number of Digits check box and then enter a value to increase the default number of positions shown when your hit counter is displayed.

9. Click the OK button and then choose File→Save to apply the counter defaults.

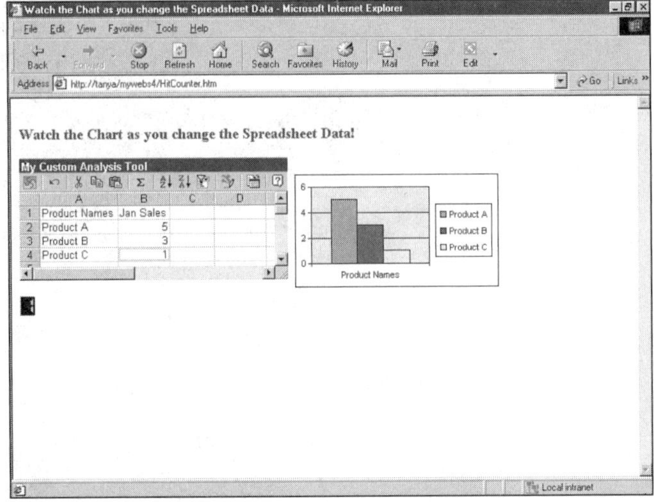

12.28

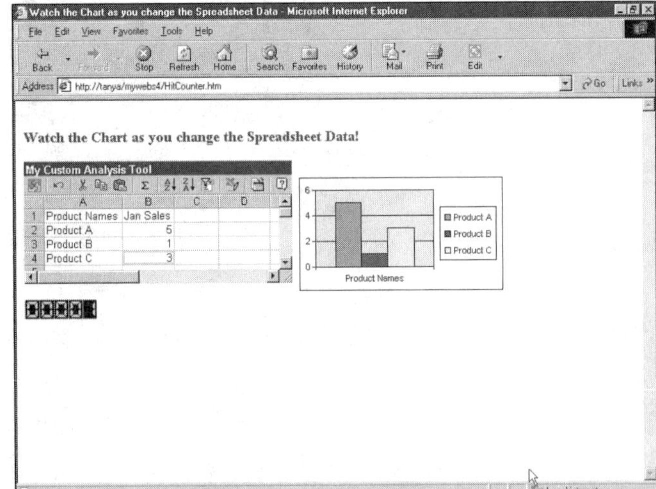

12.29

If your hit counter fails to increment when you refresh your Web page, consult the Microsoft Knowledgebase article Q208632—Hit Counter Doesn't Work In Sub Web on Netscape Servers.

 O T E

Each hit counter style displays one of its 10 positions by default (12.28). When you enter a value in the Fixed Number of Digits field—for example, 5—the number of hit counter positions displayed on a page is increased (12.29).

Creating a Hover Button

The Effect drop-down menu contains a choice of seven animation effects you can apply to a Hover button. Two of the effects affect color, three affect glow style, and two affect button bevel appearance.

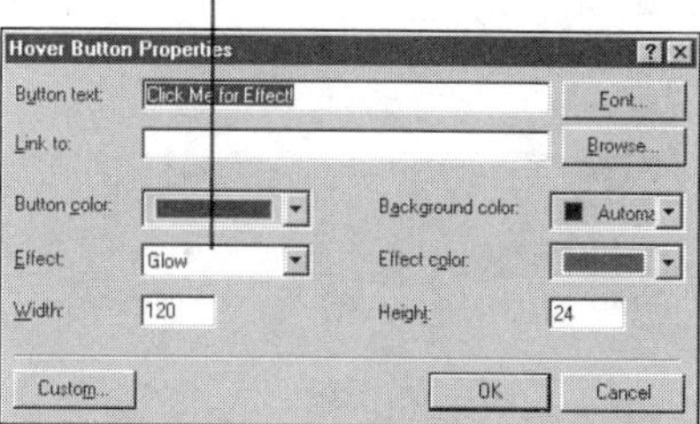

12.30

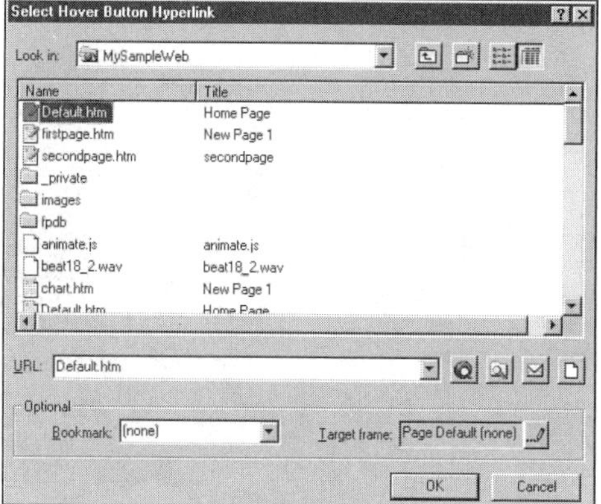

12.31

Hover buttons are FrontPage components that let you create object-based mouseover effects without programming. Like regular button objects, they are used to trigger events, such as hyperlink jumps, with the addition of effects such as color changes and label movement.

1. In Page view of an open FrontPage 2000 Web, with the cursor positioned where you want the Hover button to appear, choose Insert→Component→Hover Button to open the Hover Button Properties dialog box **(12.30)**.
2. Enter label text for the button in the Button text field.
3. Establish a hyperlink target for the button by entering a page in the Link to field, or by selecting the Browse button to open the Select Hover Button Hyperlink dialog box **(12.31)**.
4. Select the button's foreground and background colors, and an animation effect and its associated color using the drop-down lists on the Hover Button Properties dialog box.
5. Enter values in the Width and Height boxes to override the default button size parameters.

continues

 **I P**

Because Hover buttons are Java applets, sound files triggered by Hover buttons must be in the .AU file format.

Creating a Hover Button continued

6. Click the Custom button to open the Custom dialog box **(12.32)**. If you want to customize a Hover button's effect by having it play a sound, enter a sound filename in the Play sound section, or customize the button's appearance by entering a Picture filename in the Custom section of the dialog box.
7. Click OK to close the Custom dialog box, and then click OK again to close the Hover Button Properties dialog box.

Entering a picture filename in the Button field of the Custom dialog box's Custom section displays the picture when you don't move the mouse over it. Entering a picture filename in the On Hover field does just the opposite.

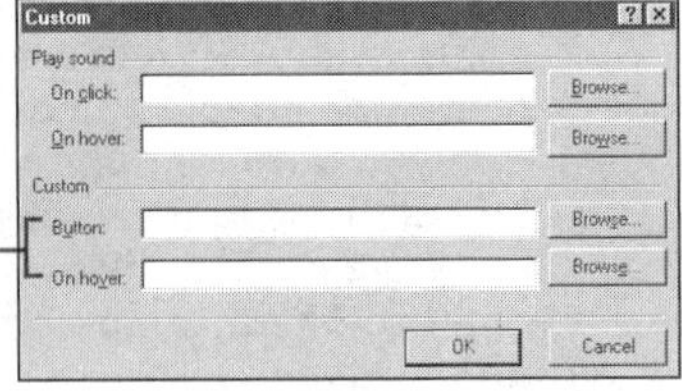

12.32

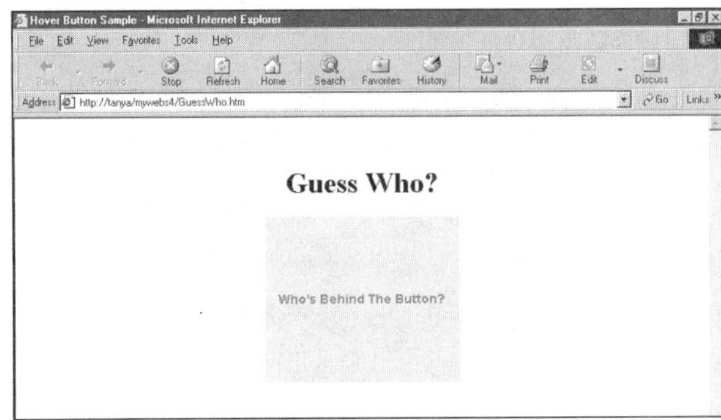

12.33

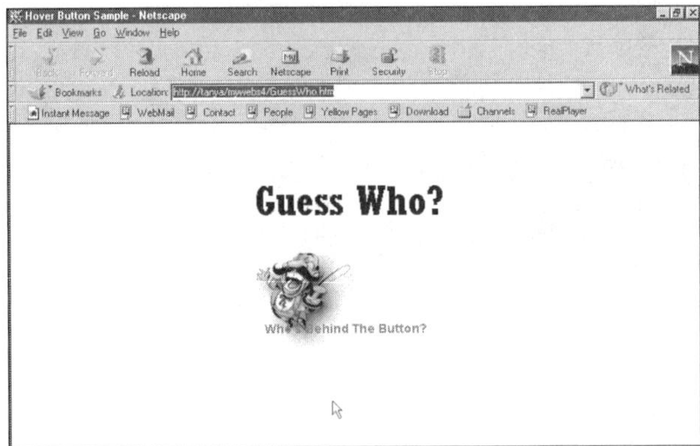

12.34

NOTE

When you set parameters in the Hover Button Properties dialog box, FrontPage 2000 uses your settings to configure the Java applet that is created when you apply a Hover button component. See Chapter 15, "Applying Special Effects".

TIP

Be aware that Hover buttons work reliably only in a controlled display and browser environment, where all users are set up with uniform fonts and font sizes (12.33). Their effect can be easily compromised when users change their display or browser fonts and resolutions (12.34).

Adding a Marquee

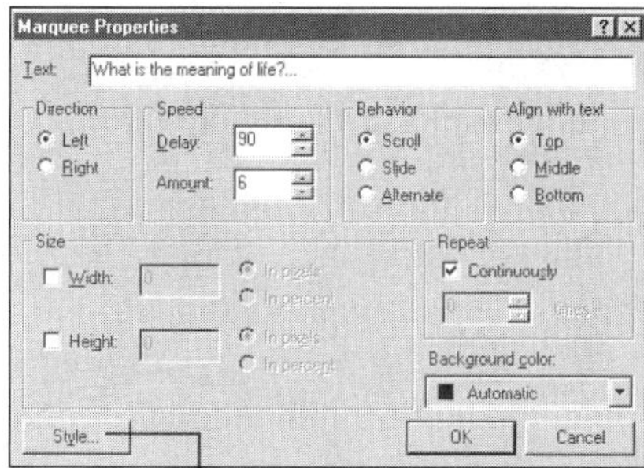

12.35 **You can change the format of the text string used for your marquee by selecting the Style button in the Marquee Properties dialog box. Also, be aware that the greater the value entered in the Amount field under the dialog box's Speed section, the faster your marquee will scroll.**

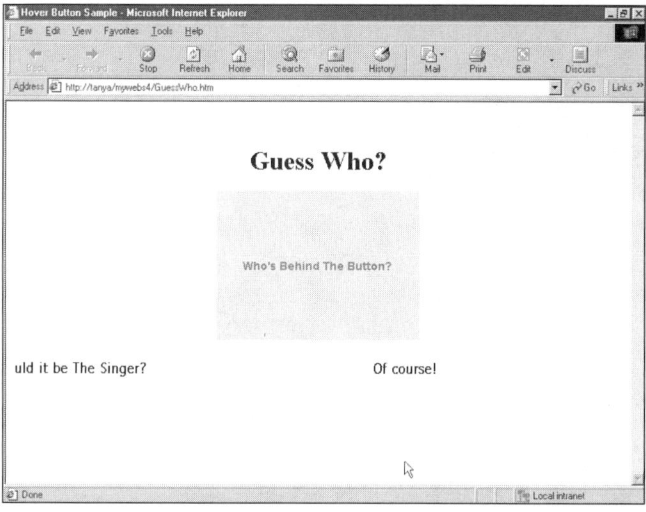

12.36

Adding a Marquee component to your Web page presents visitors with a text message that scrolls horizontally. You can control the Marquee's direction, speed, scrolling behavior, and alignment. One way to use a marquee effect is to present text-based headlines about your site, similar to the way that television stations present breaking news headlines.

1. In Page view of an open FrontPage 2000 Web, with the cursor positioned where you want the Marquee component to appear, choose Insert→Component→Marquee to open the Marquee Properties dialog box **(12.35)**.
2. In the Text field, enter the text that you want to scroll across your page.
3. Accept the default settings, or select values to establish new settings for the direction, speed, behavior, alignment, size, repetitiveness, and background marquee being created.
4. Click OK. Preview the marquee to see the results **(12.36)**.

The Marquee component can be viewed using the FrontPage 2000 Preview tab. In addition, you can use the Preview tab to experiment with different marquee speeds and display characteristics.

Implementing the Banner Ad Manager

The Banner Ad Manager is a component that lets you cycle two or more images in a specific location on your Web page. Typically, you'll notice banner ads on the Web when you visit different search engines, Web promotion sites, or corporate URLs. Using the Banner Ad Manager differs from using the Scheduled Picture component in that the former cycles and transitions between its images in seconds and the latter allows more control over the period of time for one image to replace the other.

1. Add the images that will be cycled by the Banner Ad Manager to the active Web.
2. In Page view of the active FrontPage 2000 Web, with the cursor positioned where you want the Banner Ad component to appear, choose Insert→Component→Banner Ad Manager to open the Banner Ad Manager Properties dialog box **(12.37)**.
3. Accept the default settings or enter new values for the new banner's Width and Height.
4. Preview the file in your browser to see the results **(12.38)**, **(12.39)**.

For the best results, keep your banner ad images approximately the same size.

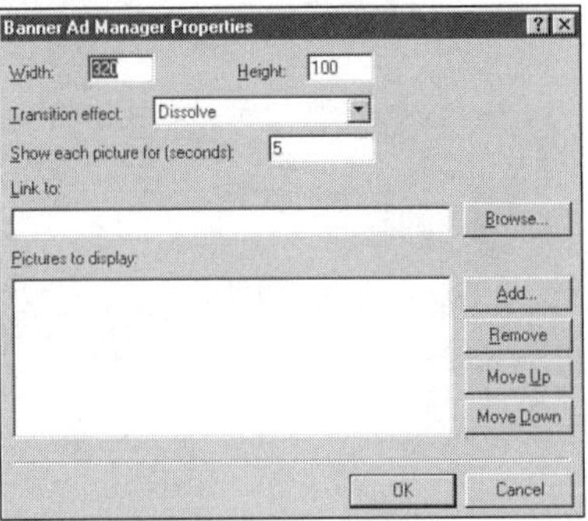

12.37

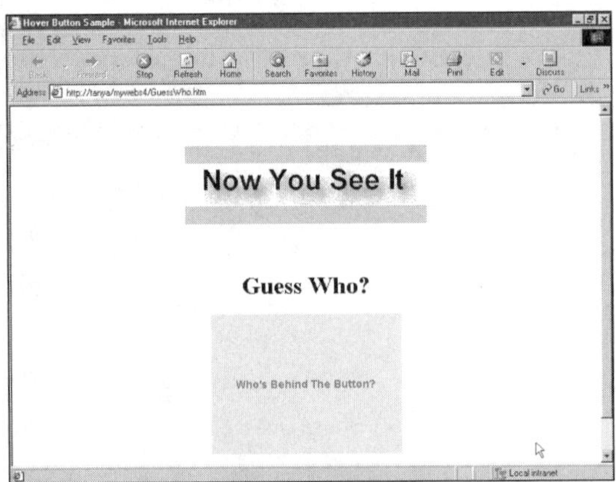

12.38

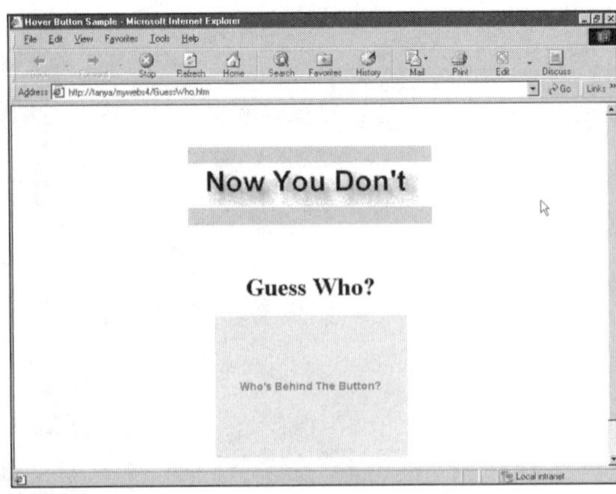

12.39

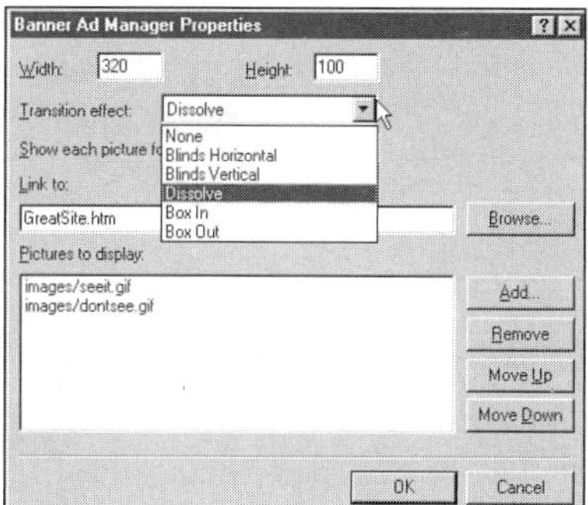

12.40

5. In the Transition effect section of the dialog box, choose a Transition effect from the drop-down menu, and enter a value for how long each banner image will be displayed **(12.40)**.
6. If applicable, enter a URL in the Link to field to make the new banner a hyperlink trigger.
7. Click the Add button to add the images that will comprise the banner to the Pictures to display list box.
8. Click the OK button.

Banner ads that act as hyperlinks can be edited only from the Banner Ad Manager Properties dialog box, or in the HTML source code between the <APPLET>... </APPLET> tag pair.

Unlike many of the other FrontPage components, banner ads created using the Banner Ad Manager can be used without having the FrontPage Server Extensions installed to the Web server. This is because FrontPage 2000 banner ads are implemented as Java applets.

Applying a Confirmation Field

Confirmation fields are used to return the values that a user has input using a FrontPage form. For this reason, confirmation fields are embedded on a Confirmation Form page associated with a given data collection form. Typically associated with customizing a Confirmation Form, confirmation fields are placeholders capable of returning each data element that you want the site visitor to confirm.

1. In Page view of an open FrontPage 2000 Web, with the cursor positioned where you want the Confirmation Field to appear, choose Insert→Component→Confirmation Field from the FrontPage 2000 menu bar to open the Confirmation Field Properties dialog box **(12.41)**.
2. Enter the name of the form field you want to confirm and then click OK.
3. Repeat steps 1 and 2 for each additional confirmation field you want to add.

Confirmation fields appear in braces when placed on a custom confirmation page (12.42) and serve as placeholders for the data submitted via an online form (12.43).

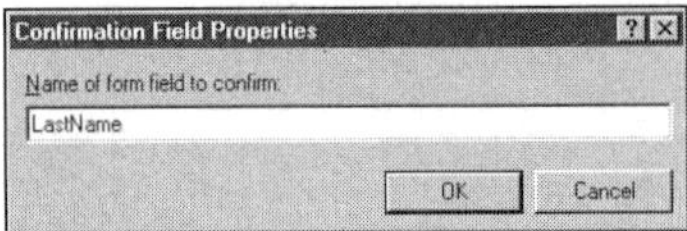

12.41

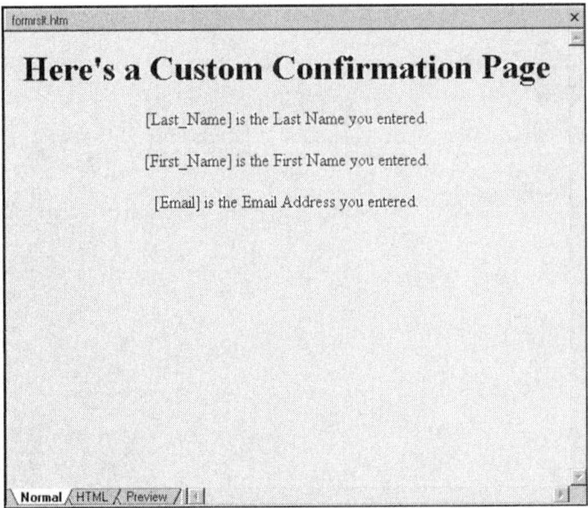

12.42

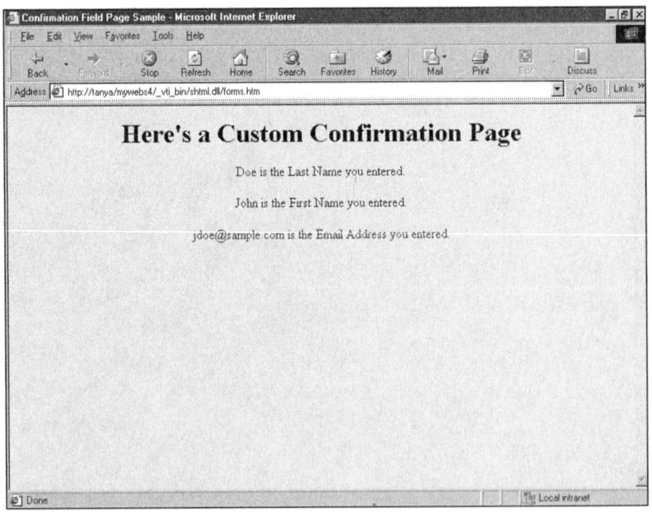

12.43

Adding an Include Page

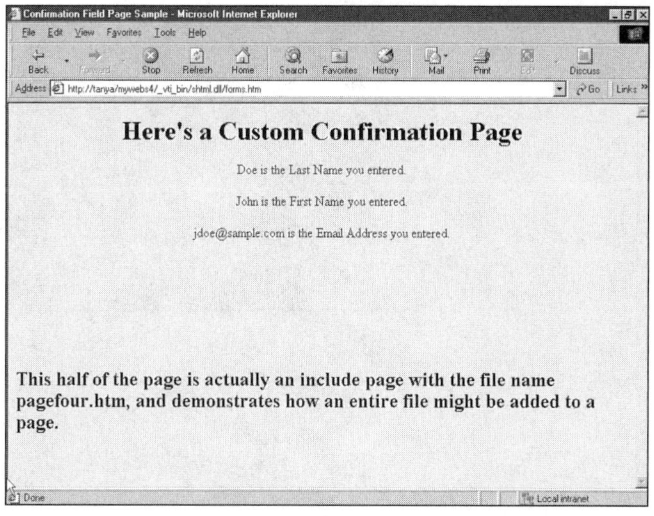

12.44

Include Page Properties

Page to include:

pagefour.htm | Browse...

OK | Cancel

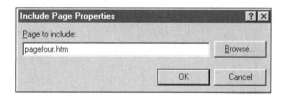

12.45

Include Pages are Web pages created to host page elements common to multiple pages in a Web site, similar to a page header or footer. For example, you might use an Include Page to uniformly apply Navigation Controls throughout a site. Include Pages are a great way to reduce your site maintenance workload, thereby making your Web design more efficient **(12.44)**. This is because you can make page updates by modifying only the Include Page and not each individual page where an Include Page component has been inserted.

1. In Page view of an open FrontPage 2000 Web, with the cursor positioned where you want to apply the Include Page, choose Insert→Component→Include Page to open the Include Page Properties dialog box **(12.45)**.
2. Enter the name of the page you want included as part of the current page and then click OK.

With FrontPage 2000, you have the option of using shared borders or Include Pages to access or display common page elements. In fact, shared borders might be considered a variation on the use of Include Pages.

Scheduling an Include Page

The Scheduled Include component works just like the Scheduled Picture component. The difference is that it lets you predefine the period for which an entire Web page will appear. This is a great timesaver when it comes to making site updates.

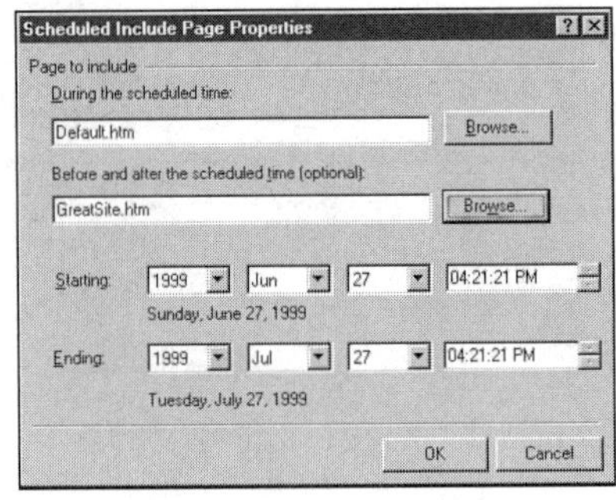

12.46

1. In Page view of an open FrontPage 2000 Web, with the cursor positioned where you want to apply the Scheduled Include Page component, choose Insert→Component→ Scheduled Include Page to open the Scheduled Include Page Properties dialog box **(12.46)**.
2. In the Page to include section of the dialog box, enter the name of the Web page file with which you want to start. As with the Scheduled Picture Properties dialog box, you can select the Browse button to choose a file from the current Web.
3. Enter the name of a file that should appear when the initial file's time period expires.
4. Enter the year, month, date, and time that the initial file should begin to appear.
5. Enter the year, month, date, and time that the initial picture should stop appearing.
6. Click the OK button to close the dialog box.

Setting Up a Scheduled Picture

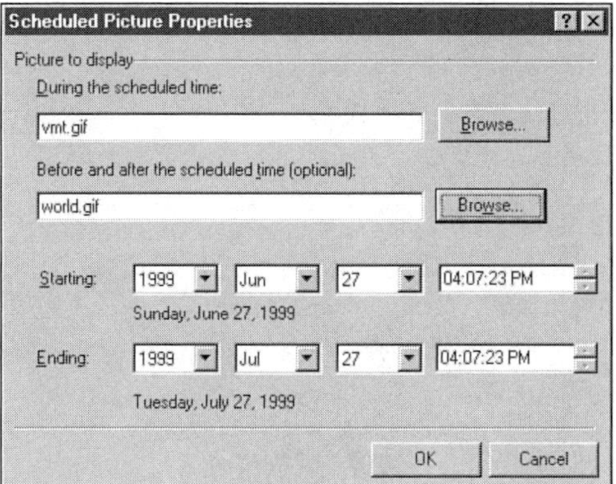

12.47

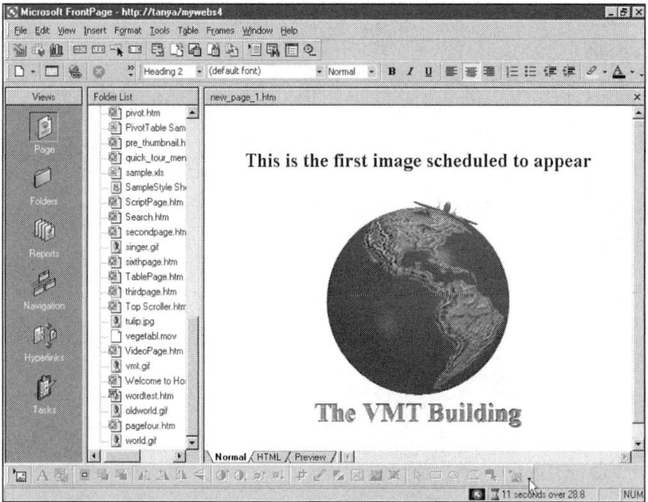

12.48

The Scheduled Picture component lets you predefine the period for which image files will appear on a Web page. This allows you to keep the picture content of your site as current as the schedule that you establish for the content's expiration. Some applications of the Scheduled Picture component might be for sales campaigns, seasonal advertising, or online catalog updates.

1. In Page view of an open FrontPage 2000 Web, with the cursor positioned where you want to apply the Scheduled Picture component, choose Insert→Component→Scheduled Picture to open the Scheduled Picture Properties dialog box **(12.47)**.

2. In the Picture to display section of the dialog box, enter the name of the picture file with which you want to begin the picture display schedule **(12.48)**. You can also select the Browse button to choose a picture file from the current Web.

continues

TIP

When you use the Scheduled Picture component, no picture is displayed on your Web page until the designated start time.

Setting Up a Scheduled Picture continued

3. Enter the name of a picture file that should appear when the initial picture's time period expires **(12.49)**. You can also select the Browse button to choose a picture file from the current Web for this option.

4. Enter the year, month, date, and time that the initial picture should begin appearing on your Web page.

5. Enter the year, month, date, and time that the initial picture should stop appearing on your Web page.

6. Click the OK button to close the dialog box.

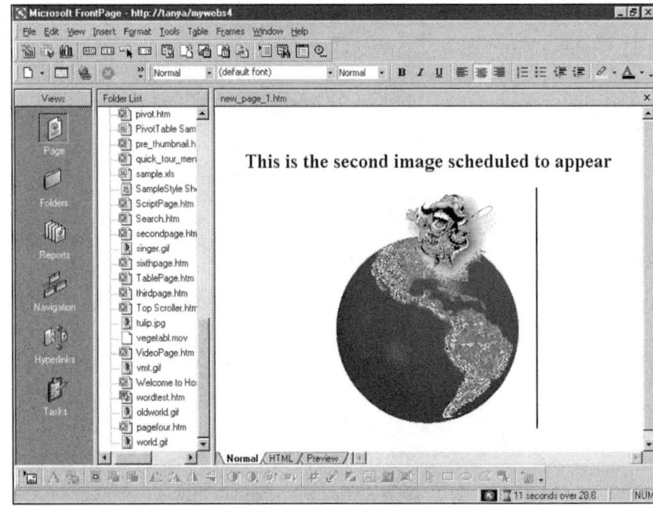

12.49

Both the Scheduled Picture component and the Scheduled Include component are based on the same concept as the Include Page component.

The Scheduled Picture component will not automatically update an expired picture unless the page hosting the component is saved and re-opened. The action invokes the FrontPage Server Extensions, which control the update process.

Applying a Substitution Component

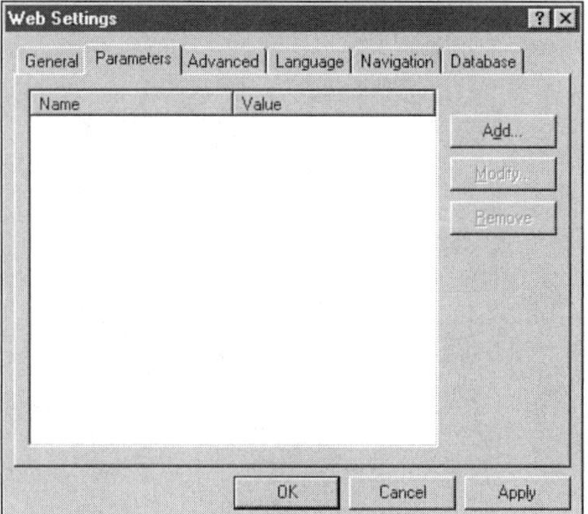

12.50

Remember—change the value of a Substitution component and not the name. If you change the name, you'll have to replace the component on every page where the old name is in use.

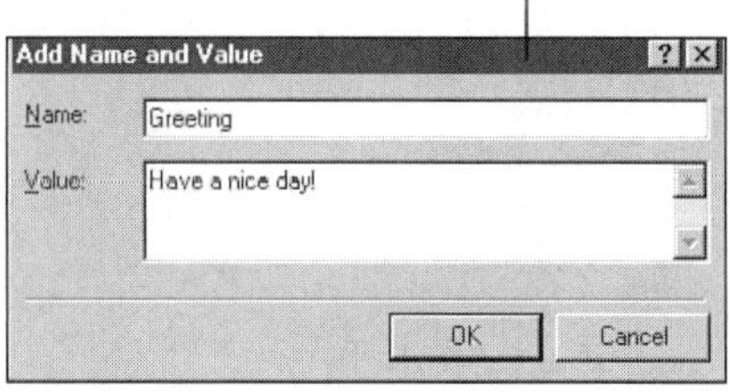

12.51

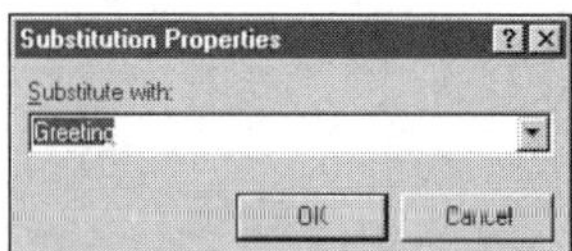

12.52

The Substitution component lets you replace named data placeholders with actual data, based on values established for variables predefined by you. The beauty of this component is that you can change the value of the variable at any time and it automatically changes on every page where the variable appears.

1. To create a substitution variable choose Tools→Web Settings. In the Web Settings dialog box, select the Parameters tab **(12.50)**.
2. Click the Add button to open the Add Name and Value dialog box **(12.51)**.
3. Enter a name for the substitution variable in the Name field, enter a value for the variable name in the Value field, and then click OK.
4. Click OK when the new substitution variable appears in the Parameters tab list box.
5. In Page view of an open FrontPage 2000 Web, with the cursor positioned where you want to apply the Substitution component, choose Insert→Component→Substitution to open the Substitution Properties dialog box.
6. Make a selection from the Substitute With drop-down list **(12.52)**, and then click OK to see your result.

Using Categories

Categories are a new feature introduced with FrontPage 2000. Categories allow you to group and manage Web pages, media files, or other content as a named collection of like items. You can then insert a Categories component into your Web page, and instantly create a list of hyperlinks to all the files belonging to the category that you selected. For example, if you had five pages that you stored in a category called Current Events, placing the Current Events Categories component on a Web page would automatically generate hyperlinks to the pages stored in the referenced category.

1. Assign a file to a category by right-clicking the file in Folder List view, and then choosing Properties from the shortcut menu to open the Properties dialog box for the selected file.
2. In the Title field on the General tab, enter a label name for the file to be categorized **(12.53)**, and then select the Workgroup tab.

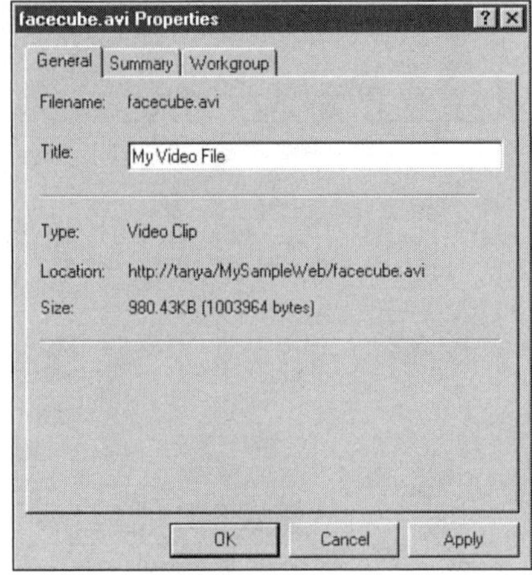

12.53

If you've assigned your Web pages to categories, you can use the Categories report to see all pages by category. All you need to do is select View, Reports, and Categories from the FrontPage 2000 menu bar.

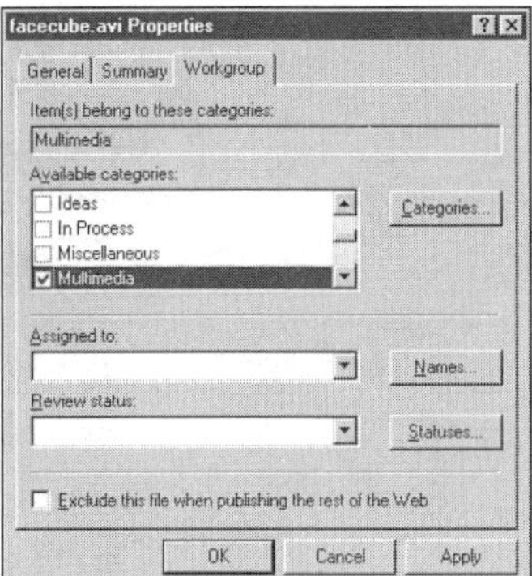

12.54

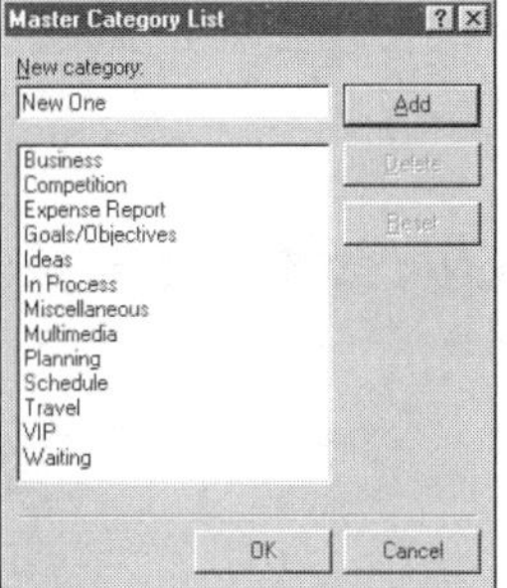

12.55

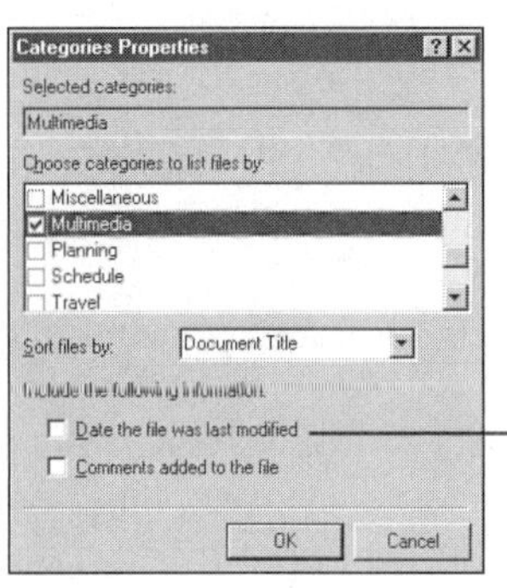

You can choose to have the file modification date and any comments about the file appear on the page to the right of the listed file title.

12.56

3. Select a category for your labeled file from the scrolling list box of Available Categories **(12.54)**. You can also create a custom category: Select the Categories button, enter a Category name in the Master Category List dialog box **(12.55)**, click the Add button, and then click OK.
4. Click OK to close the Properties dialog box.
5. In Page view of an open FrontPage 2000 Web, with the cursor positioned where you want to apply a Categories component, choose Insert→Component→Categories to open the Categories Properties dialog box **(12.56)**.
6. Select one or more file categories to apply to your page by placing a check mark next to the specific category.
7. Click the OK button, and then choose File→Preview in Browser to see your result.

TIP

On the Categories Properties dialog box, you have the option to sort the hyperlink list of categorized files alphabetically by title, or by the date each file was last modified.

Creating a Search Page

FrontPage 2000 offers the option of adding full-text search to your Web site using the Search Form component. This component gives your site visitors the ability to conduct a text-based search of your entire site, and to have results returned as a list of hyperlinks to the pages that match the search criteria. The Search Form component is designed for server-based Webs using the FrontPage Server Extensions. In this environment, FrontPage 2000 automatically creates a text index based on the words in each of your Web pages. This index is searched each time you or your site visitor submits a query using the Search Form component **(12.57)**.

1. In Page view of an open FrontPage 2000 Web, with the cursor positioned where you want to apply the Search Form component, choose Insert→ Component→Search Form to open the Search Form Properties dialog box **(12.58)**.

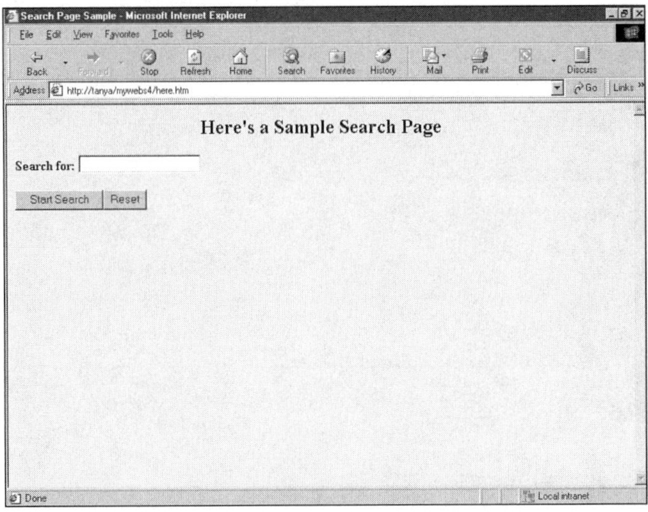

12.57

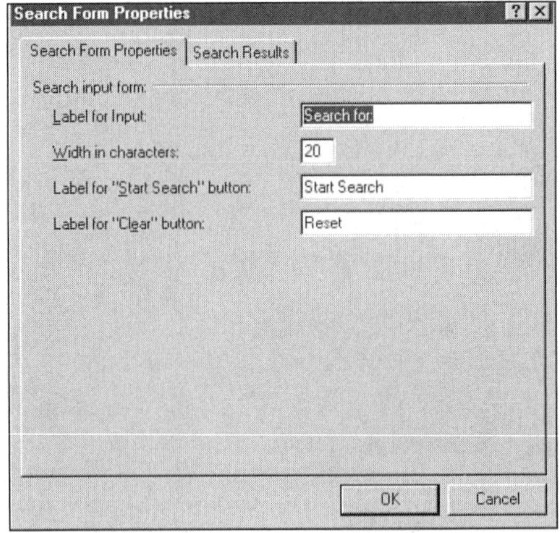

12.58

I P

You can create a new text index for a Web and purge outdated words by choosing Tools→Recalculate Hyperlinks.

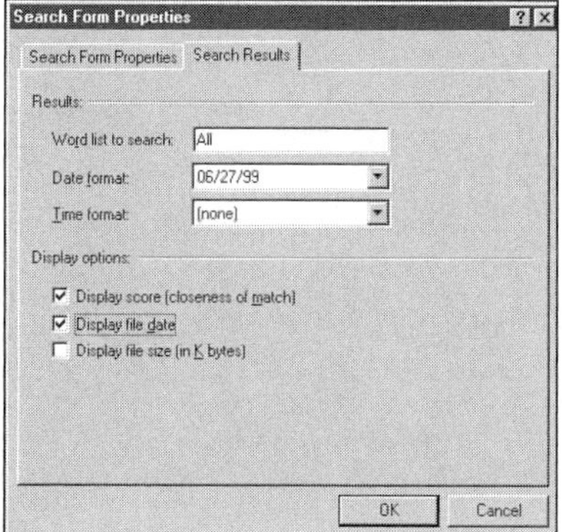

12.59

2. On the Search Form Properties tab, enter values to define how the Search Form will appear on the page. Value options include labeling the form's input field, setting the number of characters that the field will accept, and labeling the buttons to execute the search and to clear the input field.
3. Select the Search Results tab **(12.59)**, and enter values to define how your search results will be returned. Results settings include options to display a score for how close a result matches the search criteria, display the date the file was last changed, and the file size matching the search criteria. Click the OK button.

When you save a page in a Web, FrontPage adds any new words to its text index for that Web. The text index is cumulative. This means that new words are added to the index, but old ones are not removed.

Correcting Search Page Errors

If you find that after submission of a query, you continue to get the message `No documents found. Please try again.` **(12.60)**, when you know that your query should return a result, choose Tools→Recalculate Hyperlinks and then resubmit your query. If you continue to get the message, reset the dependency databases used by the Search Form component.

1. In Windows Explorer, open the folder containing your Web content.
2. Open the `\_vti_pvt` folder and delete the files Deptodoc.btr and Doctodep.btr.
3. Open the `\_vti_txt\default.wti` folder and delete the files `All.cat`, `All.dct`, `All.doc`, `All.fmt`, `All.fn`, `All.hl`, `All.idx`, `All.inv`, and `All.src`.
4. Choose Tools→Recalculate Hyperlinks.
5. Resubmit your query using the Search Form component **(12.61)**.

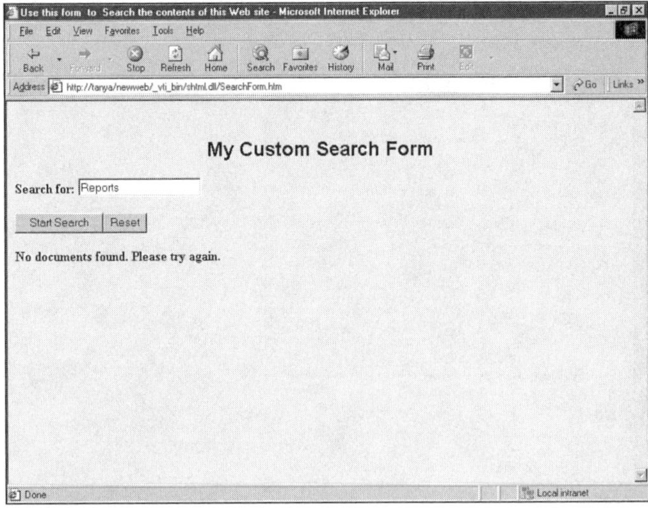

12.60

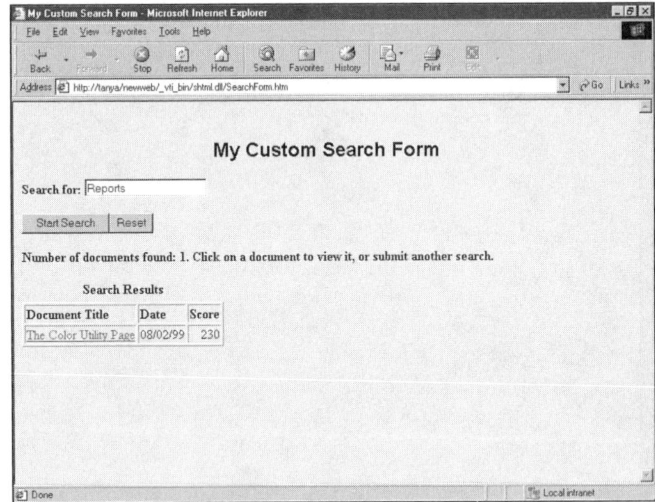

12.61

 I P

A search form component will not locate approximately 300 of the most common English words. See the FrontPage Knowledge Base article q156861 for the list.

Adding a Table of Contents

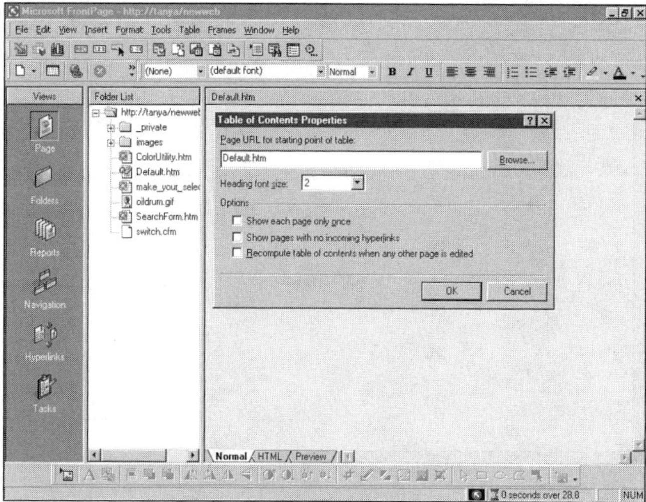

12.62

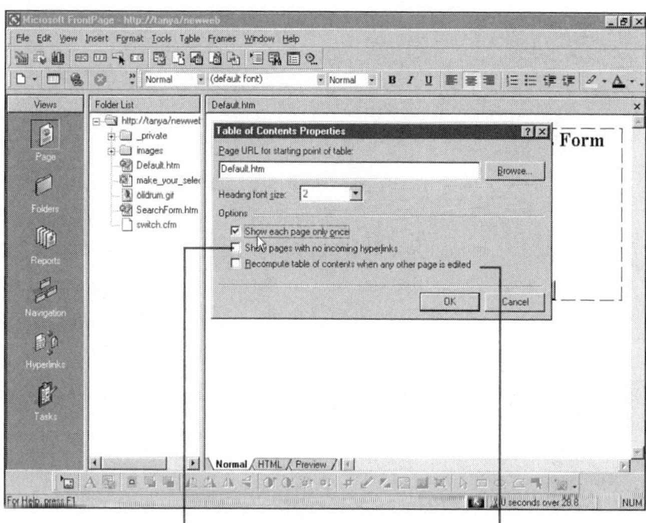

12.63 **Recompute Table of Contents causes the TOC to update automatically.**

Show Pages with No Incoming Hyperlinks tells the TOC to display all pages in the site.

The FrontPage 2000 Table of Contents component creates a hyperlink outline of each page in your Web site. This can be a time-saver; however, using the Table of Contents component is a judgment call because it might introduce a measure of redundancy into your site. If you've already established a site map or Web navigation scheme, a table of contents probably isn't necessary.

1. In Page view of an open FrontPage 2000 Web, with the cursor positioned where you want to apply the Table of Contents component, choose Insert→Component→Table of Contents to open the Table of Contents Properties dialog box.
2. Enter the URL for the page that you want to begin the site's Table of Contents or select the Browse button to select a page from the current Web **(12.62)**.
3. Choose a heading size for the Table of Contents header from the Heading Size drop-down list.
4. Select the Show Each Page Only Once check box to display a single occurrence of a page in the Table of Contents listing **(12.63)**.

continues

Adding a Table of Contents continued

5. Select the Show pages with No Incoming Hyperlinks check box to display every page in the site, even if the pages contain hyperlinks with no active destination in the current Web.
6. Select the Recompute Table of Contents When Any Other Page Is Edited check box to have the current table of contents automatically reflect any page updates.
7. Click the OK button when you finish making your selections and then check the results in your browser **(12.64)**.

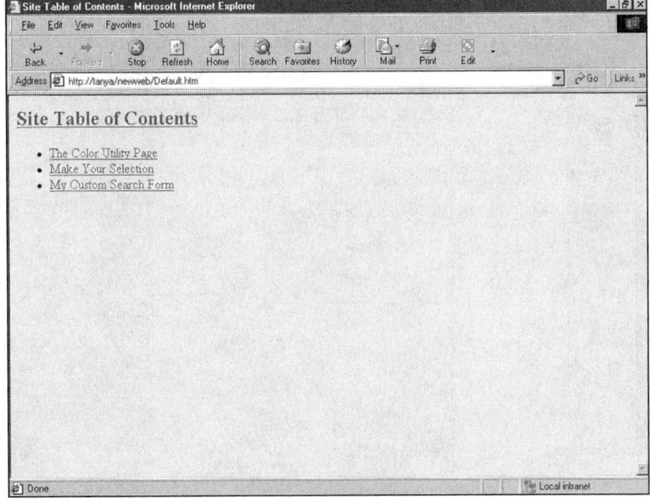

12.64

The Table of Contents component reads each of the hyperlinks in your Web beginning with the home page. It follows each hyperlink found on the home page to the next page and continues until the entire Web has been read. This process results in an ordered list of Web pages based on each page's relationship to the other. Consequently, a 200-page site could result in a 200-item table of contents. Furthermore, if your site contains frames, the Table of Contents component creates hyperlinks to the frameset pages and the documents they reference. You'll need to determine whether having a navigation tool that automatically updates each time you save a new page is worth the effort required to maintain it.

Applying a COM Component

COM components can be purchased or developed. You must have Office 2000 Developer tools installed to create your own COM Add-in components using Visual Basic for Applications.

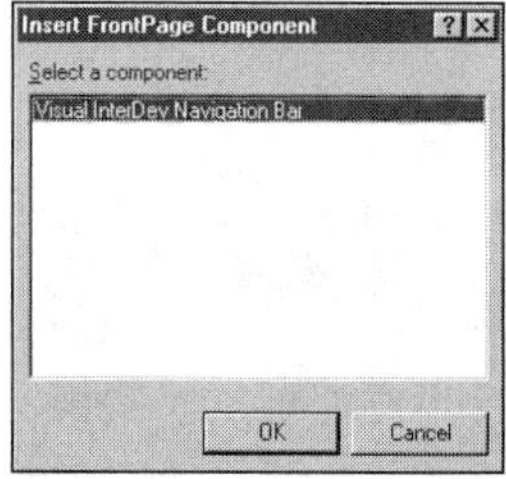

12.65

COM components are software objects created in accordance with the Component Object Model specification. This specification defines how to build components that are capable of interacting with each other regardless of language, tool, or development platform. FrontPage 2000 supports the application of COM components by making them accessible via the Components submenu.

1. In Page view of an open FrontPage 2000 Web, with the cursor positioned where you want to apply an installed COM component, choose Insert→Component→Additional Components to open the Insert FrontPage Component list box **(12.65)**.
2. Select the component of your choice from the list box, and then click OK.

You can learn more about COM and COM Add-In components by referencing the Microsoft Knowledge Base article Q232680. You can access the Microsoft FrontPage 2000 Knowledge Base by visiting `http://support.microsoft.com/`.

CHAPTER 13

In this chapter you will learn how to...

- Add a Picture File
- Position a Picture File
- Crop a Picture
- Adjust Picture Brightness and Contrast
- Create a Thumbnail Picture
- Create Transparent Pictures
- Add a 3D Effect
- Resample a Picture

WORKING WITH PICTURE FILES

Using picture files on Web pages can present some unique challenges. Applying pictures that are too large (greater than 10K) consumes bandwidth and irritates visitors who must sit and wait for the download. On the other hand, applying pictures that are small (3K-5K) can mean sacrificing picture and color quality. A few rules of thumb in working with picture files are to be mindful of image size, color, and quality. FrontPage 2000 helps you in each of these areas by providing features that make working with picture files easier than you might imagine.

Although FrontPage 2000 supports a variety of graphic formats, the formats you'll most likely use in the development of your Web pages are GIF (Graphics Interchange Format), which supports 256 colors and picture transparency; JPEG or JPG (Joint Photographic Experts Group), which supports high-resolution photorealistic pictures and file compression adjustments; and PNG (Portable Network Graphics), which supports picture transparency of photorealistic pictures. In either case, using picture files to enhance your Web pages is an exercise in subtlety. Remember that your visitors are generally looking for information, and that the use of picture files should support the delivery of that information. For example, if your site provides used car information, a small picture file of the subject automobile adds to the user's online experience. If you're interested in promoting a particular product brand, a picture file can indeed be worth a thousand words. Simplicity is the key.

In this chapter, you'll discover how to add pictures to your Web pages and customize them to meet your needs.

Adding a Picture File

Adding a picture to your Web page can be accomplished in just a few mouse clicks. If you've added pictures to your Word documents, you've got the hang of this already.

1. In Page view of an open FrontPage 2000 Web, choose Insert→Picture→From File to open the Picture dialog box **(13.1)**.
2. Select a Picture file from your local drive using the Look In drop-down menu, make a selection from the Picture dialog box list box, or enter the URL for the Picture file you want to apply.
3. Click the OK button to insert the selected picture **(13.2)**.

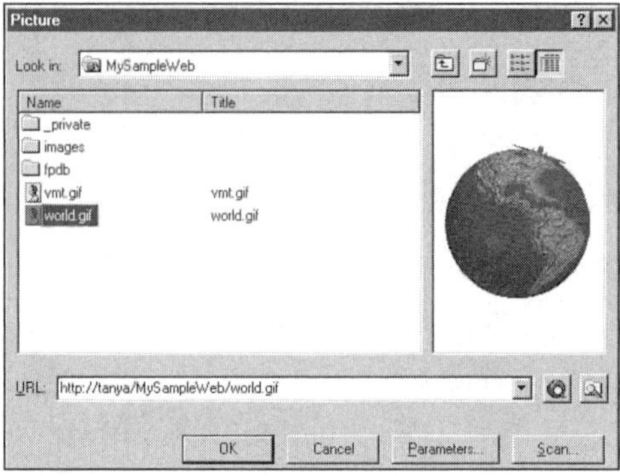

13.1

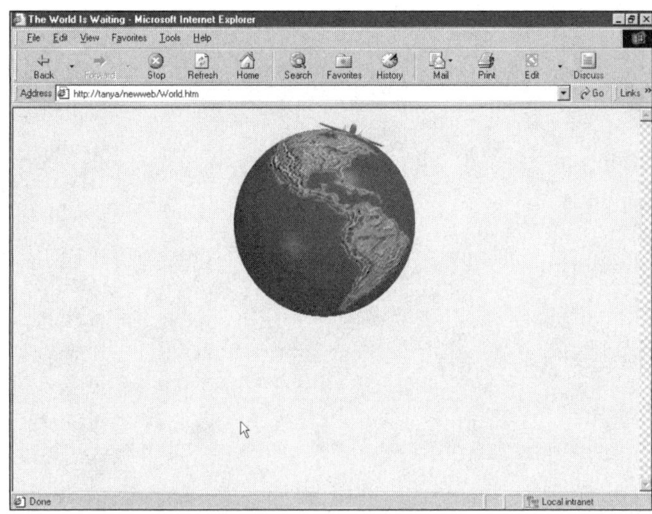

13.2

The Scan button on the Picture dialog box lets you use a digital camera, scanner, or other device as a picture source.

If you have a clip art collection installed on your machine, you can also choose Insert→Picture→Clip Art to make your Picture file selection. Just be sure that the file is in an appropriate format for the Web as noted in the chapter introduction.

Positioning a Picture File

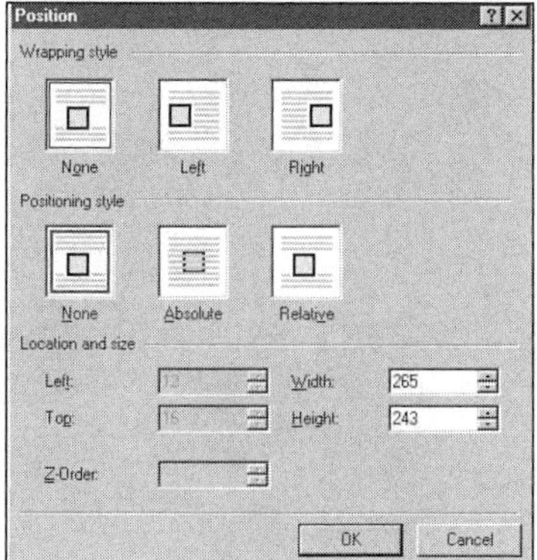

13.3

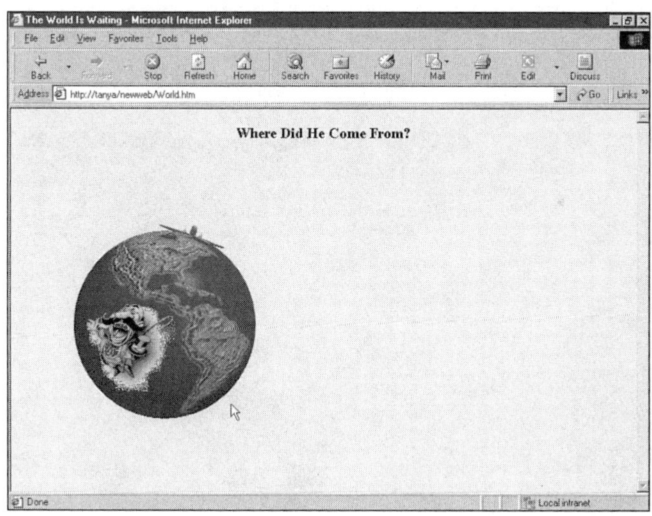

13.4

Positioning pictures in FrontPage 2000 is much like positioning text. In case you missed it in Chapter 7, "Working with Text," positioning is new in FrontPage 2000, and allows you to control how and where a page element is placed on a page and how other page elements sharing the page are displayed in relation to the positioned element.

1. Select the picture that you want to position.
2. Choose Format→Position to open the Position dialog box **(13.3)**.
3. Select a position placement option, and then click the OK button to apply the selected property to the picture.

NOTE

The z-index property is a numeric value that dictates the top to bottom order of layered page elements, and is a feature of FrontPage 2000's new Positioning feature. FrontPage 2000 gives you the option of making z-index property adjustments using the Z-order spinner on the Positioning dialog box. When you select the last item in a layered group of page elements, and you adjust its Z-order value, assigning the element a relative value of 1 places it in front of the page element preceding it (13.4).

Cropping a Picture

It seems that sometimes the best pictures are combined with others, or are simply too large to be compatible with your Web's design theme. One way to address this issue is to crop the picture to suit your needs.

1. Select the picture that you want to crop.
2. Select the Crop icon on the Pictures toolbar to place cropping handles around the selected picture **(13.5)**.
3. Drag the cropping handles toward the picture to surround the picture area that will remain.
4. When finished, deselect the Crop icon on the Pictures toolbar to see your result **(13.6)**.

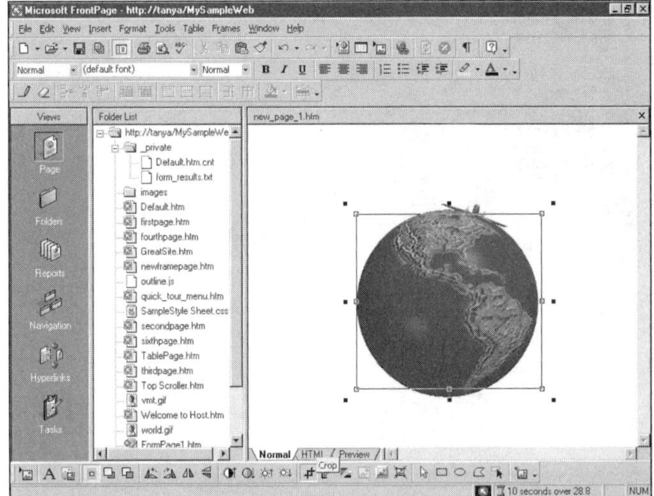

13.5

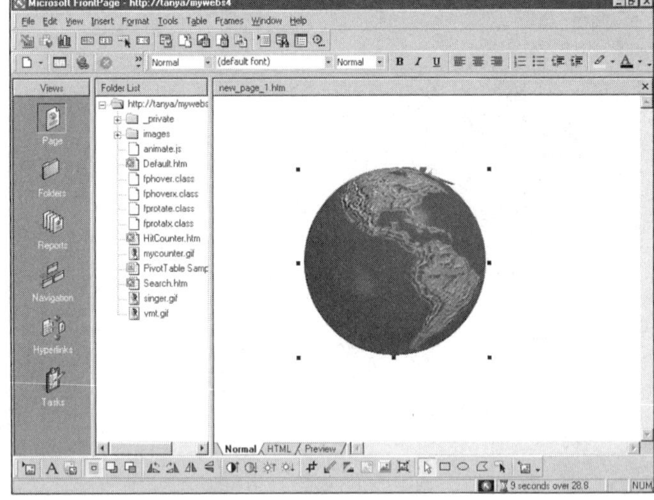

13.6

Any portions of your image that are removed during the cropping process are permanently removed from the image, not just hidden from view.

Adjusting Picture Brightness and Contrast

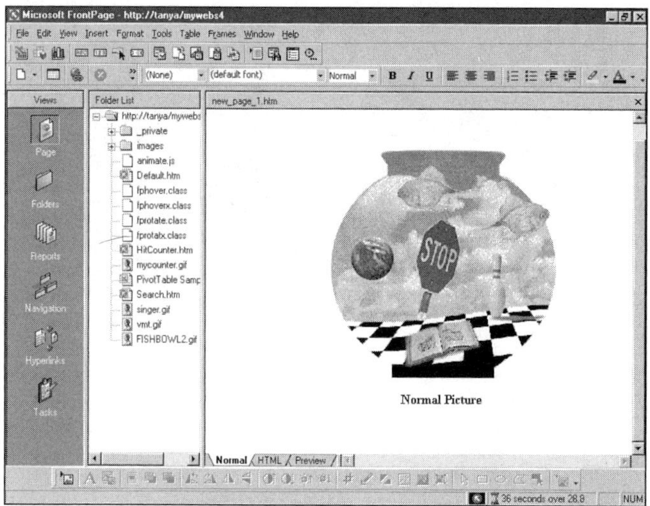

13.7

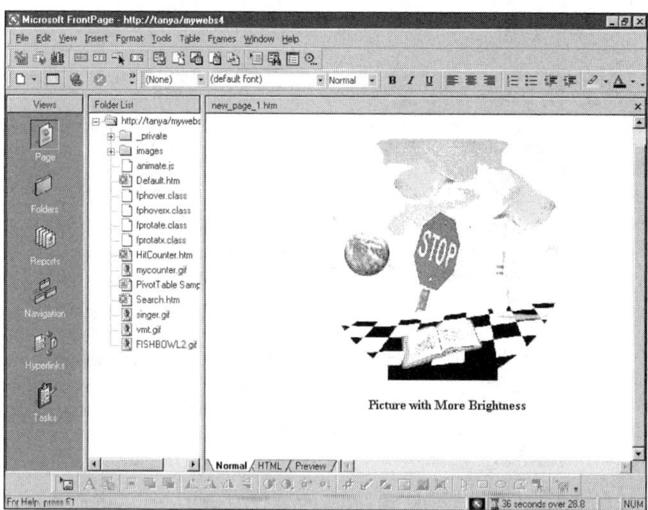

13.8

Using light as an artistic device need not be a foreign concept when it comes to Web design. FrontPage 2000 provides contrast and brightness tools on the Pictures toolbar to let you explore your creative side. For example, light is sometimes used as an effect to change the appearance of a picture's texture. You can also apply light and contrast effects to blend the pictures that you use into the overall theme of your Web page.

1. Select the picture to which you want to add brightness **(13.7)**.
2. Select the More Brightness icon on the Pictures toolbar to increase picture brightness **(13.8)**.

continues

I P

In HTML code, pictures are placed using the <IMG> tag, for example <IMG border="0" src="images/world.gif" width="265" height="243">. The SRC attribute of the IMG tag is used by the Web server to retrieve the correct picture file.

I P

If your page contains a large picture file (Not Recommended), you might want to add a pop-up warning to your page using VBScript or JavaScript to advise your visitors that they may be waiting awhile depending on their connection speed.

Adjusting Picture Brightness and Contrast continued

3. Select the Less Brightness icon on the Pictures toolbar to lessen picture brightness **(13.9)**.
4. Select the More Contrast icon on the Pictures toolbar to increase picture contrast **(13.10)**.
5. Select the Less Contrast icon on the Pictures toolbar to lessen picture contrast **(13.11)**.

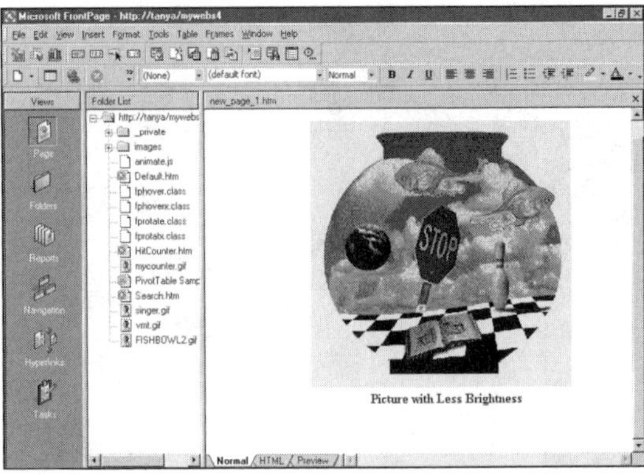

13.9

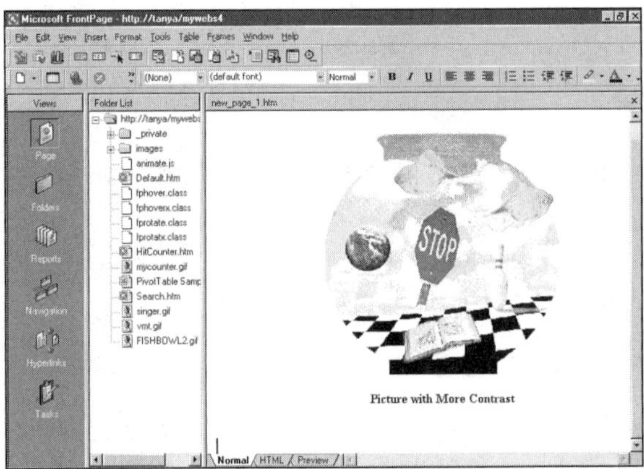

13.10

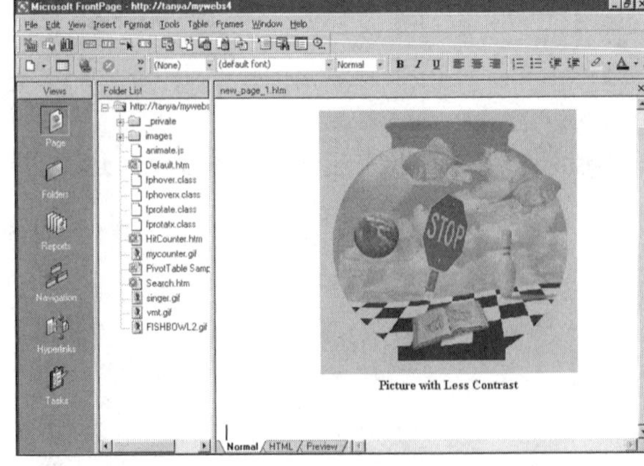

13.11

TIP

When an image is placed on a page in the midst of text, that image is referred to as an inline image.

Even though you may make adjustments to a picture with respect to brightness or contrast, you can select the Restore icon on the Pictures toolbar to return a picture to its original state.

Creating a Thumbnail Picture

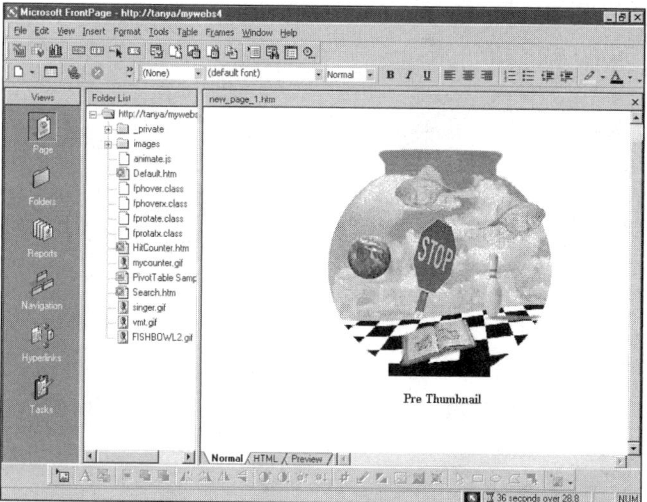

13.12

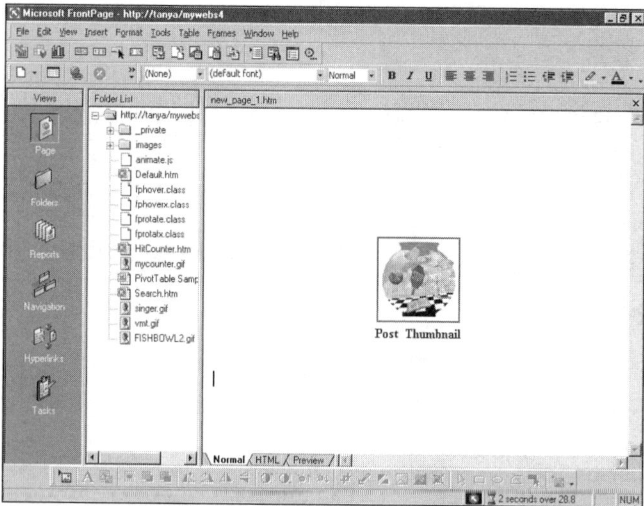

13.13

Thumbnail pictures are useful when you want to allow users to determine whether downloading a full-size picture is worth the time. In other words, using thumbnail images decrease the download time for your pages that contain pictures. This means that visitors don't spend time waiting for one or more large pictures to appear. This type of consideration for site visitors generates return visits. Consequently, thumbnail pictures are an indirect benefit to the Web developer as well. Some examples of the application of thumbnail images might include online sales catalogs, real estate sites, or auto dealership sites. FrontPage 2000 lets you create thumbnails of larger pictures using the Auto Thumbnail command.

1. Select the picture for which you want to create a thumbnail version **(13.12)**.
2. Select the Auto Thumbnail icon on the Pictures toolbar to convert the selected picture to a thumbnail **(13.13)**.

 I P

Optimize your picture files for size, color, and quality before applying them to your Web pages.

If the original picture is the size of a thumbnail picture, the Auto Thumbnail command has no effect.

Creating Transparent Pictures

The ability to make a picture transparent is a life-saver when the background of your page and the background of the picture you want to use are incompatible. FrontPage 2000 makes creating transparent pictures a breeze.

1. Select the picture you want to make transparent **(13.14)**.
2. Select the Set Transparent Color icon on the Pictures toolbar.
3. Click the selected picture to see your result **(13.15)**.

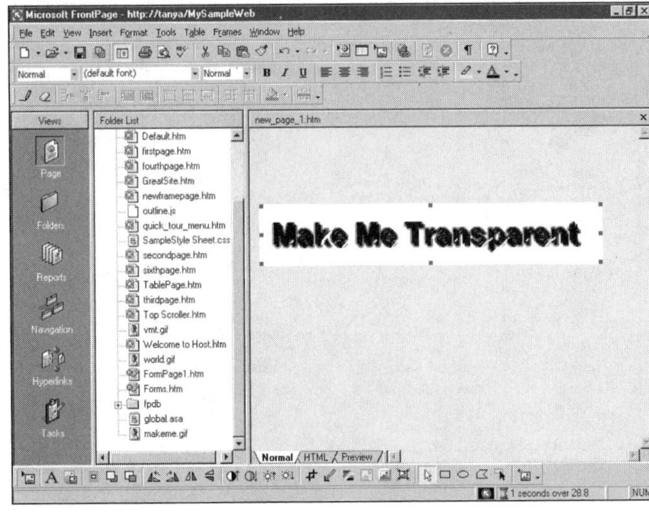

13.14

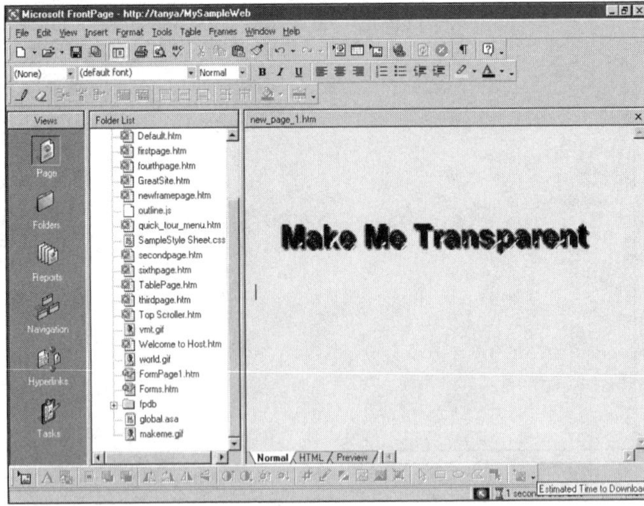

13.15

 **I P**

You can add an elementary level of animation to any picture file using FrontPage 2000's Dynamic HTML command.

 **I P**

If you've not used an image editing tool in a previous life, get to know Microsoft Image Composer. Microsoft Image Composer is a full-featured graphic design application shipped on the FrontPage 2000 CD.

Adding a 3D Effect and Resampling a Picture

Prior to resampling a picture, right-click the picture from the Folder List in Page view and select Properties to see the original file size of the picture. Open the picture's Properties dialog box again after resampling to see how much the file size was reduced during the resampling process in comparison with just resizing, which doesn't effect the file size itself.

13.16

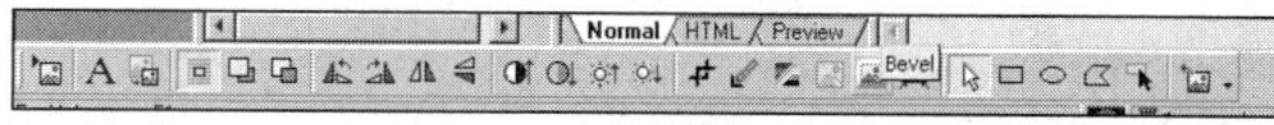

13.17

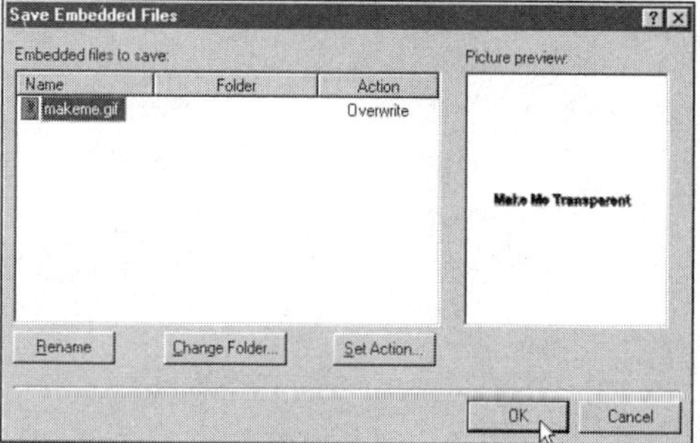

13.18

Beveling the border of a picture is a great way to add a dash of 3D effect to your page. FrontPage 2000 lets you bevel a picture with a single mouse click.

1. Select the picture whose border you want to bevel **(13.16)**.
2. Select the Bevel icon on the Pictures toolbar, and notice the effect that the procedure has on the selected picture **(13.17)**.

Resampling a picture means that you adjust the file size of a picture from its original file size to the actual picture display size. For example, if you resize a picture by 30 percent so that it appears smaller on your Web page, the actual picture file size has not changed. However, when you resample the picture, the actual picture file size is also reduced.

1. Select the picture you want to resize and resample, and then drag a corner of the selected picture inward to make it smaller. Select the Resample icon on the Pictures toolbar.
2. Choose File→Save to open the Save Embedded Files dialog box **(13.18)**. Click OK.

CHAPTER 14

In this chapter you will learn how to...

- **Add a Video File**
- **Add an Audio File**
- **Play an Audio File in a Continuous Loop**
- **Apply Animated Buttons**
- **Create Ad Banners**

Multimedia is a comprehensive term that defines the integration of information delivery mechanisms such as text, sound, pictures, animation, and video. When you include two or more of these media types in your Web design, you enhance the site visitors experience with content that is more effective, efficient, and interactive. You should be aware that FrontPage 2000 support for multimedia files is limited to the controlled insertion of various media file types into your

ADDING MULTIMEDIA ELEMENTS

pages. This limitation may change in later releases, but FrontPage is still an excellent media host now, because you can integrate third-party technologies such as Macromedia Shockwave or Real Networks RealAudio with your FrontPage developed Web. This chapter will cover various ways to use FrontPage 2000 to enhance the impact of your Web by adding and customizing different media elements leading to a rich multimedia experience on the Web.

You can download and install the Macromedia Shockwave player at `http://www.macromedia.com/shockwave/download/`. You can also download the latest version of RealNetworks' RealPlayer by visiting `http://www.real.com/products/player/index.htm.?src=hp_butn,home&hp=yes`. I highly recommend both of these sites as a starting point for exploring ways to extend your FrontPage 2000 Web with multimedia content.

Adding a Video File

FrontPage 2000 supports the addition of video files to your Web page in any format supported by the Windows Media Player. This typically means files created in the .AVI and .MOV video file formats.

1. In Page view of an open FrontPage 2000 Web, choose Insert→Picture→Video to open the Video dialog box **(14.1)**.
2. Select a video file from your local drive using the Look In drop-down menu, make a selection from the Video dialog box list box, or enter the URL for the video file you want to apply.
3. Click the OK button to close the Video dialog box and apply the video clip to your Web page.
4. Right-click the applied video clip and select Picture Properties from the shortcut menu to open the Picture Properties dialog box at the Video tab **(14.2)**.

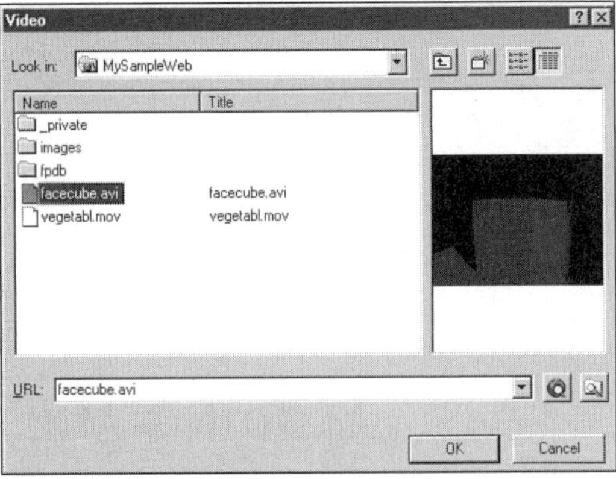

14.1

On the Video tab of the Picture Properties dialog box, you can set parameters that show playback controls in the browser, and cause the selected video clip to play in a loop of one or more cycles or perpetually. In addition, you can set parameters to have the video begin to play when the page opens, or when you mouseover.

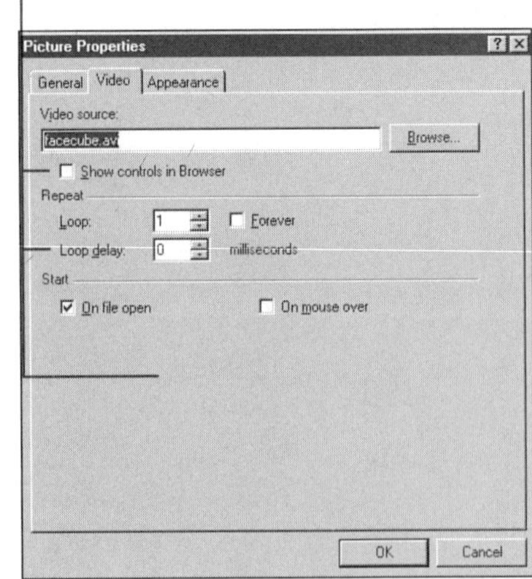

14.2

Because Internet Explorer is an integral part of the FrontPage 2000 interface, be aware that IE's multimedia format is called ActiveMovie. ActiveMovie is a streaming technology installed with IE that supports real-time audio and video playback.

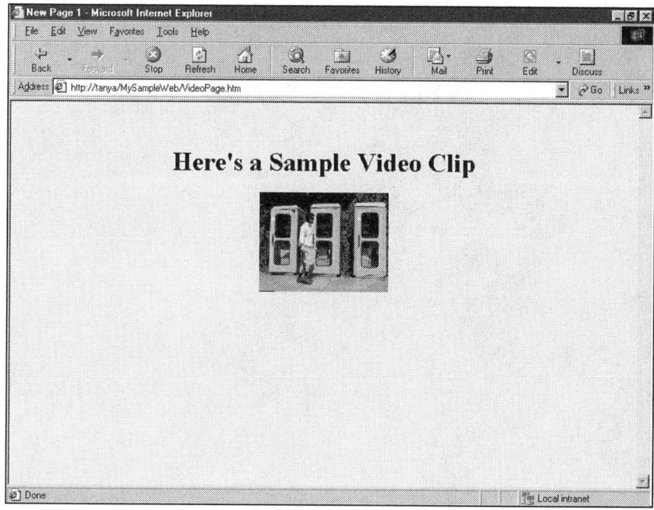

14.3

5. Set parameters for the video clip's playback cycles and the trigger that initiates playback—either when the file opens or on a mouseover.
6. Click the OK button to close the Picture Properties dialog box, and apply the settings.
7. Preview the video in your Web browser **(14.3)**.

At the time of this writing, FrontPage 2000 supports the following audio and video formats seen in Table 14.1.

Table 14.1

Audio and Video Formats

Video for Windows	.AVI	Microsoft
RealMedia	.RAM, .RA	Real Networks
Wave	.WAV	Generic Waveform
MIDI	.MID	Musical Instrument Digital Interchange Format
AIFF sound	.AIF, .AFC, .AIFF	Apple Standard Audio
AU sound	.AU, .SND	UNIX Audio Format

If you're partial to Netscape Navigator, be prepared to deal with Netscape's plug-ins for video playback support. With IE, you get the same video playback support benefits via ActiveMovie.

Adding an Audio File

Another multimedia element that adds pizzazz to your Web site is audio. FrontPage 2000 supports a variety of audio file formats including .WAV, .AU, and .RA.

1. In Page view of an open FrontPage 2000 Web, right-click the open page, and then choose Page Properties from the FrontPage 2000 shortcut menu to open the Page Properties dialog box **(14.4)**.

2. In the Background Sound section of the dialog box, click the Browse button to open the Background Sound dialog box **(14.5)**.

3. Select an audio file from your local drive using the Look In drop-down menu, make a selection from the Video dialog box list box, or enter the URL for the video file you want to apply.

4. Click the OK button to close the Background Sound dialog box and add the audio clip filename to the Location field under the Page Properties Background Sound section.

5. Click the OK button to close the Page Properties dialog box, and to apply the audio file for background playback on the Web page.

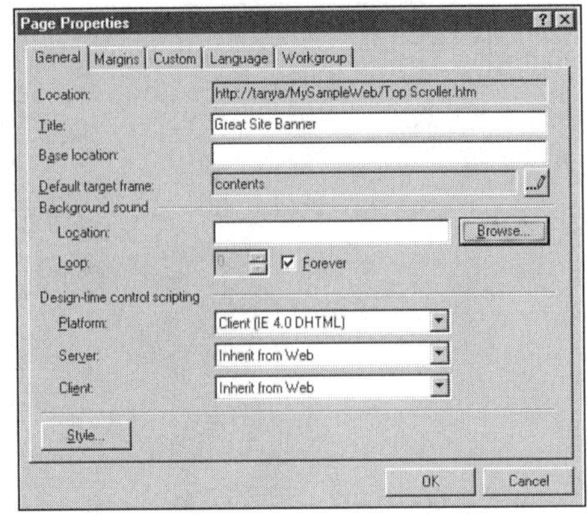

14.4

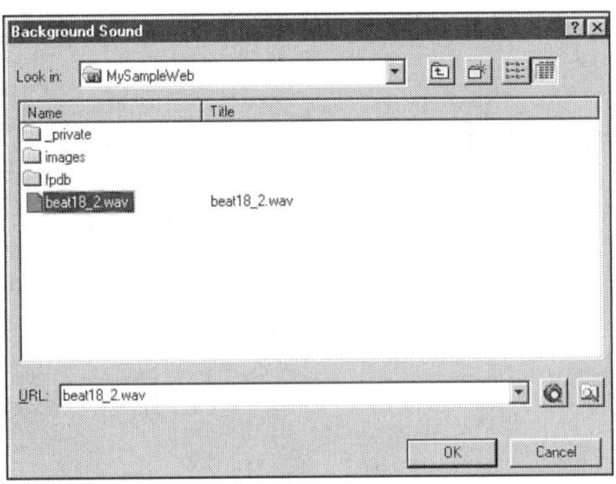

14.5

Playing an Audio File in a Continuous Loop

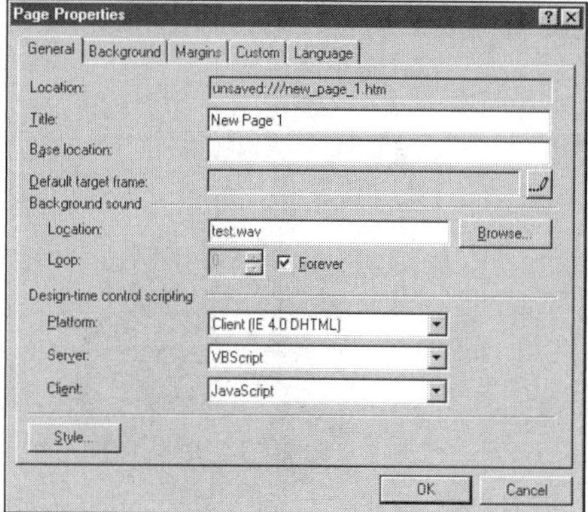

14.6

On those occasions when you want a background audio file to play continuously rather than for one or two cycles, FrontPage 2000 makes it as easy as two mouse clicks.

1. In Page view of an open FrontPage 2000 Web, right-click the open page, and then choose Page Properties from the FrontPage 2000 shortcut menu to open the Page Properties dialog box.
2. In the Background sound section of the dialog box, select the Forever check box **(14.6)**.
3. Click the OK button to close the Page Properties dialog box, and to apply the continuous play setting for the audio file.

TIP

FrontPage 2000 does not offer you the option of using playback controls on the screen. After you've applied the sound file and set its parameters, that's pretty much it, so use the forever loop option sparingly so as not to drive site visitors away rather than bringing them in.

Adding Animated Buttons

FrontPage 2000 now supports the application of animated buttons for your Web pages using Dynamic HTML. Animating your push button controls adds a flair to your pages that gives your site visitor a truly interactive experience.

1. In Page view of an open FrontPage 2000 Web, choose Insert→Form→Push Button to place a push button control on the page **(14.7)**.
2. Select the button, and then choose Format→Dynamic HTML Effects to access the DHTML Effects toolbar **(14.8)**.
3. From the On drop-down menu, select an event that will trigger the button's animation effect.

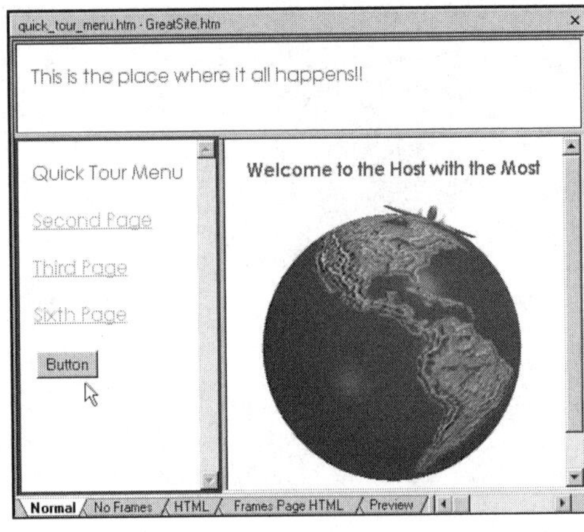

14.7

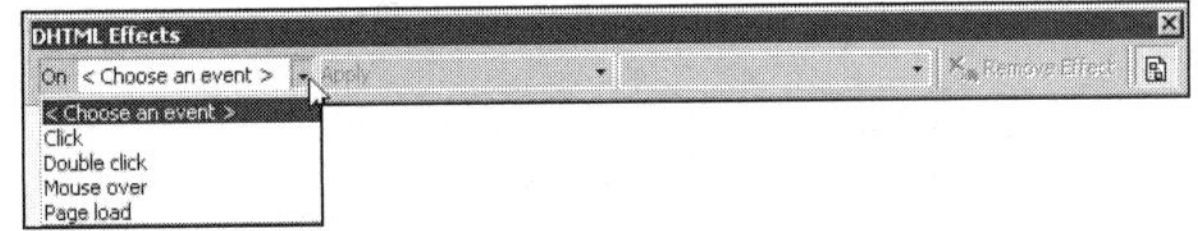

14.8

Check out some other examples of how Dynamic HTML is used by visiting `http://www.microsoft.com/ie/ie40/demos/default.htm?/ie/ie40/demos/main.htm`.

Be wary of using DHTML and style features if you're not doing so in a pure Microsoft environment. The application of these features is great; however, they may execute differently if you're partial to a Web development environment that's not Microsoft-centric.

Applying Fly out causes the button to exit the page, as specified by the selected direction on the Effects drop-down menu. Applying Formatting lets you change the way that a page element like a font or border appears in response to an event.

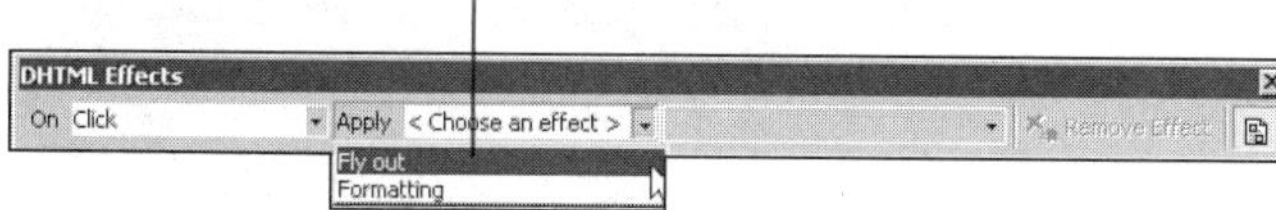

14.9

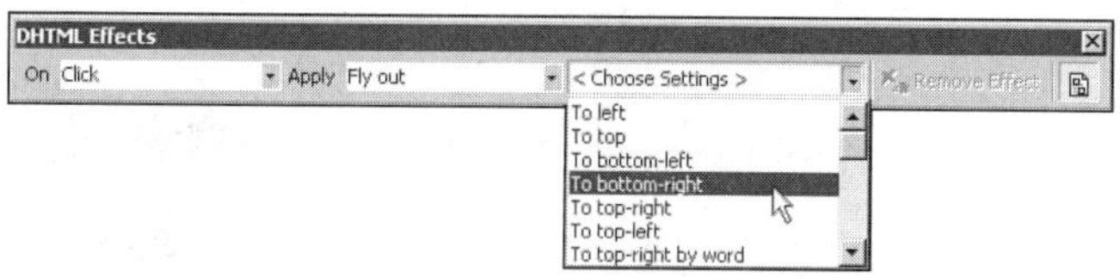

14.10

4. From the Apply drop-down menu **(14.9)**, select the effect that your event will trigger.
5. From the Choose Settings drop-down menu **(14.10)**, select the setting that applies to the effect that you selected.
6. Close the DHTML Effects tool-bar to apply the animation effect to your push button.

 **I P**

FrontPage 2000's Dynamic HTML effects only work in Internet Explorer.

 **I P**

Don't let your use of animated buttons become gratuitous. Remember, visitors to your site are there for the content.

Creating Ad Banners

Visit any search engine on the Web today, and it's hard to miss those animated banner ads. With FrontPage 2000, you can create banner ads of your own; all you need is a couple of image files.

1. In Page view of an open FrontPage 2000 Web, choose Insert→Component→Banner Ad Manager to open the Banner Ad Manager Properties dialog box **(14.11)**.
2. Enter values for the banner's Width and Height.
3. Choose an effect from the Transition Effect drop-down menu.
4. Enter a value in seconds for how long each banner will display.
5. In the Link To field, enter the filename that you want the banner to hyperlink to, or click the Browse button to open the Select Banner Ad Hyperlink dialog box **(14.12)**. In this dialog box, you should select a file from your local drive using the Look In drop-down menu, make a selection from the dialog box list box, or enter the URL for the file you want the banner to hyperlink to, and then click OK.

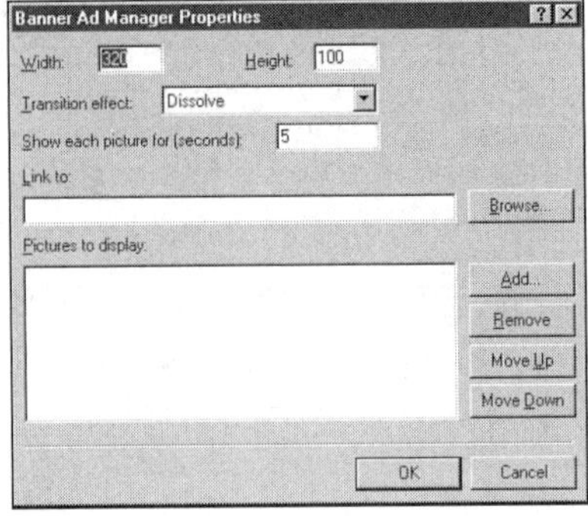

14.11

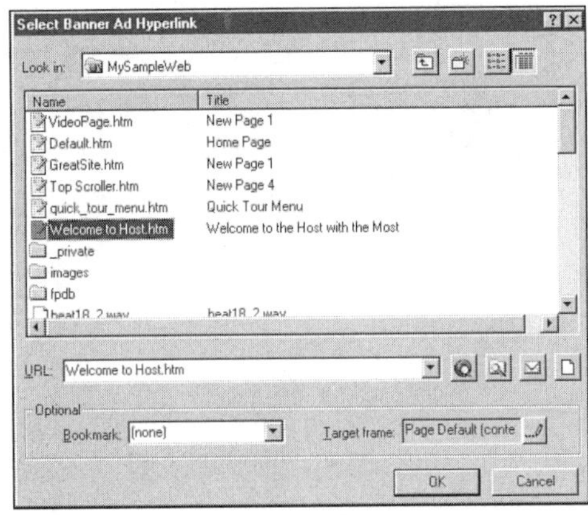

14.12

See Chapter 12, "Applying FrontPage Components," for more information about the Banner Ad Manager.

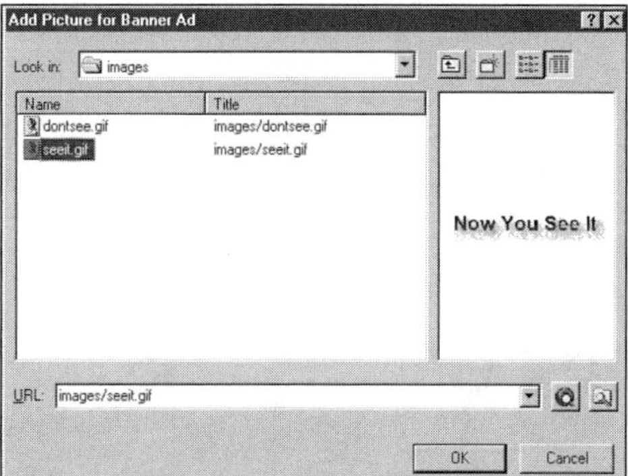

14.13

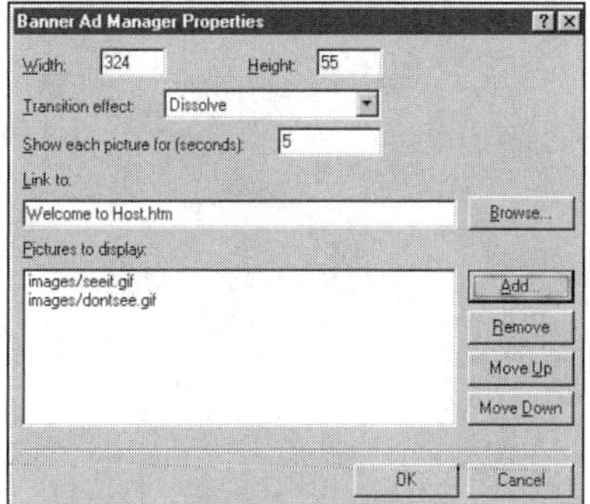

14.14

6. Click the Add button to open the Add Picture for Banner Ad dialog box **(14.13)**.
7. Select a file from your local drive using the Look In drop-down menu, make a selection from the dialog box list box, or enter the URL for the files you want as banner images, and then click OK to see the images listed in the Pictures to display list box **(14.14)**.
8. Click the OK button, and then select the Preview tab to see your dual image banner ad.

You don't need to have the FrontPage Server Extensions installed to take advantage of the FrontPage 2000 banner ad feature.

Remember, banner ads employ image files. For this reason, it's still important to consider download time. A good rule of thumb for using images in general, is to keep your images at 10K or less.

CHAPTER 15

In this chapter you will learn how to...

Apply Dynamic HTML Effects

Integrate Page Transitions

Work with VBScript

Work with JavaScript

Special effects add a visual dynamic to your Web pages that may or may not appeal to site visitors. Unless your Web page is purely for entertainment purposes, special effects such as page transitions and animated page elements can often detract from the message that your Web is trying to communicate. If you decide that razzle-dazzle special effects will improve the look of your page and are consistent with your site's image,

APPLYING SPECIAL EFFECTS

FrontPage 2000 makes it possible with the introduction of support for Dynamic HTML. Dynamic HTML is an extension of cascading style sheets (CSS), and as such supports the application of precise positioning, object-layering, and real-time animation without the need for ActiveX controls or Java applets. If you're planning to use ActiveX controls or Java applets in your pages, you'll find that FrontPage 2000 facilitates the use of both VBScript and JavaScript.

In fact, JavaScript is one of the key elements in the creation of Dynamic HTML effects. Another element behind FrontPage 2000's implementation of Dynamic HTML effects is the Internet Explorer event model. The IE event model is a framework for how scripting languages handle events like onMouseover or onClick, providing information to your Web browser such as the origin of an event trigger.

Applying Dynamic HTML Effects

Using Dynamic HTML, you can add a variety of animation effects to most any page element. For example, you can highlight text with borders that instantly appear, cause tables to fly in from the side of your screen, or make images appear to slide off the edge of your page.

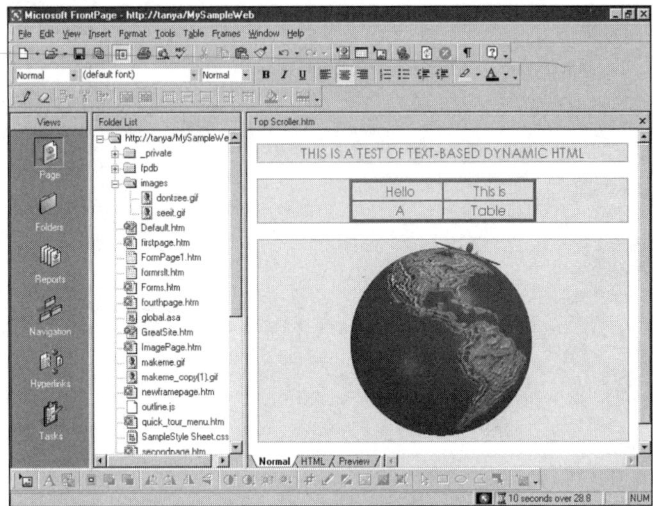

15.1

1. In Page view of an open FrontPage 2000 Web, enter a line of text, or insert a page element of your choice **(15.1)**.
2. Select the page element, and then choose Format→Dynamic HTML Effects to access the DHTML Effects toolbar **(15.2)**.
3. From the On drop-down menu, select an event that will trigger the page element's animation effect.
4. From the Apply drop-down menu, select the effect that your event will trigger.

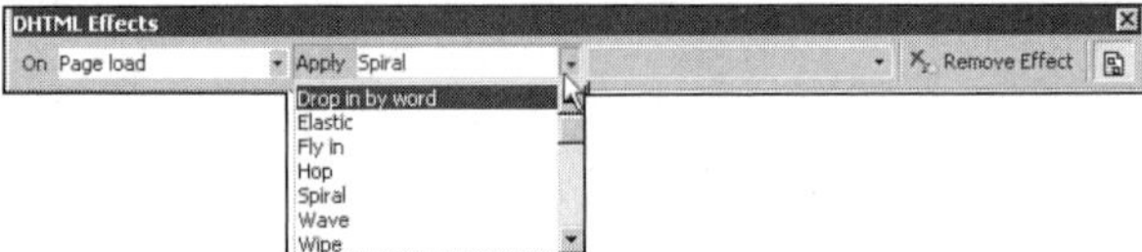

15.2

Page elements with DHTML effects applied appear on a blue background.

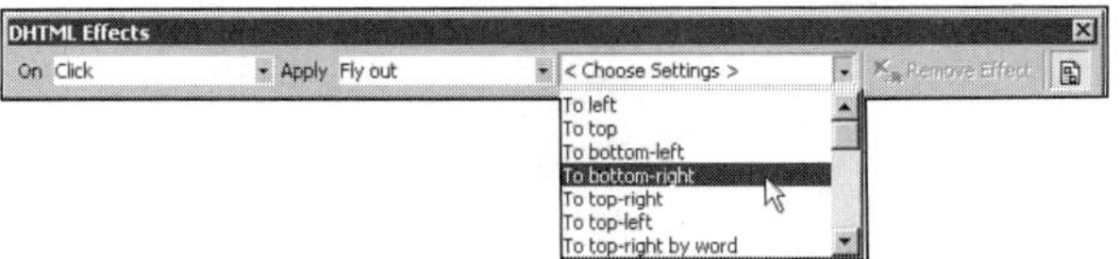

15.3

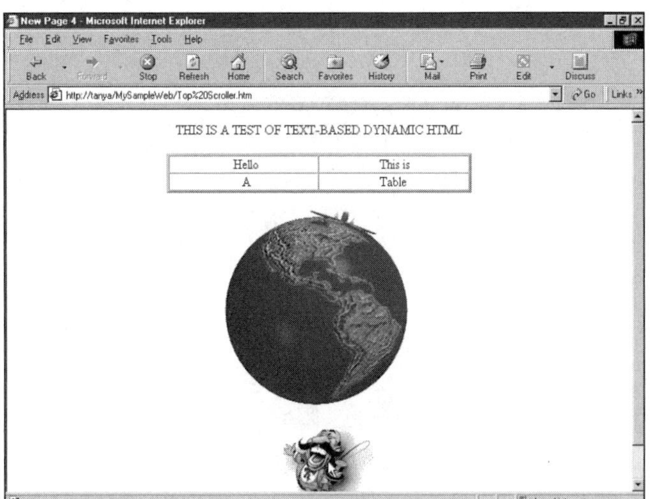

15.4

5. From the Choose Settings drop-down menu **(15.3)**, select the setting that applies to the effect that you selected.

6. Close the DHTML toolbar to apply the effect.

Although it's not obvious from the figure, the screen is jumping with Dynamic HTML effects. Each word of the title header drops in one at a time, the table spirals into the screen, and the little man slides off to the right when you click the picture (15.4).

You can delete a DHTML effect by selecting a page element and then clicking the Remove Effect button on the DHTML Effects toolbar.

Integrating Page Transitions

If you're familiar with Microsoft PowerPoint or other presentation packages, page transitions should not be foreign to you. Page transitions add a little flash when you're moving from one page to another; however, you should be aware that page transitions effects are visible only when you're using Internet Explorer 4.0 or higher.

1. Choose Format→Page Transition to open the Page Transitions dialog box **(15.5)**.
2. Select an event to trigger the transition effect from the Event drop-down menu.
3. Enter a value for the number of seconds required for the transition effect to complete in the Duration field.
4. Select a transition effect from the Transition Effect scrolling list box, and then click OK.

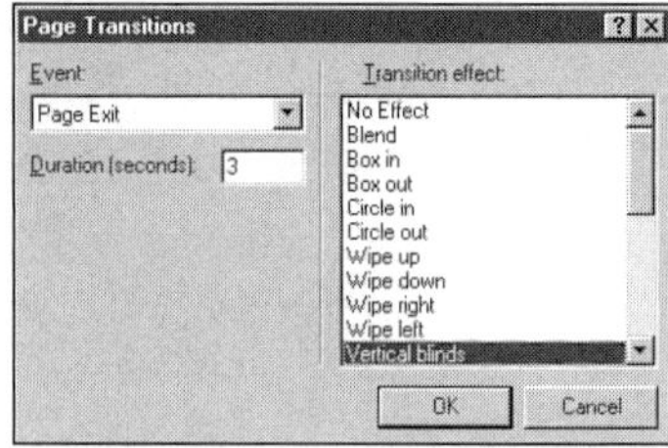

15.5

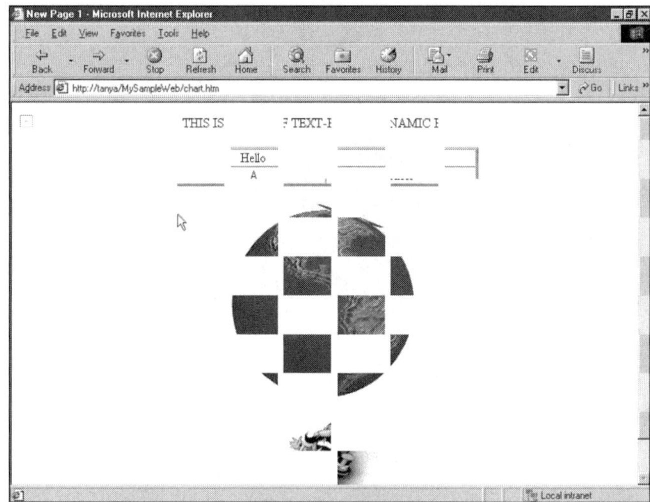

15.6

The Checkerboard transition effect is one of 25 page transitions available from the Page Transitions dialog box (15.6).

In FrontPage 2000, the page transition effect applied to a page supercedes the site transition effect applied to the same page.

Working with VBScript

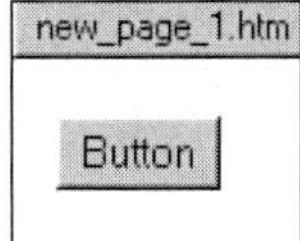

15.7

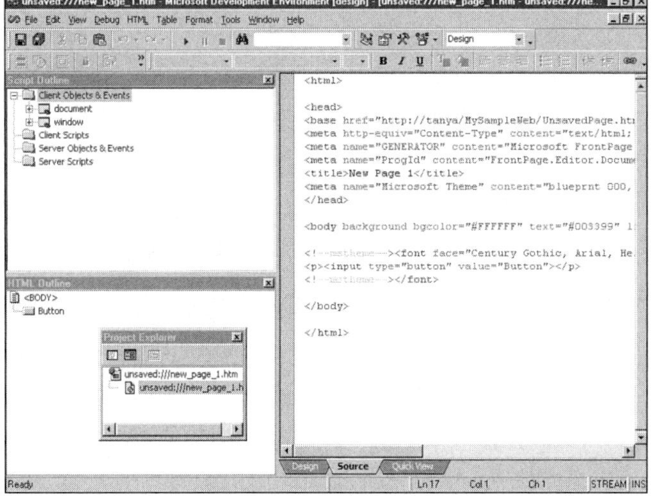

15.8

FrontPage 2000 supports two scripting languages, VBScript and JavaScript. VBScript is an adaptation of the Microsoft Visual Basic programming language. So, if you're a VB programmer, you'll pick up VBScript without a problem. JavaScript, on the other hand, is a Netscape scripting language that is supported by most standard browsers. This makes JavaScript a bit more appealing as a scripting language, because VBScript is only supported by Internet Explorer.

1. In Page view of an open FrontPage 2000 Web, insert a page element—such as a push button control **(15.7)**.
2. Choose Tools→Macro→Microsoft Script Editor from the FrontPage 2000 menu bar to open the Microsoft Script Editor user interface **(15.8)**.

continues

I P

Be aware that FrontPage 2000 supports the addition of backend scripts using either VBScript or JavaScript. It does not automatically generate scripts as it does HTML source code. If you're interested in where to acquire some VBScript or JavaScript samples, you can visit `http://www.microsoft.com/vbscript`, `http://www.vbscripts.com`, *and* `http://www.gamelan.com`.

Working with VBScript continued

3. In the Script Outline window of the Microsoft Script Editor **(15.9)**, click the document object to expand it, and then select an event trigger from the list of choices.

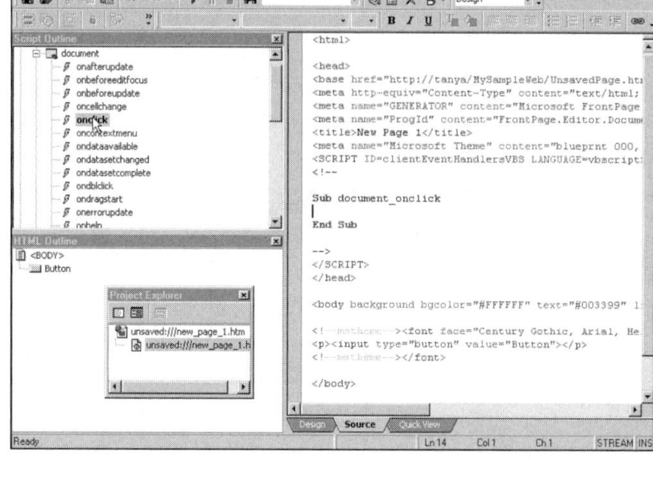

15.9

NOTE

Notice that in the Source window of the Microsoft Script Editor, selecting an event trigger adds the applicable VBScript code to the body of the HTML source code, that is `SCRIPT` *tags and* `Sub...End Sub` *statements.*

The Microsoft Script Editor, by default, displays the Script Outline window containing a tree-based hierarchy of scripting objects and events; the HTML Outline containing a tree-based view of HTML objects on the page being edited; the HTML Editing window containing three tabbed views along its bottom edge—Design view for creating pages in the Script Editor (like FP Normal view), Source view, the default view (like the FP HTML tab), and Quick view (which is like the FP Preview tab); and Project Explorer containing a list of all active Script Editor projects and the items comprising them.

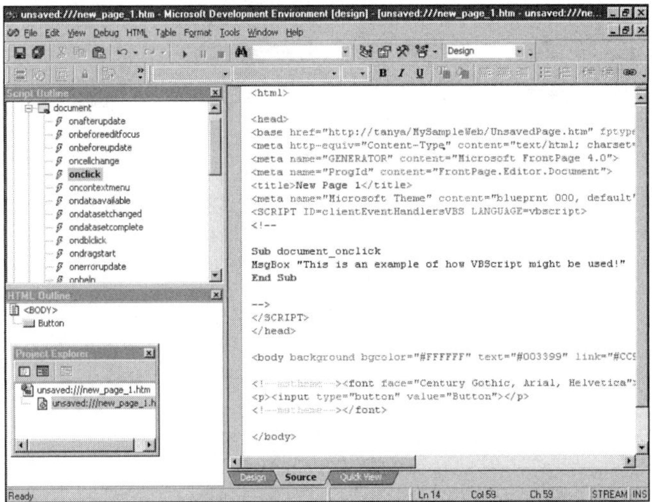

15.10

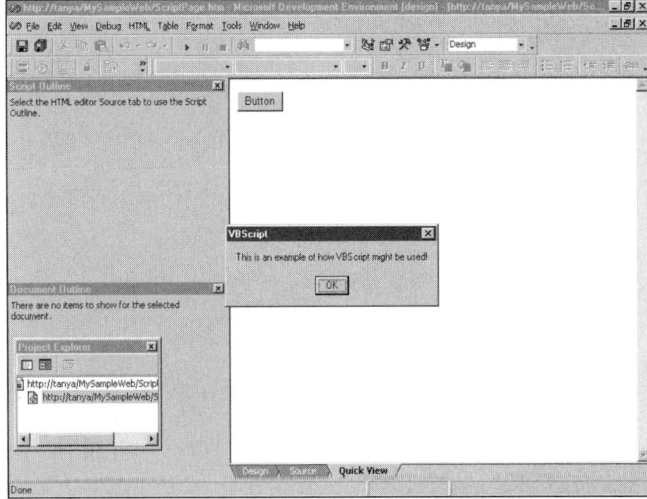

15.11

4. In the Source window of the Microsoft Script Editor, place your VBScript code between the Sub and End Sub statements **(15.10)**.

5. Select the Quick View tab in the Microsoft Script Editor and click the applied control to see the result **(15.11)**.

6. Choose File→Save, and then File→Exit to save your work and close the Microsoft Script Editor.

 I P

Using scripts in your HTML pages allow you to add interactivity to your Web, which facilitates a more dynamic user experience.

 O T E

The Microsoft Script Editor is new in FrontPage 2000, replacing the FrontPage 98 Script Wizard. You should be aware that the Microsoft Script Editor is a separate application that may be installed separately from your FrontPage 2000 installation. If the Script Editor feature is not enabled, you'll need to install the application from your CD-ROM.

Working with JavaScript

An alternative to using VBScript is to use JavaScript to enhance the capability of your Web. The scripting language you use is largely a matter of preference. However, if you want your scripts to be cross-browser compatible, JavaScript is the scripting language of choice.

1. In Page view of an open FrontPage 2000 Web, insert a page element, such as the push button control shown earlier in Figure 15.7.

2. Choose Tools→Macro→Microsoft Script Editor from the FrontPage 2000 menu bar to open the Microsoft Script Editor user interface as shown previously in Figure 15.8.

3. In the Source window of the Microsoft Script Editor, place the cursor just above the opening HTML tag and then choose HTML→Script Block→Client to insert a script block **(15.12)**. Be sure that you change the Language parameter in the script block from VBScript to JavaScript.

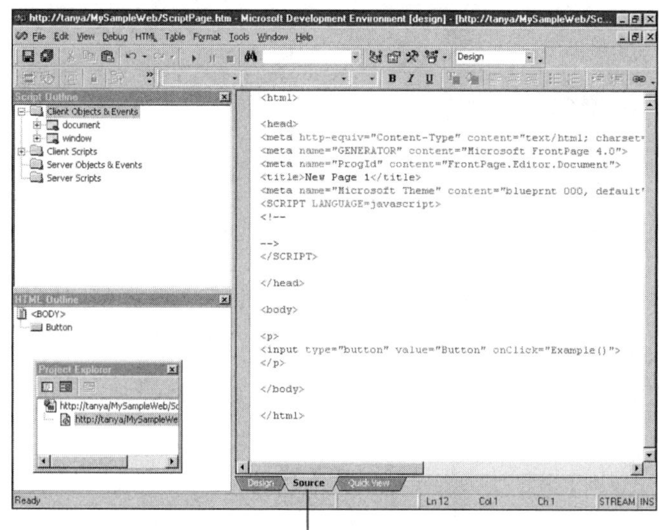

15.12 **Use the tab at the bottom of the document window to access the Source view.**

Take a look at the VBScript sample, and the JavaScript sample provided in this chapter. Notice how the language parameter is different in each script. This parameter allows the browser to identify the scripting language that it must interpret.

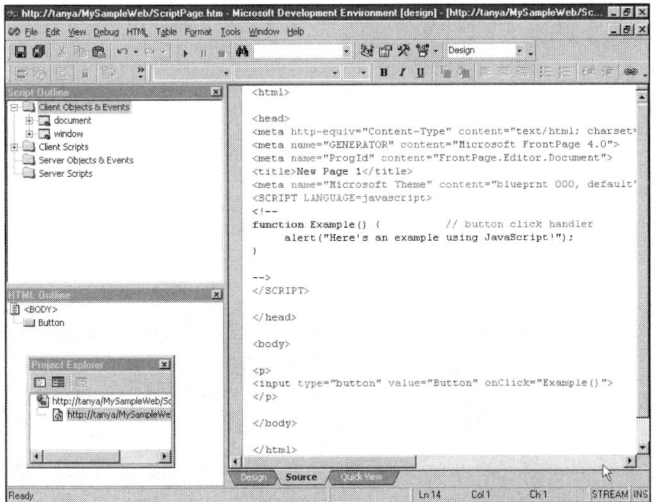

15.13 **If you're familiar with scripting syntax, you can bypass the Microsoft Script Editor and enter your script directly into your HTML source code using the FrontPage 2000 HTML tab.**

```
<SCRIPT LANGUAGE="JavaScript">
<!—
aWindow=window.open("javascript.htm",
"thewindow","toolbar=no,width=360,height=400,status=no,
scrollbars=yes,
resize=no,menubar=no");
//—>
</SCRIPT>
```

15.14

4. In the Source window of the Microsoft Script Editor, place your JavaScript code between the <!— and — > **(15.13)**.
5. Select the Quick View tab in the Microsoft Script Editor and click the applied control to see the result of the script.
6. Choose File→Save, and then File→Exit to save your work and close the Microsoft Script Editor **(15.14)**.

I P

Here's an example of a JavaScript you can apply to your HTML code. This script causes a new 360 × 400 window to open that displays the page referenced in the script. Don't put line breaks in the code. Make sure the script code is all on one line.

CHAPTER 16

In this chapter you will learn how to...

- **Import Files from Other Office Applications**
- **Apply Design-Time Controls**
- **Add ActiveX Controls**
- **Apply Java Applets**
- **Add HTML Source Code**
- **Add Database Connectivity**
- **Add Plug-Ins**
- **Address Cross-Browser Compatibility**
- **Insert a Date and Time Component**
- **Create and Run Macros**

The day of the static Web page is quickly coming to an end. With the evolution of the desktop client/server application model to a more Web-centric model, the demand for Web pages that provide desktop application functionality is on the rise. For this reason, FrontPage 2000 is designed to support the use of tools and technologies like scripting languages, back-end databases, ActiveX controls, and Java applets.

EXTENDING WEB PAGE FUNCTIONALITY

ActiveX technology is based on a software specification that defines how to develop object-based software components capable of providing functional services to other client applications. The basic software specification is called the Component Object Model (COM). Software components that are compliant with the COM specification are called COM objects. As such, COM objects are capable of exchanging data with each other, regardless of the programming language used to develop them. This chapter describes the use of FrontPage 2000 as an enabler for the application of these tools and technologies, thereby allowing your Web to be more functional and your users to be more productive. For example, scripting languages let you add intelligence to your Web pages through the application of embedded programming logic. Back-end databases, ActiveX controls, and Java applets extend your Web's capability to interact with users by collecting and responding to data entered in real time. In addition, these technologies support popular features such as online chat and data presentation using charts and graphs.

Importing Files from Other Office Applications

FrontPage 2000 is designed to integrate seamlessly with the other applications comprising the Office 2000 Productivity Suite. This is demonstrated by the fact that although Office 2000 files can be saved as HTML files and imported into FrontPage, selecting these files in FrontPage 2000 launches the source application used to create them. In FrontPage's Folder List view, files created in other Office 2000 applications are identified by a document icon containing the logo of the source application used to save the file as a Web page.

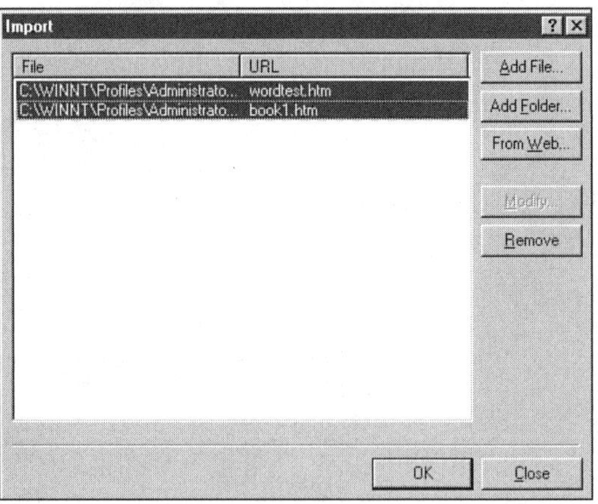

16.1

1. Save an Office 2000 application file, such as a Word document or an Excel spreadsheet, in .htm format.
2. Choose File→Import to open the Import dialog box **(16.1)**.
3. Select the Add File button to locate the saved Office application files on your local drive, and then click OK.
4. Notice how the files appear in Folder List view **(16.2)**.

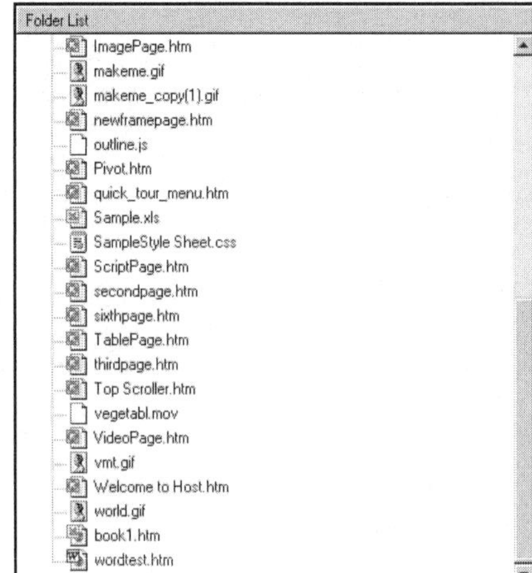

16.2

Copying and pasting cells of an Excel spreadsheet into a FrontPage Web page converts the spreadsheet cells and values into table cells and values. Double-clicking the Excel file in FrontPage opens the file in Excel, if the application is installed on the Web host.

Applying Design-Time Controls

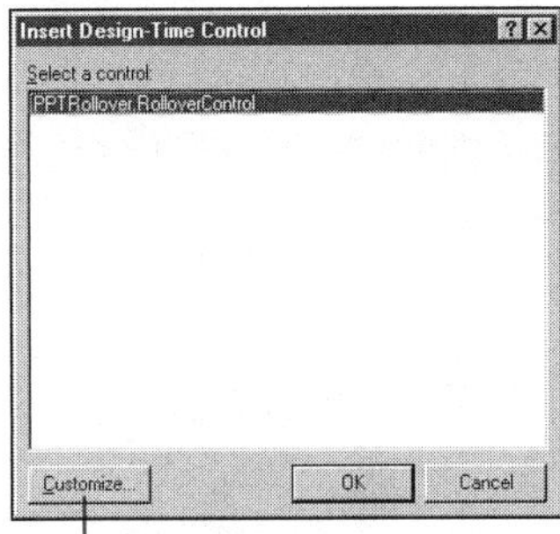

16.3 If no control appears in the list box, click the Customize button to see if there are any design-time controls registered on your machine. If so, check the item listed and click OK.

Design-time controls are server-based ActiveX controls that, like FrontPage components, are used to extend the functionality of your Web page. Design-time controls produce server-generated HTML source code and scripting logic to support a desired capability, based on the ActiveX standard. Consequently, unlike FrontPage components, they are not dependent on the FrontPage Server Extensions. By way of origin, design-time controls, also known as server-side ActiveX controls, are usually developed by Web programmers using C++, Java, Visual Basic, or some other programming language. For this reason, design-time controls are not visible to the user, but rather are referenced within the context of a script embedded in your HTML code and then executed on the Web server to produce the desired result. This differs from client-side ActiveX controls, which are downloaded as part of the Web page and then interpreted and displayed by the browser.

1. In Page view of an open FrontPage 2000 Web, position the cursor where you want to apply the Design-Time Control. Choose Insert→Advanced→Design-Time Control to open the Insert Design-Time Control dialog box **(16.3)**.

2. Select a control appearing in the list box and then click the OK button.

Adding ActiveX Controls

ActiveX controls are software objects designed to be the Microsoft response to Java applets. However, unlike Java applets, ActiveX controls are browser-dependent by design. In other words, ActiveX controls are designed to run in the Internet Explorer environment, and although third-party plug-ins exist to allow ActiveX controls to run with Netscape, suffice it to say your best results are garnered by sticking with IE.

1. In Page view of an open FrontPage 2000 Web, position the cursor where you want to apply an ActiveX control. Choose InsertfAdvanced→ ActiveX Control to open the Insert ActiveX Control dialog box **(16.4)**.
2. Select a control appearing in the list box and then click the OK button **(16.5)**.

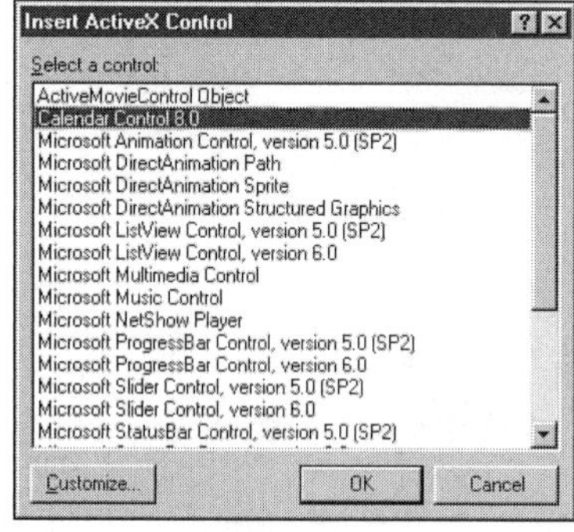

16.4

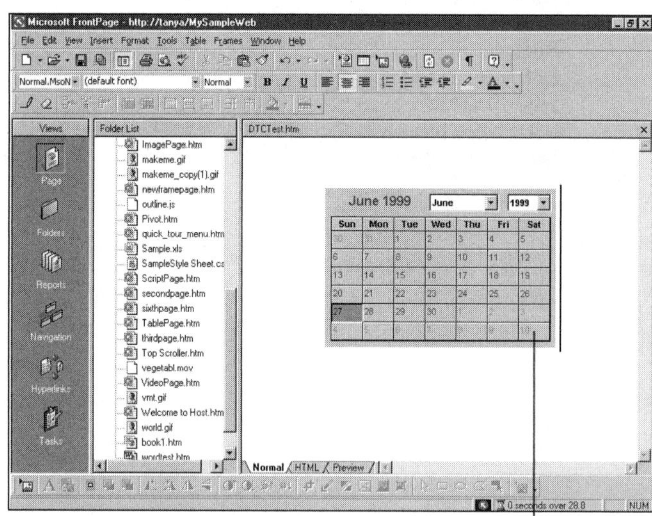

16.5

This is an example of the ActiveX Calendar control applied to a page.

The capabilities of some ActiveX controls are obvious from their title; however, if you're curious about what a particular control does, you might try applying it to your Web page and taking a look at its properties to find out its purpose.

Applying Java Applets

Applet Source takes the name of the Java applet class file.

Applet Base URL takes the URL or directory path containing the class files that support the applet.

Optional field in which you can enter a message to display to users that don't have Java-compatible browsers.

16.6

Like ActiveX controls, Java applets are software objects designed to add functionality to your Web pages. However, Java applets carry one important distinction—they are typically browser-independent. In other words, their functionality can be applied and run on Web pages viewable in any Java-compatible Web browser.

Java applets are available to support a variety of capabilities such as pop-up menus, vertical scrolling text, timers, and chat-clients—just to name a few. A source for Java applets and information is `http://www.gamelan.com`, `http://www.jars.com`, or `http://www.sun.com`.

1. In Page view of an open FrontPage 2000 Web, with the cursor positioned where you want to apply a Java applet, choose Insert→Advanced→Java Applet to open the Java Applet Properties dialog box **(16.6)**.

continues

The Layout Section of the Java Applet Properties dialog box lets you apply values for horizontal and vertical spacing, as well as applet alignment. In the Size section, you can set applet Width and Height values.

Applying Java Applets continued

2. Consult the documentation associated with the applet you want to apply to configure the Java applet's parameters on the dialog box, and then click OK. (Java applet documentation is typically a ReadMe file that is found among the applet class files delivered with a packaged or downloaded Java applet.)

3. In Page view, you can see how a Java applet appears in the FrontPage editing window after being configured **(16.7)**.

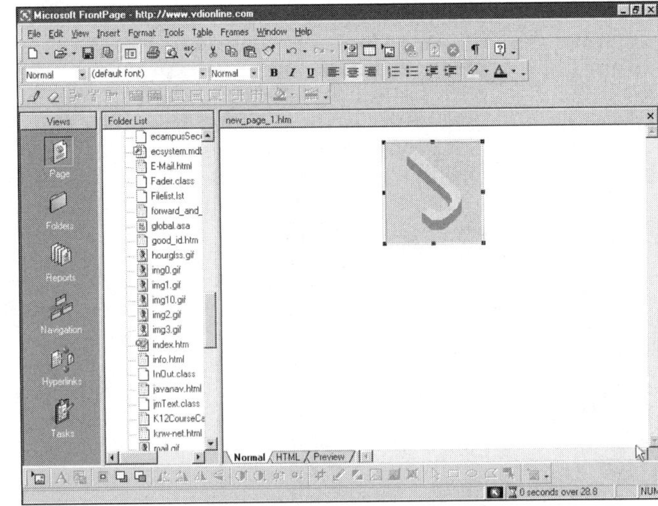

16.7

NOTE

Because Java applets are compiled into what's known as bytecode, which must be interpreted by a program installed with your browser called the Java Virtual Machine (JVM) or the Microsoft Virtual Machine, they are platform-independent. Consequently, the applet runs the same way whether it's served via an NT, UNIX, or Mac.

TIP

In the Applet Parameters section of the Java Applet Properties dialog box, you can add, remove, or modify an applet's configurable parameters such as Font size, Font Style, and Background Color. FrontPage Hover buttons are Java applets. Apply one to your Web page and select the HTML tab to see an example of configurable parameters (16.8).

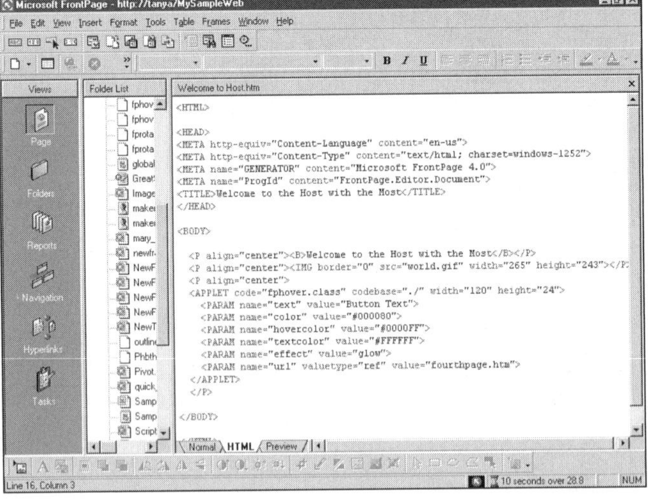

16.8

Adding HTML Source Code

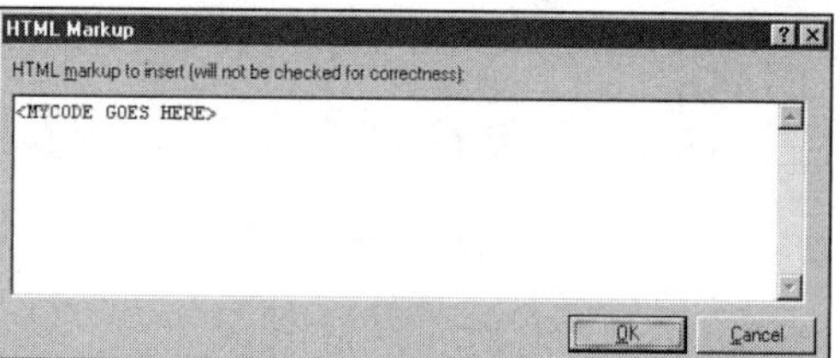

16.9

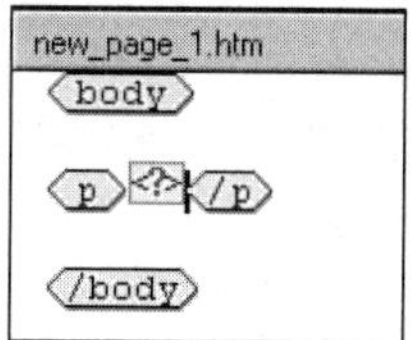

16.10

Although FrontPage 2000 lets you access source code directly via the HTML tab in Page view, there may be occasions when you want to apply HTML source that you don't want reinterpreted by the WYSI-WYG editor. For example, you might want to experiment with Extensible Markup Language (XML), or you may make up a tag of your own to test its effect in your Web page. FrontPage 2000 gives you an alternative method of applying nonstandard HTML using the HTML Markup component.

1. In Page view of an open FrontPage 2000 Web, with the cursor positioned where you want to apply your nonstandard HTML, choose Insert→Advanced→HTML to open the HTML Markup dialog box **(16.9)**.

2. Enter your nonstandard HTML, and then click the OK button.

 I P

Choosing View→Reveal Tags after applying an HTML Markup component reveals a yellow box containing a question mark. This box is called an HTML Markup icon and indicates that HTML has been inserted that FrontPage does not recognize (16.10).

Adding Database Connectivity

Database connectivity and the Web is the future. With the advent of e-commerce and the ever-increasing requirement for real-time information updates, the capability to collect, retrieve, and manipulate data over the Web is changing the Web-based brochure site to the Web-based business application site.

1. In Page view of an open FrontPage 2000 Web, with the cursor positioned where you want to apply results of a database query, choose Insert→Database→Results to open the first of five Database Results Wizard panels **(16.11)**.
2. Select an option for your database connection, then click the Create button.
3. Select the Next button to establish your database connection.

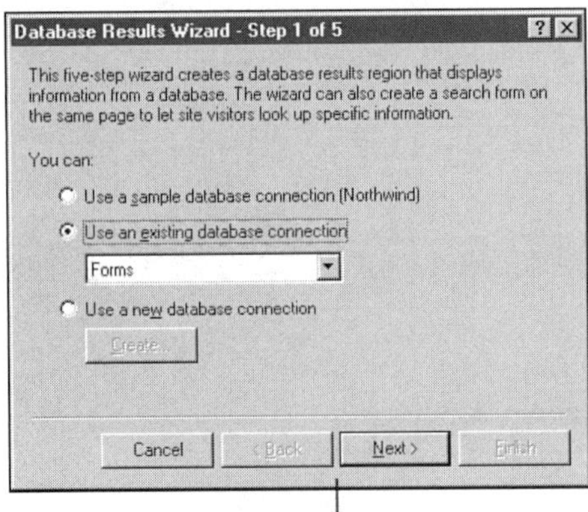

16.11 **FrontPage 2000 enables you to establish a database connection as a Web Settings option; however, you can also use the first panel of the Database Results Wizard to accomplish the same result.**

The ability to securely manipulate data over the Web has led to the advent of e-commerce. FrontPage 2000 is excellent for developing commercial and informational sites with no more than simple ODBC data retrieval. Although you could typically support your database interaction needs using Microsoft Access, be aware that more advanced database transactions might require using SQL and ASP or other database-specific strategies.

Adding Plug-Ins

Enter a message to display to users who don't have browsers that recognize the plug-in tag <EMBED>.

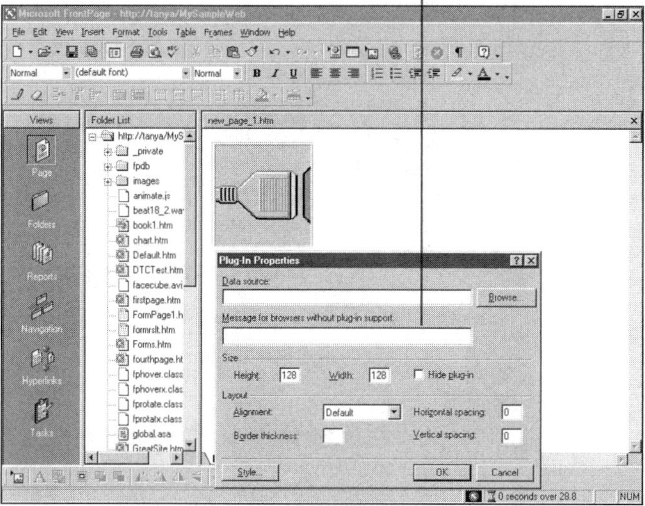

16.12

Plug-ins are proprietary applications designed to enable browsers to support proprietary file formats, such as those supporting RealPlayer, Shockwave, or Flash. FrontPage 2000 makes the application of plug-ins a breeze. All it takes is a few simple steps.

1. In Page view of an open FrontPage 2000 Web, with the cursor positioned where you want to apply the plug-in, choose Insert→Advanced→Plug-In to open the Plug-In Properties dialog box **(16.12)**.
2. Type in the name of the file to be displayed by the plug-in in the Data Source field.
3. In the Size section, enter values to set the Width and Height for the plug-in in pixels.
4. Add values for alignment, spacing, and border thickness in the Layout section.
5. Once you have configured the plug-in parameters, click OK to accept the selections.

The Hide Plug-In check box is selected when the plug-in to be rendered has no visible component.

Addressing Cross-Browser Compatibility

FrontPage 2000 now offers support to help you address the issue of cross-browser compatibility. This ability allows you to tailor the delivery of your Web site's content by disabling those features that are not compatible with different browser types. Commands not supported by certain browser technologies appear dimmed on FrontPage 2000 menus when you begin Web development.

1. Choose Tools→Page Options, and then click the Compatibility tab **(16.13)**.
2. From the Browsers drop-down menu, select the specific browser or browsers of your choice **(16.14)**.
3. From the Browser versions drop-down menu, select the specific browser versions of your choice.

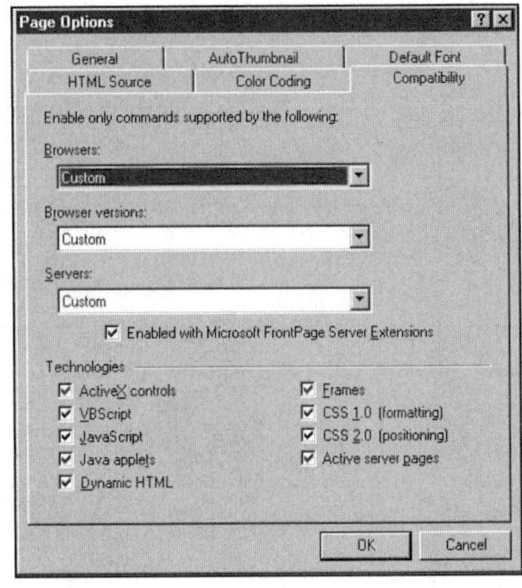

16.13

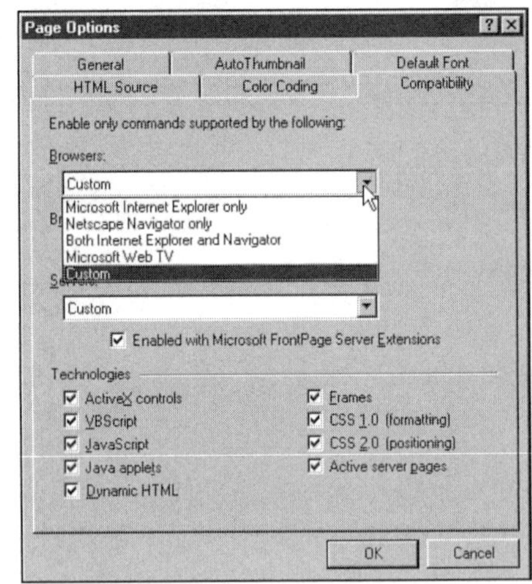

16.14

See Chapter 1, "Configuring a FrontPage 2000 Working Environment," for additional details concerning the Compatibility tab.

Inserting a Date and Time Component

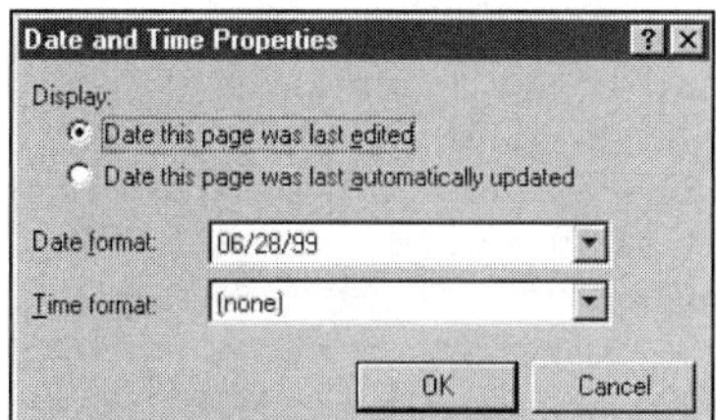

16.15

16.16

One of the best ways to keep visitors coming back to your Web site is to keep the information fresh by updating frequently. FrontPage 2000's Date and Time component gives you the ability to let your visitors know how current your site's content is.

1. In Page view of an open FrontPage 2000 Web with the cursor positioned where you want to apply the date and time, choose Insert→Date and Time to open the Date and Time Properties dialog box **(16.15)**.
2. Select an option to display the date and time the page was last edited or automatically updated.
3. Select a date format from the Date Format drop-down menu.
4. Select a Time Format from the Time Format drop-down menu, and then click OK.

The Date and Time component is useful when working in Web development teams because individual team members can determine when specific Web content was last updated (16.16). This component also lets the user validate the timeliness of the content presented.

Creating and Running Macros

Macros are programming devices that let you consolidate the execution of multiple tasks by initiating a single command string. They are typically defined by you, the Web developer/programmer, to save a few keystrokes or to simply execute a utility program of your own design. FrontPage 2000 supports the creation of macros using the Visual Basic Editor. Consequently, this will be your starting point for developing the tasks that your macro will trigger. FrontPage 2000 macros are not exposed to site users and are typically created and used as a development-enabler by the Web designer/programmer. In the following example, you'll build a macro called ColorSwitch. Executing the ColorSwitch macro opens a form that enables you to preview several background colors without having to open and reopen the Page Properties dialog box. This little utility can be quite handy if you want to quickly try different background colors as you develop your pages.

1. Choose Tools→Macro→Macros to open the Macro dialog box and then enter a name for the macro in the Macro Name field **(16.17)**. The name used for this example is ColorSwitch.

2. Click the Create button to open the Visual Basic Editor **(16.18)**.

Select Run to start macro execution. Select Step Into to see the macro code execute one step at a time in the Visual Basic Editor. Select Edit to edit the macro code. Select Delete to remove the macro from the list box. Select Cancel to end the entire macro selection and execution process.

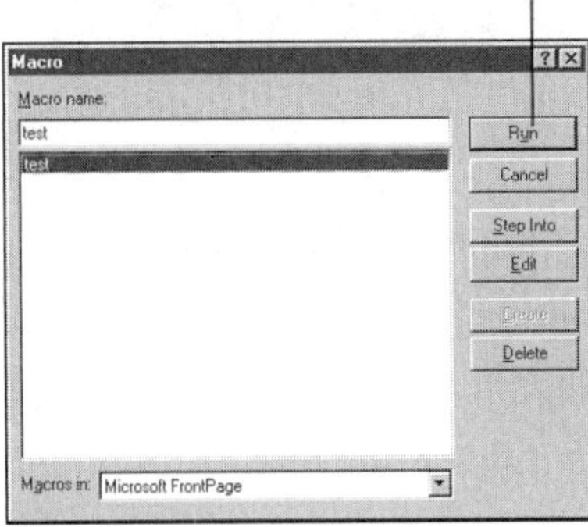

16.17

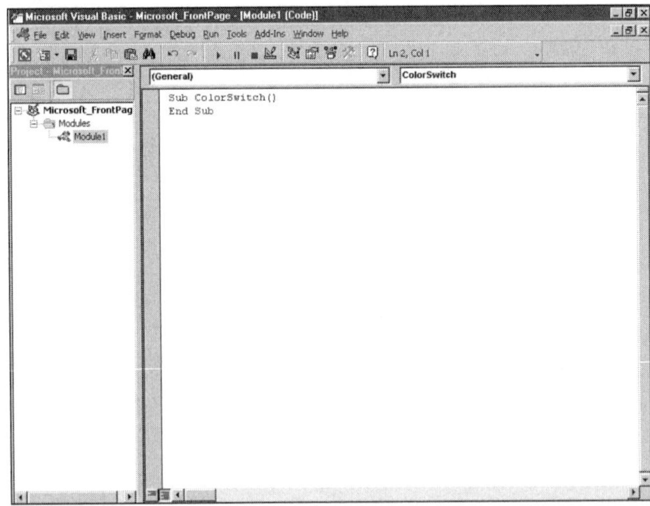

16.18

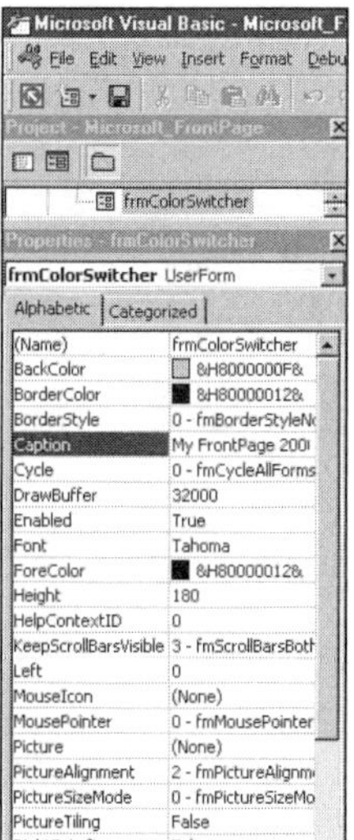

16.19

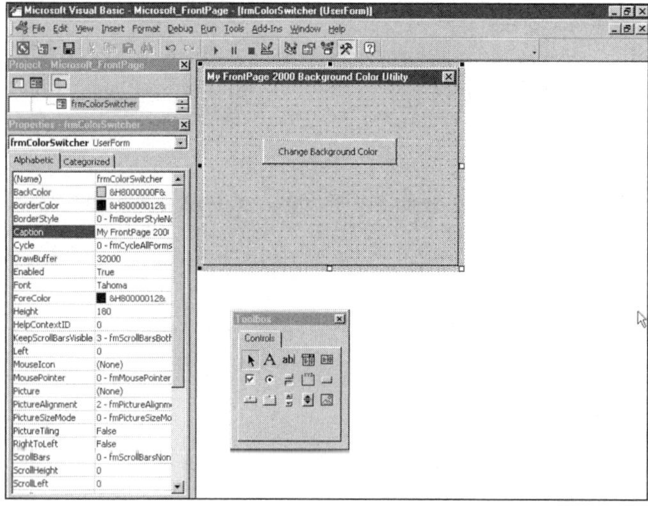

16.20

3. In the Visual Basic Editor, select Insert→Userform to open a blank user form along with the Visual Basic Controls toolbox.

4. Select View→Properties Window to open the UserForm's property listing, replace the name UserForm with the name `frmColorSwitcher` in the Name field of the Properties window, and then in the Caption field enter `My FrontPage 2000 Background Color Utility` **(16.19)**.

5. Select the My FrontPage 2000 Background Color Utility windows and then the CommandButton control on the Toolbox, draw a button in the middle of the form, give the button the name `cbColorSwitcher` in the Properties Window Name field for the newly created button, and then enter `Change Background Color` in the Caption field **(16.20)**.

continued

 **I P**

Macros created using the Visual Basic Editor are for use by you, the Web developer, only. VB macros are not intended for interactive use by site visitors.

Creating and Running Macros continued

6. Select the CommandButton control on the Toolbox again, draw a small button beneath the first button, give the button the name `cbExit` in the button's Properties Window Name field, and then enter `Exit` in the Caption field **(16.21)**.
7. Double-click the top button to open its coding window, and then enter the following lines of code between the `Sub` and `End Sub` statements **(16.22)** and **(16.23)**.
8. Choose File→Save Microsoft_FrontPage and then close the button's coding window by selecting the window's close button in the upper-right corner.

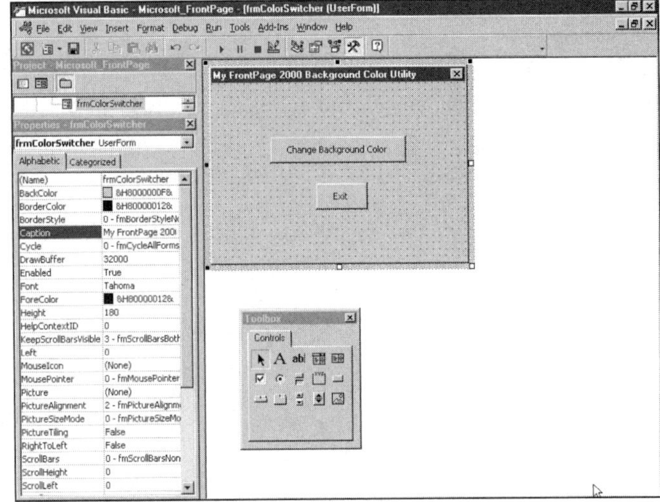

16.21

```
Dim NewColor As Variant
    NewColor = InputBox("Enter a color:")
    ActivePageWindow.Document.bgColor = NewColor
```

16.22

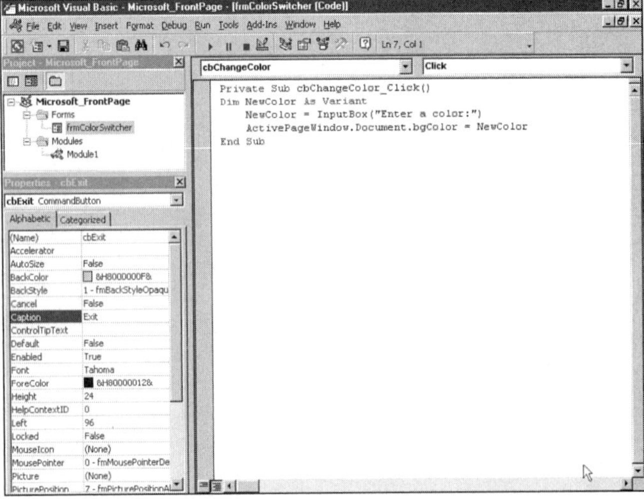

16.23

You must be working in an active page in Page Normal view, or you will get errors.

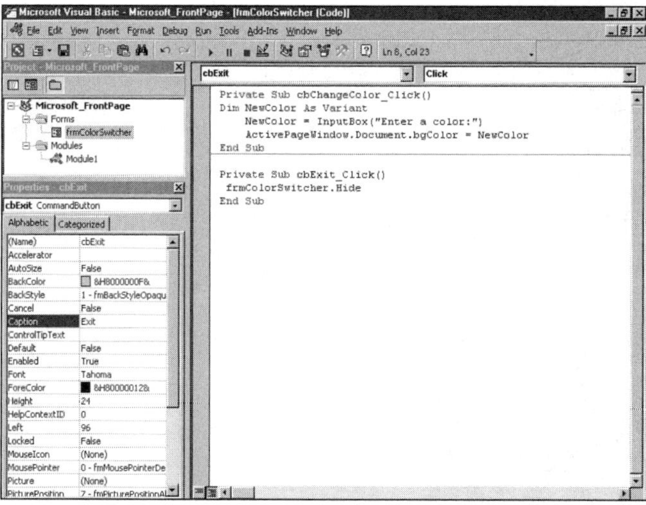

16.24

9. Double-click the bottom button to open its coding window, and then enter the following line of code between the `Sub` and `End Sub` statements **(16.24)**:

   ```
   frmColorSwitcher.Hide
   ```

10. Again, choose File→Save Microsoft_FrontPage and then close the button's coding window by selecting the window's close button in the upper-right corner.

11. In the Project window of the Visual Basic Editor, double-click the item labeled `Module1` and then enter the following line of code between the `Sub` and `End Sub` statements:

    ```
    frmColorSwitcher.Show
    ```

12. Choose File→Save Microsoft_FrontPage.

13. Choose File→Close and return to Microsoft FrontPage.

continues

The example that follows was developed using Visual Basic code, as it applies to interacting with FrontPage. You might want to take a moment to review the basics of Visual Basic for Applications in FrontPage 2000 Help to gain a better understanding of the concepts covered in the example.

Creating and Running Macros continued

14. Choose Tools→Macro→Macros to open the Macro dialog box and then double-click the macro named ColorSwitcher to open your new utility in FrontPage **(16.25)**.

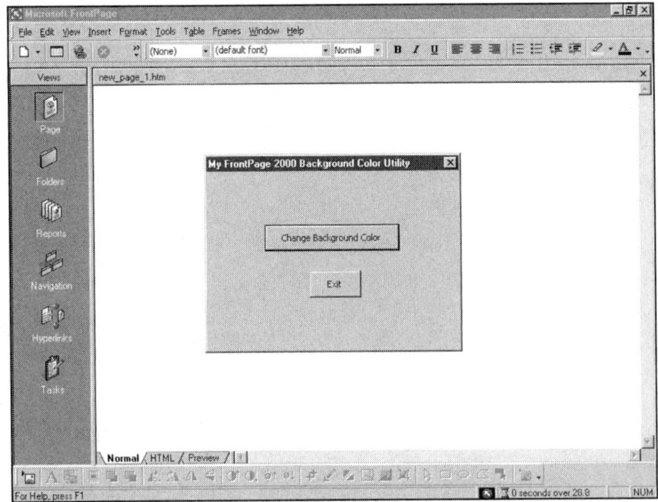

16.25

(N) O T E

`ActivePageWindow` is a property of the FrontPage `Application` object. The Application Object Model is the top level of the three FrontPage programming models available through the Visual Basic Editor; it allows macros to interact with the `CommandBars`, the FrontPage Application Object itself, and the second-level model—the Web Object Model. The Web Object Model allows macros to engage FrontPage Webs and their content. The third-level model is the FrontPage Document Object Model, which makes design-time objects accessible within FrontPage 2000. For detailed information about the FrontPage object models, consult the FrontPage 2000 Help files under Visual Basic Reference for Microsoft FrontPage.

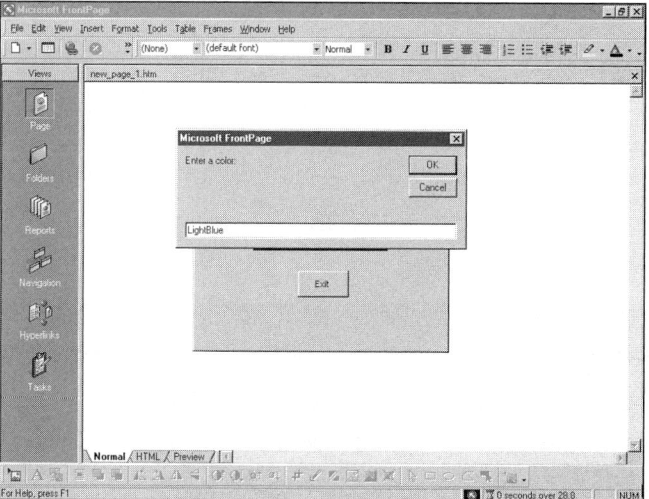

16.26

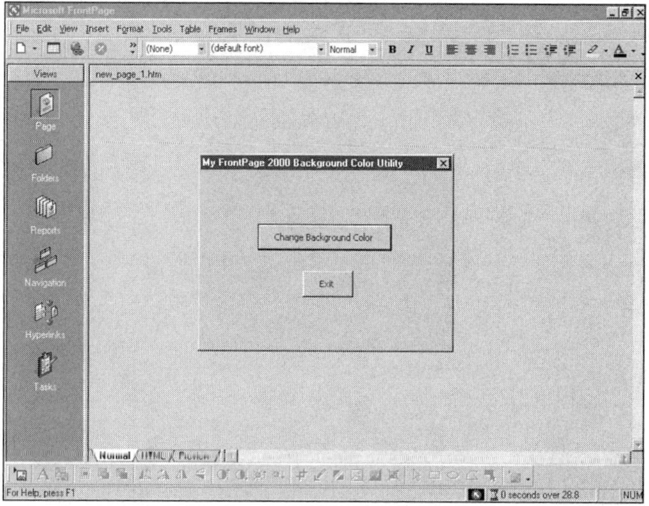

16.27

15. Click the Change Background Color button on the form you created, enter a color when prompted **(16.26)**, and then click OK to see your result **(16.27)**.

16. Click the Exit button to close your utility.

Because FrontPage 2000 uses Active Server Pages (ASP) to interact with the ODBC data source, you'll need to be sure that your Web server has the Active Server Page extensions installed. If the ASP extensions are not installed, the Database option under Insert is disabled. If your current Web server does not have the ASP extensions installed, you can add the extensions by upgrading your server to IIS 3 or better under Windows NT or upgrade to Personal Web Server 4.

INDEX

SYMBOLS

A

B

C

D

E

F

G-H

I

J-K

L

M

R

S

T

U-V

W-Z

Other Short Order

Short Order Adobe Photoshop 5.5

By Michael Lennox
ISBN: 0-7897-2044-2
$19.99
2-color with a full-color insert!
Available October 1999

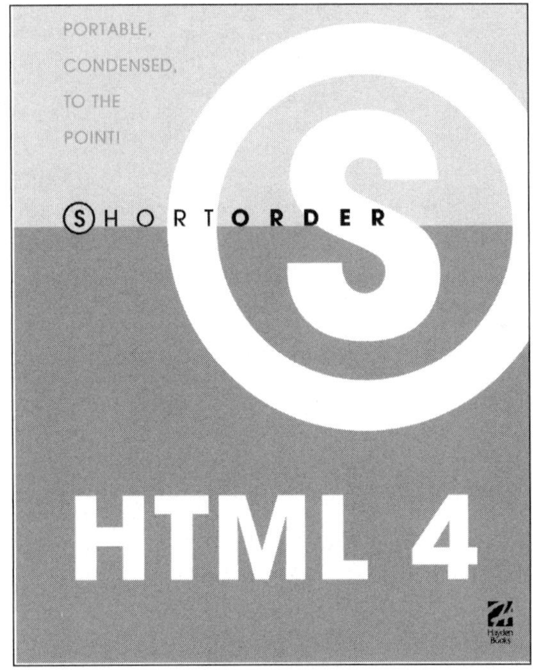

Short Order HTML 4

By Molly Holzschlag
ISBN: 0-7897-2049-3
$19.99
Available October 1999

Books from Hayden

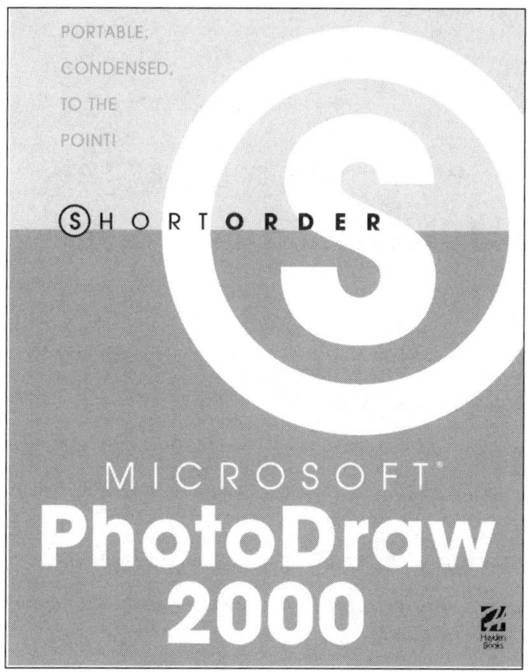

Short Order Microsoft PhotoDraw 2000 v2

By Molly Joss
ISBN: 0-7897-2048-5
$19.99
Available November 1999

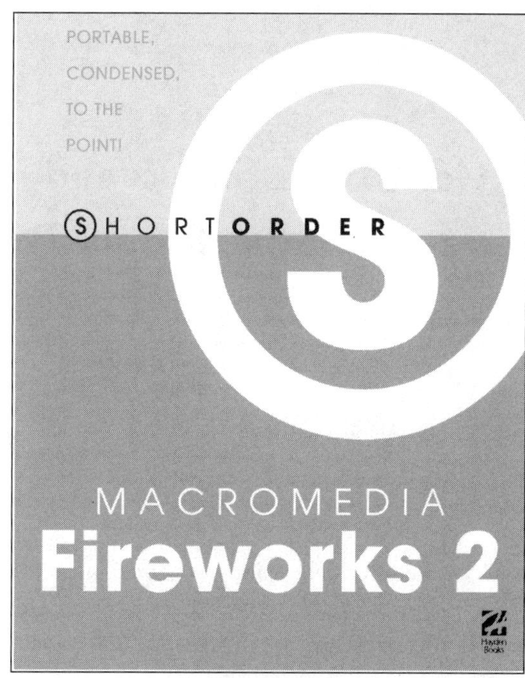

Short Order Macromedia Fireworks 2

By Nancy Martin and Ronnie Sampson
ISBN: 0-7897-2043-4
$19.99
Available December 1999